Working Class Hero

John St. John

DEEP WATER PRESS
NELSON, BRITISH COLUMBIA
CANADA

National Library of Canada Cataloguing in Publications

St. John, John, 1949-
Working Class Hero/ John St. John.

ISBN 0-9731795-4-6

1. St.John, John, 1949- 2. Working Class--Canada-Biography. 3.
Working Class--England--Biography.
4. Chauffeurs--Canada--Biography. 5. Chauffeurs--England--
Biography. I. Title.

HD8107.S28A3 2005   305.5′ 62′ 092   C2005-903491-2

Book Layout: M. B. Wallis/C. L. Hunter
Cover Design: M. B. Wallis/ K. Dodds

Deep Water Press
Box 964
Nelson, V1L 6A5
British Columbia
Canada

*This book, on request of the author, John St. John, has been printed
on recycled eco-friendly paper. Save our trees!*

Dedication

This book is dedicated to Mary.
My partner, wife, best friend, soulmate and saviour,
whose love and light never failed to illuminate my path.

And to My Family,
Samantha, Julie, Michael, Lyndsay, Leah and William.
May they all learn something from this, and
never have to endure the constant circle of repetition.

With grateful acknowledgements to;
Harald, Flo, JB, Tela, Jackie and Raili.
For their faith in me and making the Millennium a reality.

In loving memory of:
My mother Doris, Debbie, Ronnie and David.
Until we meet again.

And finally to all the working class heroes

Thank you,
because without your input, this world could never
work ANYTHING!

Bless You All.

Introduction

Ever ask yourself, "Why was I born?" I bet you have… and over the last fifty years it's been a question that's constantly bugged me. Not just 'Why,' but 'Who on earth am I and what am I doing here?'

Ever since the age of ten, when my father died, I've felt like a square peg in a round hole, where nothing seemed to fit. For years I drifted from job to job, having over fifteen different employers by the time I'd reached twenty. *Maybe that in itself is some kind of record, who knows?*

What I did know, is that I couldn't seem to find anything in common with those around me. I may have been on the world, but I definitely didn't feel of it! My impeccable lifestyle kept getting in the way. I didn't drink, I didn't smoke, I didn't do drugs and I detested swearing. And if that wasn't enough to be a party-pooper, I was honest, dependable, hard working and conscientious! "Bloody Hell," some of you may say. With traits like that, it's a wonder that I had any friends at all, and I couldn't agree more. I hated being like this and I had to take a lot of flack because of it. Many branded me a snob and a prude, which, as you can imagine, did wonders for my self-esteem… In reality, they couldn't have been further from the truth.

I've always had a *'live and let live'* philosophy, with a compassion for the plight of others that could bring me to tears just by watching the evening news. This rejection by my friends and workmates manifested into an extreme lack of self-confidence, making me strive harder and harder to please people, even to the extent of working for little to no money just to prove myself worthy. Continuously moving from place to place to fit in, my life became one adventure, or miss-adventure, after another, which has accumulated over the years into a story that makes the movie "Forrest Gump," look like a three-hour preview. Like the character, my life experiences also epitomized the life and times of the period; and boy, what experiences they were! I've had over forty jobs, thirty-five cars, four kids, three careers, two marriages and a leopard in a pear tree, and moved house thirty-three times! I've witnessed events and situations that most people could only ever dream about, involving hundreds of Movie Stars, Pop Stars, Rock Musicians, Sports Celebrities, Politicians, Ambassadors, CEO's, Corporate Executives and Royalty! And all of my experiences are fact, not fiction.

Forty years and never a dull moment, and as interesting and exciting as my life has been at times, it was no picnic. Due to my inept self-worth, I managed to work my way up from nothing to virtual poverty, with an anxiety level that's been up and down more times than a whore's drawers. How, I managed to get through it all and still stay sane, God only knows. Like the way money seems to come to those that don't need it, I found myself mixing with "The Rich and Famous," and not wanting to be there, while others would have given their right arm to be in my shoes. Constantly I cursed fate for thrusting me into arenas to which I didn't belong.

"Why Me?" I'd ask. I'm the last person on Earth you'd expect to be associated with these people. I had absolutely nothing in common with them, and how on Earth I ended up to my neck surrounded by Sex, Drugs and Rock 'n' Roll, frankly amazes me. With age comes wisdom, and to every rhyme there is a reason, and I now believe that the purpose of my life was to write this book.

In truth, it's not who I met that's important, it's what I discovered while working with them. That's what I wish to reveal here, as I take you into a world that many rarely see, and we journey behind the scenes to uncover the real life personalities of some of them. A thousand and one stories of 'the Good, the Bad and the Ugly,' that will make you laugh, cry and outraged, as you wake up to the reality of what these people really think and do... Don't worry, it's not all doom and gloom, there's also a lot of humour. I'm not here to praise Caesar or to bury him; I just want to make those who work for him more accountable, and if I ruffle a few feathers along the way, then so be it.

Although, most of my life has been spent surrounded by the wealthy, none of their money ever came my way. In fact, throughout my life, my family and I have never had more than a few hundred dollars in our bank account, and that's what makes my story so unique. "I did it all on nothing!"

That's why I chose to write an autobiography rather than just cut and thrust to the 'meaty bits,' because I believe it's important for you to know who I am and where I came from. Then, by experiencing my colourful and incredible background, you will see that I did everything from the perspective of the 'ordinary person,' and that's probably why all the extravagance never sucked me in. No matter what the circumstances, I always tried to keep my head, whilst those around me lost theirs- and it's because I succeeded- that I was able to write this book.

Whoever it was that said, "Truth is stranger than fiction," was right. I've spent a lifetime witnessing it first hand. Which brings me to one other saying, this time from my mother, who definitely hit the nail on the head when she told me, "I may never have had any money, but I've certainly seen life!"

So move over Forrest Gump. It's time to tell my story.

John St. John

Chapter One

Oh, No! Not Another Boy

*"Just when you think you can make ends meet,
somebody moves the ends!"*

That saying could probably sum up most of my life, and I guess that many people would agree with the sentiment. I know my father would have.

At the time of my birth, George Bell and my mother, Doris, ran a local convenience store in Birmingham, England. Dad had built it from scratch, starting with a small greengrocer cart at the end of the garden that eventually evolved to the single story Mini Mart that served the neighbourhood. Everything in my father's life epitomised the classic middle-class family of the 1950's. A loving wife, nice house, own business, new car every year and three children, all boys. The only thing missing was a daughter.

When my mother got the news that she was expecting again, it must have been quite a surprise for her, considering that her youngest was then 10 and she herself was 41. What-the-heck, this had to be the girl they'd always wanted, and so everyone waited with eager anticipation for my birth.

On a beautiful Tuesday morning in June of 1949, I arrived into this world, probably followed by a resounding chorus of "Oh, No! Not another boy!" Poor mom, what a shame, and it must have been quite a blow to my father and brothers too.

At least everything else in dad's life was going great. Not only was his business booming, but his expertise as a repertory theatre actor was at long last being acknowledged. He was being offered bigger and more important roles and he'd also been accepted as a member of London's famed Variety Club, an honour in itself. Not bad for the butler son of a disinherited Scottish heiress. ("Och-aye we lost out on the family fortune there laddy").

The story being: my grandmother's family had cast her out because she married a mere 'Master Bricklayer', a man well below her station in life, (I believe her parents were shipyard owners). So after marrying my grandfather they packed up and moved to England to start a family of their own, and eventually ended up with four boys, my father being the oldest.

Funny how history has a way of repeating itself; years later my father, who after attaining the prestigious rank of Butler to a large household, fell in love with the lowly upstairs maid, and this outraged my grandmother so much, that she refused to give her consent to their marriage.

It would appear that she had learned little from her own experience, because she never attended my parents' wedding (a five shilling affair with no guests and a pork pie reception at the local pub) and flatly refused to help them in any way. Amazing isn't it- you'd think she would have been more understanding after losing everything for love herself, but no! My mother's punishment for her seduction was to be confined to the kitchen whenever they visited my grandparents' home, never being permitted to enter the parlour and have tea with the rest of the family! Mother must have been pretty lonely, that is until she had children, as they too became confined to the kitchen. My mother never complained though; she knew her place only too well, having been one of twelve children, from one of the poorest areas in Nottingham. Her father was the local 'Rag & Bone' man (scrap dealer), trading in anything he could find, and was quite the character by all accounts. Often his horse would be seen late at night making it's own way home with my grandfather lying dead drunk on the back of the cart. Although the street mom was born in did acquire fame of it's own later, being featured in a famous English movie from 1960's called "Saturday Night & Sunday Morning," which launched Albert Finney into stardom. Even the house they used in the movie was only two doors away from my parent's first home.

Anyway, though she was from a poor family, mom was of strong stock and had survived many tribulations, including WW1, so coping with my grandmother wasn't so bad. It's a good job she was tough, because over the next 20 years she would have to suffer the great depression, another world war, and a barrage of marital problems that were more suited to the pages of a 'Charles Dickens' novel. Slowly but surely she and dad clawed their way up through amazing poverty, with George being frequently out of work, which probably accounted for his lack of patience and extremely bad temper. Often he would throw my mothers lovingly cooked meal across the room and on occasions her along with it! But eventually, still together they made it through, and were now living in Birmingham with their own business and a good life, and this is where my story begins.

Although I remember very little of my childhood, my carefree youth seemed to be like that of an only child, due to the vast age difference between my brothers and me. My clearest recollections of each of them are in uniform while doing their National Military Service. My brother Ronnie, who was my peer by 18 years, chose the Army as did Gordon, who was ten years older than me. However, it was my brother David (14 years older) whose service I remember the most, as he'd joined the Royal Air Force and I was far more interested in that. I still have fond memories of dressing up in various

9

parts of his old uniforms to play with my friends, his peaked cap giving me an air of importance as commander of all I surveyed. I'd wait with eager anticipation for his visits home to see what new toy plane would be concealed under his coat or hiding in the depths of his knapsack.

Other memories of my brothers during my youth are pretty sparse. My brother Ronnie's wedding, when I was only 5, (fig.1) put an end to his participation with my youth and as for my brother Gordon whose place I had taken as being the baby of the family, we never did get along. Reluctantly, he had been given the job of my care and welfare while mom and dad were busy in the shop, a job he hated and resented, since he was seriously courting at the time and didn't want to be bothered with a little kid brother. Subsequently, he and I got into numerous scraps. Once I ran into the shop with my head cut and bleeding three times in one day. On another occasion my brother begrudgingly took me with him to a local pond to play 'war' with his mates, I was six, and yes, I soon became the first casualty when a .22 pellet hit me square in the forehead and once again I was dragged into the shop bleeding and crying, the pellet caused a scar I still have to this day. Honestly it's amazing that either of us grew up. Because my father's short temper was renowned, Gordon had been the target of many a flying fist, and often ran away to hide until things cooled down, which of course meant that he wasn't watching me. Left to my own devices I would then go on one of my frequent walk-abouts, following a Fire-engine or similar distraction and end up lost miles away from home, until the neighbourhood call went out to look for a boy and his dog. (Peter, my constant companion).

This is where having the shop came in handy because customers would come in and say to my mother "Did you know that your John and Peter are down by the railway bridge?" or wherever, after which my mother would run out of the shop to find me. This of course, would make my father lose his temper and he would go after my brother who would then run and hide again, leaving no one to look after me when I got back and … 'Well you get the picture.'

Besides losing his temper and running the shop, my father was quite the thespian and frequently appeared in local theatrical productions. Though an accomplished actor, he was also a very good stand-up comedian and, on one occasion after participating in a talent contest at a holiday camp we were at, he was invited to stay another week with the family for free, if he agreed to perform some of his comedy sketches for them, which of course he did. (fig.2) That week's performance when I was eight was the only on-stage recollection of him that I can remember, other than the way he used to rouse the house each morning with his renditions of famous monologues and Shakespearean prose. He was truly a master of the spoken word and loved to be the centre of attention and was loved by all, including quite a few ladies, as I found out later from my mother. He was also sought after by his past employer, 'The Ruberoid Roofing Co.,' who with the offer of a management position, eventually managed to coax him to give up the shop and work for them again. So the shop was sold and dad bought a beautiful detached house for the three of us, because if I remember correctly Ronnie and David were married by then and Gordon was away in the Army.

Within a year of moving, my father was offered the opportunity to join something that appeared to be a growing market, 'Television.' He was so delighted that after his audition with the BBC, he visited the annual 'Motor Show' and ordered himself a new Vanden Plas car to celebrate. At last the long hours of working in the shop were behind him, life was good and he was now making ends meet! Until something moved the ends...

A few months later he was admitted into hospital with a suspected slipped disc. After his examination, the Doctor asked all the family to attend a meeting at the hospital for some bad news- my father had got cancer! I can still vaguely remember my mother and brothers' wives all crying, as they came out of his office after hearing the news, (I had been allocated to wait in the hallway). Everyone was in such deep shock and so busy comforting my mother, that no one bothered to explain things to me, and little did I know it then, at age 10, how much my life was about to change. My father had always been a heavy smoker and the cancer was extremely advanced, so there was nothing they could do for him, and everyone (except me) knew that he was dying. I just thought he was ill and then a few weeks later when he returned home, I saw a bed appear in the parlour and I was told to be very quiet and keep out of the way, while the endless droves of well wishers came to visit him. I know now that they were probably paying their last respects, but at the time I really had no idea what was happening, as again my family told me nothing. Then as the months went by, my mother became more and more preoccupied with looking after my father, and frequently I would see her crying, but again I just thought she was tired. The morning came when she entered my bedroom and woke me to tell me that my dad had gone. Gone where? I really had no idea! My family shipped me off to school as usual that day and when I returned home the house was full with people, and once more I was told to keep out of the way. Even on the day of the funeral, I was kept out of things and sent to school again. It was while sitting in class that I remembered that on Remembrance Day, people held a one minute silence for those who had died, so that's what I did with my friends at 11 o'clock, coincidentally the same time my dad was going to be cremated. (Whatever that was). Never being allowed to say good-bye to my father was to have a negative affect on my health from then on, but that was just the beginning of my troubles!

My mother was extremely naive when it came to matters of money, and knew nothing of maintaining the house and its finances. Everything had been the responsibility of dad, and so my brothers and their wives stepped in and took complete control over everything, putting the fate of mom and me totally in their hands... "The Vultures descend." To give dad his credit, he had left my mother very well off, the house was paid for and she had money in the bank. 'Oh,' and just for the record my father had also won the Premium Bonds (British form of lottery) a week after his death, but sorry to say, mom couldn't claim anything as it was in his name only... C'est la vie! Despite the fact mom was financially okay, my brothers decided that there was only one thing to do, and that was to sell the house and split all the money *four ways*, between the three of them and my mother. What of me? I was to get a new bike! I suppose none of my brothers had ever heard of the words "to be held in trust?" So let it be written, so let it be done!

Good-bye home and good-bye Birmingham, because my mother was also coaxed to move back to her hometown of Nottingham. I have no idea why; I think they just wanted to get her and me out of the way. So mom bought us a tiny house and my brothers moved us in. The strange thing about this is, as I look back, I remember that our old house was full of objects and antiques that my father had accumulated over the years, but none of these items ever appeared in our tiny Nottingham home??? In fact, I wasn't given a single thing that had belonged to my father, and all I had to prove that he ever existed was a few photographs and his signature on my birth certificate, and even that was to be stolen a few years later!

Now on our own, my mother who had a quarter of the wealth was forced back to work and she fell back on the only thing she knew, the service trade. She became a canteen assistant at the Raleigh Bicycle Works, in Beeston. As for me? Here I was in a strange city, about to enter Secondary School for the first time, with people who spoke what appeared to me to be a different kind of English, little knowing then how my own Birmingham accent was to become a constant source of ridicule itself, even from my teachers. If all that wasn't bad enough, I'd also gained over 20 pounds in weight due to a glandular problem, which the doctors said was due to the anxiety of my fathers' death...

'Heck!' I was just a kid and knew nothing of life's traumas and yet here I was up-to my neck in five of them! I was a fat kid, about to enter high school, in a strange city, with no father and no friends! 'Oh,' and just to rub a bit more salt into my wounds, a few weeks later my dog Peter died! (The only friend I had) "Sometimes Life Just Sucks."

Well, as you can probably guess my high school years were no picnic. Four years of being picked on, spat on, and constantly called names; children can be so cruel sometimes and these were certainly no exception. Depressed and unhappy I had to walk five miles to school each day, uphill both ways, with bare feet, in a foot of snow.... of course I might be exaggerating things a little, but it certainly felt like that! They say time heals and as the years went by, I did manage to accumulate a few close friends and I also joined the local 'Boy's Brigade,' to become a drummer in a Scott's pipe band, (probably an hereditary thing). Perhaps grandmother's parents would have been proud, whoever they were. At fifteen I began to feel a little more confident, having managed to shed the extra pounds, so together with a few friends we formed a 'Pop Group' (The Interns) and starting playing at school dances and the local youth centre. "Perhaps life isn't so bad after all," I thought, as at last, I too was now making ends meet, but again somebody was about to move the ends! Little did I know then of the drama that was unfolding in Birmingham.

My brother David had been caught having an affair, and his marriage was in trouble, plus he'd lost all the money from dad's estate, and now in big financial doo-doo, was about to lose his house! His only hope of survival was to persuade mother to sell our house and move back to Birmingham, so that she could buy another house for all of us to live in, and thus save his marriage. Oh, and mom may as well lend him the money to pay his bills, while she's at it! Of course, she did all of the above and I was forced to do my last three months of high school back in Birmingham, which did wonders for my exam results! Yeah right! 'What a frigging mess'.

While David and his wife were busy trying to save their marriage, I had to rebuild my life once again and my first thought was to find all my old friends, but even that didn't work out. The years of high school had changed us in so many ways and now, I was the one with the strange accent, having picked up the Nottingham dialect at last...

I tried in vain to start a new pop group but none of my friends were musicians, so that put an end to my music career, and being fresh out of school I had other, more pressing concerns, finding a job. One of my other talents was technical drawing and I managed to get myself an apprentice draftsman's job, and although the wages were lousy, a mere £4 ($8) a week, at least I was living at home. Over the next fifteen months things didn't seem too bad. I had a good friend called Tony, and I even acquired something new in my life 'a girlfriend' Debbie, who lived in the next road and we all started going around together. Then as soon as I was seventeen, I took my driving test and passing first time, I traded in my old motor-scooter and bought my very first car, a 'German Gogomobile.' No kidding, that's what it was called! Life was good and again I was making ends meet.

You can guess what happened next. The woman that brother David had been having the affair with was pregnant, and it wasn't her husband's. Suffice to say the "S**t hit the fan" and that's putting it mildly, all hell broke loose! Her husband became so angry that he tried to set fire to David's car one night, and Joyce, my sister-in-law, who had believed David when he had said the affair was over, was totally devastated! But there was more to come; trying to keep the two women happy had proved expensive for David, and again he was deep in debt and owed money everywhere...

Here we go again. Personally, I felt sorry for the children, David's two, the woman's two and the one on the way. I knew this time that things had gone too far to save either marriage. Funny, this was to be my second example of how people can suffer from the consequences of another's actions, just like the way a stone is thrown into water. After the initial splash, the ripples begin to drift out in all directions, and one of those directions was mine. Once more, David decided the only way to get the money he needed was to persuade mom to sell the house and again he succeeded. Mom was shipped off back to Nottingham again, but this time she was accompanied by my brother Gordon and his family, they had convinced her to put all the money she had left into leasing a grocery store with (for) them, as they too had used up all dad's money and were now in need of some financial help themselves. {Oh' just for the record, if you're wondering what happened to my brother Ronnie's money, he too put his into a restaurant business which also failed and very nearly cost him his marriage!} I, on the other hand, had no money to lose and being only seventeen, I wasn't married either. I was old enough to know that if I moved back to Nottingham, I stood a good chance of losing the girlfriend I did have, Debbie! There was only one thing to do, get myself an apartment.

"Get myself an apartment," sounds so grown up, doesn't it, but in reality my £4 ($8) a week just didn't cut it. Bang went my apprenticeship, and I had to find myself a higher paying job. I ended up as a delivery driver for 'Halfords' a store similar to 'Canadian Tire' which paid the princely sum £10 ($20) a week, which enabled me to rent a one room bed-sit, pay my electricity and buy food, though only just!

With our house gone, David had also moved into a rented house together with his new girlfriend Brenda and their now three children, (the baby was a boy, by the way.) Joyce (his ex) had taken their two boys, George and Robert, and moved to Devon in the south of England, to get as far away from David as she could, but she still made sure that David didn't get off lightly and hounded him with a continuous barrage of custody battles. Now on my own and having to pay for everything, I was pretty 'pee'd off' about the way things had turned out, but with Debbie's help I struggled through, having to constantly change jobs to keep up with the rent increases and the accumulating bills. This was truly my initiation into working life, from which I would gain a wealth of practical knowledge as I went from one job to another; Auto parts delivery, carpet sales, tire fitting, laundry work, air cargo, kitchen designing, bowling alley controller, soft drinks delivery, car and truck sales, gas attendant, shop assistant and selling encyclopedia's were just some of my work experiences. I'm sure time went slower back in the Sixties because I can remember each job vividly, as if I worked there for years and not just the few months it must have really been. On the positive side I did manage to have a little spare money, which would always be spent on upgrading whatever car I had, something else that I changed every three months or so.

At the ripe old age of twenty and having had over twenty different jobs, I decided it was time to settle down. I knew that eventually Debbie and I would end-up getting married, so I needed to find a nice stable job, one that paid well and would last. Although David was the one who had caused me a lot of heartache, I still felt sorry for him and over the past few years I'd done what I could to assist him through his divorce, and now he was in a position to return the favour. A driving job had become available where he worked and so he offered it to me, and I eagerly accepted, of course. It was to become one of the most interesting jobs of my life.

It was during the era when many of 'England's Stately Homes' were having financial problems, and had to sell off some of their ancient treasures, mostly to foreign traders, and the company David worked for were the people who packed and shipped these speciality items. My new job was to drive to these historic places, and collect anything that had been sold to these overseas buyers, then take it back to the warehouse, where, together with David and the others, I would carefully pack the items into large wooden crates for shipment abroad. It would be a book in itself if I went into every detail about all the amazing things we saw and handled, items collected from all corners of the globe, covering every

17

era of world history, all accumulated over hundreds of years and stored in the hallowed halls of the British Aristocracy. (Some items were actually returning back from whence they came). What an array of treasures: Prehistoric weapons, flintlock rifles, swords of every shape, size and description, suits of armour, western peacemaker's, tomahawk's, ships cannons, Zulu spears, Roman weaponry and the full range of world military uniforms. Not just a cornucopia of warfare, but all kinds of things, including lots of safari trophies. You should try wrapping a stuffed tiger... it's great fun!

On occasions, we struck it lucky and the inventory would state something like, 'Winchester 44/40 with various rounds of ammunition.' The word various could mean any number, so it was our invitation to use a few (just for test purposes only of course) and for some strange reason the back of our warehouse was riddled with bullet holes. I wonder how that could have happened? Sometimes we'd even put a one eighth powder charge in the old flintlock's, thus decreasing their power and then have wars on our lunch breaks, literally shooting each other, as the ball just had enough strength to hit us. (We must have been frigging crazy.) But what a dream of a job, everyday was a new adventure. Off I would go to yet another Castle, Stately Home or Arms Auction, always wondering what new treasures lay in store for me to pick up. The intricate detailing of such ancient weaponry always amazed me, and the beauty of some of the Arabian jewelled daggers was breathtaking, (if a dagger can be called beautiful). Other items were mechanical marvels, where at the push of a button, extra blades would shoot out and impale the victim. Aagggh! Definitely not for the squeamish. I loved to show off some of the more unusual items to family and friends, and on one memorable occasion my best friend Bob and I, dressed up in full German SS officers uniforms, loaded my trunk with various goodies including a set of 'Buffalo Bills' hand guns and drove off to Debbie's house to show her parents, (in an attempt to impress my future father in-law.) On the way back, we ran out of petrol and having no other clothes with us, we had to walk the three miles to the next open gas station in full SS uniform! 'Thank God' it wasn't a Jewish neighbourhood, as we might have given someone a ruddy heart attack. (No offence intended.) Later, after putting everything back, we decided never to do anything like that again. Yeah right! It's a pity Halloween wasn't a big thing in England at that time, because imagine the costumes I could have worn: a Crusading Knight, a Kings Musketeer or even a Japanese Samurai with an original sword! If you want to make a real impression at a party, try arriving clothed in an old diving suit complete with lead boots and solid brass helmet. (Phew!) Not the best outfit to chat-up a girl in, but then, I was engaged and now ready to take the next step.

Chapter Two

Love Beads to Fashion Craze

A turtle only makes progress when it sticks its neck out!

The year was 1970. Debbie and I were now twenty and had been together for over four years and I guess everyone knew that one day we'd get married. So, to prove them right, we set the date, February 21st. Mr. & Mrs. Jones, Debbie's parents, supplied everything we needed for the wedding and Debbie and I took care of the honeymoon arrangements, skiing in Mayrhofen, Austria. The location was my choice because I'd been skiing there 5 years earlier, on a school trip and really enjoyed it, plus this was a great opportunity to take Debbie somewhere exotic, as she'd never been abroad before. On the day of our wedding, everything went as planned and although it was the middle of winter, everyone turned up and a good time was had by all. Then after the reception Debbie and I spent what was left of the night at the hotel, before being whisked away in the early morning to catch our flight.

Going from an industrial city in the middle of a dull overcast English winter, to a picturesque alpine valley with clear skies and sunshine was quite a shock and although I'd been to Mayrhofen before, everything appeared different; this time I was viewing through the eyes of an adult married man. To Debbie it was all totally new and probably felt as if she'd landed on another planet. Everything around her was alien, the country, the language, the money and the culture, but although strange, it was exciting and invigorating at the same time. We booked into our hotel, dumped our luggage and went off to explore this new world. February is a great time to visit Austria, everything is so breathtakingly beautiful, and it's no wonder that Debbie was blown away by it all. Just ordering a meal became an adventure in itself, from deciphering the menu to the taste of the food.

There's something about this part of Europe that's so phenomenal when it comes to eating. They make every meal seem like a gastronomic feast, each dish is a masterpiece deserving nothing but the best in service and presentation, something that, in my opinion, is sadly lacking in mainstream Britain and North America. We're always so busy; we never take the time to appreciate our food. Instead we look on it as putting coal into the furnace, and just swallow down so that we can get back to whatever we were doing as fast as possible. Pity though, that in our mentality we put our work first and our metabolism second!

"But not here" and it wasn't only the food that people took their time over, it was everything. Everybody appeared a lot more relaxed and content than the people back home, with an appreciation of life that was so contagious, that Debbie and I couldn't help but feel welcome regardless of the language difference. As neither of us could ski, we spent the majority of our time sightseeing and on a day trip to Salzburg, we even got to visit Mozart's birthplace & the Von Trapp house, (from the Sound of Music). Salzburg's a city steeped in history and character that was overwhelming to visit. But all too soon, it was time to leave the hospitality of Austria behind and return to the mundane reality of home, which was by then, a two-bedroom apartment that I'd moved into (move #9) a few months earlier. It was to be our new love nest, but sorry to say we were not alone, my mother was there too! Mom, (who as you may recall had been shipped back to Nottingham a few years earlier to open a grocery shop with my brother) was now back in Birmingham and knowing her luck, you can probably guess what happened! But I will digress and tell you anyway.

As planned they opened, their shop right in the middle of Nottingham's busiest industrial area, a perfect location, especially as they offered a variety of fresh cut sandwiches, a hit with the lunch crowd and a great opportunity for growth. For some unknown reason, mom was sent back to her old canteen job at the Raleigh Bicycle factory, leaving Gordon and Stella (his wife) to run the shop by themselves and here's where things get interesting! Stella didn't like serving customers and hated making sandwiches for them! Every time Gordon went out, she'd begrudgingly serve anyone who came into the shop and would even lock the door, if she got the chance, to keep them out! Grocery was not her bag... get it, grocery bag... never mind.

What she really wanted to sell was 'Baby Clothes' ("they'd attract a better kind of clientele" she said) and although it took her eighteen months to do it, she eventually succeeded in persuading Gordon to agree with her. They got rid of all the food and grocery items and restocked the shop with an assortment of baby clothing and accessories instead! 'Not surprisingly' six months later they were holding their "Closing Down" sale, having failed miserably! They were deep in debt and tied to a five-year lease, with three years still to go, but lucky for them the lease was in mom's name only, so she was the one that got stuck with having to pay it off over the next three years. Gordon and his family however, managed to move back to Birmingham and get themselves a little house, while mom on the other hand was now totally penniless and without a home, so the only thing she could do was to move in with me. Now back to my story...

With the honeymoon over, life returned to normal. Debbie went back to her job at the hairdressers and I went back to packing our Nation's history. Besides all the treasures at my place of work, the building itself contained another place of interest, the rehearsal studios for one of Britain's favorite 'Soaps' at that time "Crossroads" (similar to Coronation Street).

Often the stars of the show would pay us a visit; Noele Gordon, Benny and Miss Diane etc., extremely well known actors in Britain. They came to see all the fascinating items we had waiting to be shipped and, boy, we all felt extremely privileged to be able to chat so informally with them. For me it was my first close encounter of the 'celebrity kind' and little did I know then, but this was just the beginning of many more to come! "Yep" life was perfect – I was happily married, had a nice car, a great job and was again making ends meet, etc., etc... Then came the bad news.

The company I worked for had been taken over and the new owners had decided to centralise everything into their London office, which meant closing down the Birmingham branch, and so we were all given our three months notice. Another job bites the dust! Luckily for me, one aspect that I had gained from my job was a keen interest in antiques and history. Often Debbie and I ventured to London on weekends, accompanied by my friend Bob and his girlfriend Judy, to visit some of the museums. One visit of note was the famous 'Tutankhamen' exhibition at the British Museum, which was truly magnificent and left a lasting impression on my mind. It also began a future fascination with Egypt and its history. Besides visiting the museums, we always made time to visit the trendy places too, especially the famous Carnaby Street and it's unique boutiques. After all, this was the "flower power" era and 'Beatle mania' was in full swing.

I'll side track again for a minute, to tell you about the time we were parked outside the 'Beatles' recording studio in Savile Row. We all froze when a taxi pulled up and Ringo got out. The four of us then watched in awe as he proceeded through the studio's front door, none of us having the nerve to get out and ask him for his autograph. We did, however, find the courage to rummage through the garbage cans outside before we left, and found a letter that had been sent to John Lennon from an Arabian Prince, and would you believe, it was scribbled all over with John's doodling. Unfortunately for me I can't remember what I did with the thing, sob! I still have a photo somewhere of me walking across the pedestrian crossing in Abbey Road, without shoes of-course, so that I could copy Paul from the famous Abbey Road album cover. But I'm digressing, so lets go back to Carnaby Street and the point of my story.

One of my favourite stores was number 9, "Lord Kitcheners Valet," and throughout our numerous visits we had become friends with Simon, one of the managers there, and this is where the luck comes in! After being given my notice at work, Debbie and I decided to have one more trip to London, which of course had to include Carnaby Street and we arrived at #9 just as Simon was on his way to lunch at 'Cranks' a trendy vegetarian restaurant of high repute, and he invited us to join him. We eagerly accepted, as this was a new experience for us, we'd never been to a totally vegetarian restaurant before and we couldn't wait to see what it was like. We weren't disappointed. Regardless of the food the atmosphere alone was well worth the visit, everything about the place epitomised the swinging sixties and early seventies. I didn't see Austin Powers there, but did spot one of Britain's top comedians Dick Emery, quietly dining at a corner table and again I was too timid to approach him for his autograph, something that would be rectified in my future.

Thankfully, the food was as good as the surroundings, and it was while we were eating that I informed Simon I was about to lose my job, and the dilemma I had of what to do next. To my surprise, he suggested something that seriously aroused my attention!

Knowing how much I loved his shop, Simon explained how things had slowed down considerably in London and because of it; he had a lot of surplus stock that he would be willing to sell to me at very good price, if I was interested in opening a store of my own. 'Absobloodylutely - I was interested,' and I couldn't get the thought of it out of my mind. All the way home, I dreamt how great it would be to open a Carnaby style store in Birmingham. The only problem was how could I buy the stock, when we'd just spent all the money we had on our honeymoon. I needed money and fast, but from where? What were my options? My mother was now broke so that was out, I had no collateral to get a loan and I couldn't mortgage my house as I didn't have one, so what did I have of value? The two things I treasured most were my wife and my car, I couldn't sell Debbie; I'm not that kind of guy, so the only thing left was my car. "Gulp." It had taken me three years to build my way up to a fairly new and expensive model and now if I wanted to work for myself it had to go.

So go it did. Now I had the money, my next step was to find a shop and of course I mustn't forget those three important points, location, location and location. Thanks to Debbie's little Austin Mini, I still had wheels to get around and I set off to explore the trendy areas of town for any 'For Rent' signs. After the usual disappointments such as places being too expensive or in the wrong area, I heard of a unique complex being built right in the centre of downtown, called the 'Oasis', which would be comprised of individual shops inside one large four floor building, something that is quite common in England today but back then it was the first of its kind in Birmingham. On further investigation I discovered the building was to be portioned into sixty units of approximately 300 sq. ft. each, that would then be rented out to small retail businesses, as long as they complied with the criteria laid down by the building's owners. Each tenant would be required to build their own store front and interior, in-keeping with the concept of an up-scale market of individually crafted boutiques. This was only a slight drawback, considering how the rent was affordable and the location was fantastic. After meeting with the manager I signed my lease and became the proud owner of unit G40.

My timing was perfect; being one of the first people there I was able to obtain a prime position right next to the coffee bar. Waiting for the building itself to be finished and the remaining units let seemed endless, but eventually we were given the go-ahead to commence construction of our own stores. This was the green light we had all been waiting for and hundreds of people suddenly descended on the complex. Like ants in a colony, everyone got busy doing their our own unique piece to complete this giant puzzle. Quickly the labyrinth of stores and corridors took shape, each store's design was a statement to the world of who they were, as like myself, most were venturing out on their own for the first time and they were all determined to make an impact, by being as creative as they could. What a cosmopolitan group we were; Market Traders, Craft makers, Artists, Hippies, Designers, Tinkers, Tailors and Candlestick makers, plus of course the all important 'Poster & Novelty' store, my contribution to the mix.

For once I must admit that my transition into self-employment had been considerably smooth and everything had fallen into place perfectly. My job had come to an end a few weeks prior to the completion of the Oasis, allowing me the time to acquire the stock that I needed, and the sale of my car gave me £500 ($1000) to buy it with! {Not bad considering that you could buy a new Mini back then for £700} After paying £107 to cover my deposit and the first month's rent, I was off to London to see what I could get, and with Simon's help I was able to obtain most of my merchandise on a consignment basis, (sale or return). He also introduced me to numerous other stores in Carnaby St. that also had surplus stock, and they too assisted me in my venture. I struck gold, when another store I loved closed down and I managed to grab lots of great stuff from them, including a printing press to do mock 'Wanted Dead or Alive' posters and comic newspapers that were great fun!

Now that I had all my stock, I began the construction of my storefront. The years of working in a variety of jobs had paid off; now a jack-of-all-trades, I knew where to obtain all the items I needed at the lowest price and I had the know-how to assemble it all. Slowly but surely the store took shape and I was fortunate in finding a classic Victorian bay window amongst the bric-a-brac at a second-hand yard, to use for my shop window, then some wood, nails and elbow-grease completed the package and finally the store was finished! 'Trouble was' there were now only 3 days left to the grand opening and I still had to install, display and price all the stock! Two 18-hour days and one all-nighter soon took care of that and I was ready on time, well the shop was ready,

I on the other hand looked like crap!

The opening day was a "Grand event" with one of the BBC's top radio and T/V personalities, Pete Murray there to cut the ribbon. Once cut, our celebrity then entered the building accompanied by the management and a host of interested media, with hundreds of would-be customers hot-on-their-heels, and all of them were heading in my direction! Tired and nervous I prepared a 'Wanted Poster' to give to Pete Murray when he came into my shop, but sorry to say in my haste I spelled his name wrong, (Pete Murry fig.3).

Luckily for me, he cordially accepted it anyway and after a polite bit of chit-chat he was off to the next shop. 'Posterity Posters' (as I called myself) was now officially open for business! Looking back, what a day it must have been, everyone there had worked all through the night on last minute details, leaving no time to shave, change or put on make-up - what a way to meet your first paying customers!!! The long days, little sleep and endless trips to London were finally over, and it was time to knuckle-down to the reality of running my own business. One of the conditions of the lease was to ensure that your shop was open and staffed during the stores scheduled hours of operation, 6 days a week, which meant that on Debbie's day off, she would have to run the store while I went to London to purchase whatever stock we needed. In addition to Debbie, I also required extra help for the busy periods like lunchtime and weekends. This I accomplished with the recruitment of friends and family; a good thing too as most of my time was taken up on the printing press, doing 'Wanted Posters' and the 'Comic Newspaper Headlines' that had become such a great success.

Only I soon found out, that it wasn't such a "good thing" after all, when a progression of theft and cash shortages finally made me realise that familiarity really does breed contempt and hiring family and friends just doesn't work. (If only I had remembered that in the years to come.)

It seemed the only true friend I had was Bob who'd helped me with the construction, but he already had a job and I couldn't afford to give him the full-time position he needed, so I decided to advertise and eventually I ended up with good part time staff that enabled me to expand. Within a year I managed to acquire the lease of another unit and opened my second store. 'Posterity' became dedicated to posters and printing which also included T-shirts, and everything else was put into my new shop 'Odyssey' which had a great window position next to one of the main entrances.

They say hard work never kills anyone, but it was beginning to take its toll on the two of us. I hardly ever saw Debbie, as we were both so busy working and on her days off I was always in London. Even on a Sunday you'd find me in the shops decorating and re-arranging displays, and when the cat's away the mice will play! Little did I know, but one of my other 'so called' friends, Tony, was using this time to his advantage. You can probably guess the rest and you'd be right!

Though only married two and a half years, Debbie and I had been together for seven and it was time for the inevitable seven year itch! Sorry to say, I too was no angel and prior to being married I had strayed a few times myself, so now I suppose it was Debbie's turn. On returning home one night, the only welcome I got was from our dog, Judy, (my mother had since moved into a pensioner's apartment). Then I found the note, Debbie had gone and was not coming back! Honestly, I hadn't got the foggiest idea of why and my first thought was to call her parents, but they were as much in the dark as I was, so next I called my friend Bob, who then informed me about the gossip he'd heard but hadn't paid much attention to. This I needed to know more about and I immediately went to see him. Once there, Bob explained to me about the affair between Debbie and Tony and after my initial denial, rage set in and I had to find out more. All my other friends only confirmed Bob's story, complete with all the gory details –I might add. Whether driven by love or ego, I was determined to find her.

My only clue was that she'd quit her job and was working in a Pub somewhere, Tony being too scared to join her in case his parents found out. (Poor widdle guy!) For 3 days I searched every possible lead without success. I wasn't eating and had hardly slept, I was also in trouble at the Oasis for not opening my shops correctly, but this I managed to fix by giving the staff overtime and I continued on in my quest... Debbie, in the meantime, had heard of my frantic searching and decided to give me a call. She told me she was a barmaid at a small hotel in Knowle (a small village near Birmingham) and that she was alone and just needed some time to think about her future. What she didn't know, was that Mr. Jones (her father) and my brother Ronnie, had already paid Tony a visit and he'd denied all knowledge of their relationship. Obviously only in it for what he could get, he had no intention of standing by her.

Although Debbie had asked me to stay away from her, I just couldn't, so one night, my dog Judy and I decided to go for a drive and we just happened to be driving through Knowle when Judy thought it would be good idea to look through the pub windows of Debbie's work, something I was reluctant to do, but the dog talked me into it. There, to our surprise, was Tony sitting by the bar and to make matters worse, Debbie was sitting on his lap! "Pow" the next thing I remember was knocking Tony to the floor, throwing Debbie over my shoulder and walking back to the car, while Judy ran around us barking frantically. I thrust Debbie into the car losing one of her shoes, dumped Judy on her lap and drove home... Later that night Debbie's father came to see her and informed her of his meeting with Tony, and after a few phone calls Debbie was able to see for herself that everything Tony had promised her had been nothing but a pack of lies. After a lot of tears and deliberation, we decided to start afresh and a few weeks later things returned to normal, with one exception- now we both worked together in the shops. (fig.4)

Back to my old routine again, occasionally on my weekly excursions to London I would go by train, something I enjoyed immensely, especially having a meal in the dining car. On my return to Birmingham's New Street Station after one of these trips, I noticed a street trader selling 'Indian love beads', his arms full of hundreds of the tiny bead necklaces. "Get your love beads 20 pence each," he cried. Twenty pence, that's exactly what I was paying for them wholesale! This required further investigation, I thought, and I persuaded him to join me for a coffee. Whilst chatting he seemed very interested in the Oasis, so I invited him to visit my shops and off we went.

On the way, I discovered his name was Jerry and, from Ireland, he'd come to England to seek his fortune, where with his love of life and gift of the gab he'd managed to wheel and deal his way into some of London's cheapest importers. From them he was able to buy large amounts of stock to sell on the streets for a quick profit, hence the love beads! He was certainly right about one thing, he had a personality that could charm the birds from the trees and that was something that I sadly lacked.

I'd become so bogged down with running two shops, buying goods, scheduling staff, bookkeeping, repairs and fixing my marriage that I'd lost my personality completely. In fact, I was now so stressed about the amount of theft I was having in my shops that I'd become quite paranoid too, and it wasn't just stock. After returning from an earlier buying trip I discovered the whole day's proceeds had been taken from the cash register. In its place was a note from one of my brothers, saying that he'd taken the cash to buy an exhaust system for his car as he couldn't tell his wife that he needed one, due to their financial problems! So something had to be done. Perhaps meeting Jerry was an opportunity to do just that; maybe it was time to take a partner? The idea of combining my retail stability with his contacts thrilled Jerry, and partners we became. Jerry's love of people prompted him to continue some street trading, but this time he was also promoting our shops, plus now I had the added bonus of alternating the weekly buying trips to London with him, taking the burden of buying everything off my shoulders.

By now the Oasis was at its peak, attracting more and more of Birmingham's fashion conscious trend setters who thought the store was incredible, as did I, so let me take you for a quick tour...

Upon entering the complex, your nose was instantly assaulted by the myriad of perfumed aromas pervading up from dozens of burning incense-sticks. Before your eyes, lay a conglomeration of handcrafted oddities that we called shops, each one different, from the sublime to the ridiculous, each making a statement of what was concealed inside. Walk into a giant boot to find the cobbler's array of platform shoes and thigh length boots and across from him there's a giant lizard made of paper-mache, where inside you'd find leather clothes and bags made from alligator skins, the latest rage!

Next, you could enter a cave to experience the wonders of aromatherapy and essential oils, and then into an enormous stereo system, where you could purchase the latest Beatles album or get a cool tattoo from his neighbour and so it went. Each boutique carried the latest in outrageous clothing, from cheesecloth shirts, mini skirts, hot pants and bell bottom hipster's to elaborate sari's, goodies of every kind, hats, pottery, tie-dye fashions, woodwork, plants, books, handmade jewellery, decorative artwork, posters, sew-on patches, handmade candles, chainbelts, lava lamps, uni-sex hairdressing and used clothing-to-die for. (fig.5)

A 'Hippies' paradise to put it mildly, but for those of you who are prudish, beware... we broke all the traditional boundaries with our healing work, reflexology, reiki, yoga, massage therapy and tarot card reading, which also opened us up to rumours of immorality, drug trading and sex orgies (if only). Thus, we were given a wide berth by the narrow-minded and most senior citizens! I never saw any orgies but some of the drug trading stories may have been well founded. If so, they were done covertly; however, drug use itself was not. The rampant use of drugs led to dozens of humorous and embarrassing incidents and the adjoining clothing store next to mine was no exception, a double unit specialising in the latest and most outrageous fashions. It was staffed by a continually changing array of scantily clad young females, who would often call upon me to assist them as they were frequently stoned; one of them had probably fainted or was going though the trauma of a bad trip. My sober personality came in handy then and I was always the one they came to in times of trouble. Even out of work I was frequently being phoned in the early hours of the morning, to rescue someone that had woken up to find themselves miles from home, or had been in an argument with their lover and needed a place to crash for the night. Unfortunately, the next morning I'd awake and find them gone along with my stereo or some other valued possession. (You're supposed to live & learn, but I never did.)

Most days at the 'Oasis' were like observing scenes from 'Rowan & Martins Laugh In', constantly hoping that nobody was going to sock it to me!

Somehow underneath all this psychedelic hullabaloo it was business as usual and things were going great for me. I started working on Sunday's, selling at outdoor festivals and markets. Jerry too, including selling 'Love beads' at the British version of Woodstock! Having joined forces we were able to double the size of the 'Odyssey' shop to incorporate cheesecloth shirts and also open a third smaller unit specialising in hand made jewellery. Also, there was a craze at the time for girls to wear giant multicoloured plastic bead chokers and on one of Jerry's field trips; he met a guy who owned a plastics factory. He discovered his new friend could manufacture these large beads at an incredible low price, so subsequently we entered into the manufacturing business.

There was only one little problem, we needed someone to drill a hole through the plastic beads and thread them onto the elastic, so another new word entered my vocabulary "out-worker". This was someone who was willing to assemble our product in the comfort of their own home and get paid a fee on the quantity they produced. Then within a short time we had enough orders to keep eight families busy constructing our chokers, (including my brother Gordon's). On completion, the chokers were separated into their individual colours and bagged into dozens, and then Jerry or I would pick them up and deliver them to various wholesalers around the country.

But since fashions come and go, six months later our large

bead chokers had gone the way of the Do-do. Not wanting to lose our new found status we tried a succession of other weird and wonderful jewellery items, including bending horse shoe nails and forming them into pendant's, which we would then chrome plate and hang on leather thronging. These were quite successful, but hard to make in enough quantity to wholesale.

Then we had an IDEA! Why don't we make smaller plastic beads and thread them onto thonging instead of elastic. 'Brilliant!' So we made several dozen samples and gave them to our wholesalers to see what the reaction would be and within a few weeks we had our result. People loved the beads, but found the fastening system of tied sliding knots inconvenient and awkward, our new invention was halfway there. - 'What to do?'

While at home one night, I was putting some quartz pendants onto silver chains and wished that the leather was as easy to fasten as the chains were. I had tried putting a procession of hooks, split-rings and other fasteners on the leather, but it always ended up splitting, but that night I tried crimping tiny springs onto the end of the leather, and bent the other end of the spring up so that I could attach a hook and 'Hey Presto' it worked!

My next step was to find a manufacturer that made springs the size we needed, and as luck would have it, there was one in Birmingham. Jerry and I went to see them and as usual Jerry managed to get them to supply us with just what we needed and at a good price.

With the fastening problem solved, we had another idea! Instead of the small plastic beads, why not put on wooden ones, they look more classy. While we're at it, let's make the thonging just choker length. We also placed small metal washers between the wood beads to achieve different effects and guess what, it worked. They looked terrific! Off Jerry went again to find a supplier of washers, which of course he did, then our next step was to take the bags of springs and washers to the factory that plated our horseshoe nails and get them nickel-plated. It looked better and stopped the metal from tarnishing. For nights we toiled, designing and making dozens of samples, then off Jerry went to give them to our wholesalers and once more we waited to see what the reaction would be. But not for long! Phone call, after phone call confirmed we had a winner, (the choker was born!) and a few weeks later we had twenty families of out-workers, working around the clock to keep up with the demand. DEMAND was an understatement - we had inquiries from all over the United Kingdom!

We were so busy that Bob and I took a trip over to Holland to obtain a new supplier of wooden beads as we were exhausting all the ones we had in England. Even getting the leather was becoming harder, we were using leather shoelaces as they were the right length for chokers and had little plastic ends that made it easier to thread on the beads. Jerry and I ended up working flat out to keep the production going! But hang on a minute, if Jerry and I were working flat out on the chokers, who was minding the store? A good question, considering that Debbie was now five months pregnant!

A year had passed since her little adventure and we both had agreed it was time to have a baby, so it wasn't right to expect her to run everything at the Oasis, so something had to go! 'Odyssey' went first and 'Posterity' scaled down dropping the 'Wanted Posters' and concentrating on the T-shirt printing and a new addition 'Photo Badges' (your image on a badge), while our little store concentrated on selling just our chokers. With one shop less to worry about, Jerry and I concentrated more on the chokers and the sales went through the roof. Everyone was wearing them, we even saw people on television wearing them, maybe it was thanks to my old friend from 'Crossroads', Noele Gordon, who had also become one of our happy customers by then. Occasionally I would personally make up unique designs for her and some other celebrities. For instance I made some for the members of the 'the Move' and 'ELO' as their drummer Bev Bevan owned a record store across from us in the Oasis. Others of note were ones I made for the famous Welsh singer, Ivor Emanuel (a cousin of Debbie's father). He loved them, but I had to use leather sewing machine belting to make his, as it was thicker and more masculine and instead of wooden beads, I used things like gold and silver plated metal balls. - I believe he even sent one of them as a gift to his friend Harry Belafonte.

With sales skyrocketing you'd think we would be living the good life, but not really. Neither Jerry nor I were having much of a life at all, constantly travelling around Britain we had little time to stop and smell the flowers. We were getting physically worn out and I, for one, needed a break. I decided it was time to take a holiday. 'Budget Rent a Car' was advertising something new in England, motor-homes (RV's) and I managed to rent the largest one they had to take Debbie and my mother on an adventure touring Europe. Everything was arranged, Jerry would look after the production side and we employed a manager to look after the shops. Just prior to leaving, Debbie and I decided to go to the movies, stopping on the way at the stores to collect the day's cash. I put the £180 in my briefcase, then after a bite to eat we were off to see 'The Exorcist.' I parked my car outside the cinema and being a convertible I took great care to hide my briefcase in the boot (trunk) for safety. I didn't want to forget it, by leaving it on the floor of the cinema. After the movie as we walked back to the car, I noticed that the trunk didn't seem to be closed properly and sorry to say I was right, it had been prized open and my briefcase was gone. Not only was the money gone but our birth certificates, passports and travel tickets too, plus some other cherished personal items. This is where I lost my birth certificate, the only thing I had with my father's signature. This, of course, created another problem; since we were due to leave in 5 days! And I don't know how I did it, but miraculously I managed to get copies of everything we needed and we got away on time...

Starting in France, we ventured out to visit Germany, Belgium, Luxembourg and finally Holland from which we took the ferry back to England and although Debbie was over seven months pregnant, we all had a fantastic time and a well-needed rest! It was pretty late when we finally arrived home, so we went straight to bed. The next morning I was awakened by a 'phone call from the manager of the Oasis complex, who was calling to complain that our shops were not open and that the staff were standing outside, unable to get in! That's weird, I thought, and with Jerry busy in London, I immediately set off to find out the problem. Once there I soon discovered that the guy we had employed to manage both stores had disappeared, together with a week's cash, which he should have banked while we were away. I couldn't believe it, the holiday had ended the way it began, with us being robbed! I swore then and there, that I would never watch 'The Exorcist' ever again.

Besides having to cope with the loss, I wondered who was going to manage the stores now? Debbie was heavily pregnant and regrettably Jerry couldn't do it as he'd decided to go off on his own again. He was missing his carefree life and wanted to explore pastures new. Don't worry, we hadn't fallen-out, it was just time for him to move on; his restless spirit had been confined long enough! Now back on my own again with no Jerry and no manager, I wondered what the hell was going on, it couldn't be because of the movie could it? Anyway, I had to make changes and fast. After closing down the small shop, I tried looking after the last remaining store myself, but I knew with all my wholesaling commitments, I would need to find some extra help. I invested some money into a hippy friend of mine and bought him a used car, so that he could help me supply the out-workers and do some deliveries.

Things settled down once more and on the 11th of October, 1974, Samantha was born! (After a seven-hour labour). Mother and baby were fine and the proud daddy got busy driving around to tell everyone of our new addition to the family. This also gave me the opportunity to show off my other new addition to the family, my beautiful new 'E.type Jaguar! I was so overjoyed and preoccupied with the new baby, (and new car) I'd forgot to watch my back. Unfortunately, I discovered that my hippie friend had been stealing half my supplies to give to his friends, who would then make chokers to sell and split the money between them to buy drugs. This was getting bloody ridiculous. Who the heck could I trust?

I was in need of help again. "How about Bob?" I said

to Debbie, and as we hadn't seen him for weeks, we decided to visit him at his parents. When we got there, I was surprised by the solemn attitude of his father, but I soon discovered why when he informed us that Bob was dead! "Pull the other one – its got bells on," I said, but he wasn't kidding. Bob had died a week earlier of a drug overdose. 'Boy when it rains, it pours!' We were dumbstruck! How come no one told us? It appeared that they couldn't find our new phone number, as we had moved into a new house a month earlier and since Bob was the only one who knew where we lived, there was nothing they could do.

Losing Bob was the final straw. I decided to close Posterity and my days at the Oasis were finally over. The Oasis itself had become a huge open planned market by then anyway. Most of the unique and individualistic shops had gone, having lost their struggle to keep up with the ever increasing rent. So had the flamboyant store fronts. They had been ripped down by the hordes of market traders who were now moving in. Posterity closing was just one more casualty of progress. With the shops gone, I put all my attention into manufacturing the chokers, which were still selling well having incorporated many new designs, including ceramic beads from Greece, glass beads from Italy and amazing money beads from Africa. (Money beads are the beautiful glass beads that were used by the slave-traders to purchase slaves.)

Because of their continued success, it didn't take long before I was burning the candle at both ends again. Each morning and evening I would visit the out-workers to give them supplies and pick up finished stock. During the day, I had to buy any materials needed and get anything metal plated, then I'd do all the deliveries, to cities like London, Manchester and Bristol.' Phew' and I was just about to crack-up when along came Mr. Singh! Mr. Singh was a middleman, who said that if I would lower my price, he would buy everything I produced and do all the selling himself. Lower my price? It was already pretty low, averaging out about £2.00 a dozen, though it was costing me a lot in expenses to deliver everything and it would be nice to just concentrate on the manufacturing. "It's a deal," I said, and I decided to give him a try. Things turned out extremely well and I loved having time to spend with Debbie and Samantha. So well, in fact, that Debbie and I had time to go on an amazing adventure!

It was a once in a lifetime opportunity. Nigel, another close friend of mine, had a brother called Ivor, who was a little mentally disabled. Ivor, who was a movie fanatic, had been in correspondence with the people at 'Pinewood Film Studios' for many years and because of it, he'd received an invitation for him and three friends to go on a personal guided tour of the entire studios!!! So he asked Nigel, Debbie and me to join him. (Thank-you, thank-you!) Arriving by train, there was a car waiting for us at the local station to take us to the studio. Once there, we were greeted by the head of security and together we went off to explore every aspect of film making, from set-building, wardrobe, cinematography to editing- everything.

The film sets were fantastic! First we found ourselves surrounded by the world of 'James Bond (007)' and various bits of Bond movies lay all around us. From space rockets to fake Islands, it was all there. Next we were taken onto the giant film set where 'Chitty Chitty Bang Bang' had been made, a few years earlier. Then it was off to 'The Battle of Britain' set, which was littered with pieces of old Spitfire aircraft, that had been left over from the epic. Next we were taken to a personal favourite of mine, the famous English comedy film classics of the 'The Carry On' movies. There I was. Standing in one of the very doorways from 'Carry on up the Khyber.' I could hardly believe it myself. But that was nothing compared to the biggest set of them all, as we entered the world of 'Sherlock Holmes.' (fig.6) Who by the way, is in some way related to me!

My father told me that the character of Sherlock Holmes, was based on a past relative of ours. It seems that when Arthur Conan Doyle was learning medicine in Edinburgh, one his professors was a Dr. Bell, and Dr. Bell had an amazing power of deduction. He could deduce everything about a student just by looking him over. This ability fascinated Conan Doyle, and he thought what it might be like if a crime detective, had the same powers of deduction as Dr. Bell, and from that Sherlock Holmes was born! (The rest is history.) But fictitious or not, I now found myself standing in the doorway of number 221b Baker Street, which by the way, is just a tiny section of a gigantic Victorian set the size of a small town. Faithfully reproduced and complete with genuine cobblestone roads, it has been used for hundreds of period movies, by film companies from all over the world. "Absolutely magnificent to see."

Our next stop was the prop department, equal in size to an aircraft hanger and then after one final stop at the editing rooms it was back to 'Pinewood House' for tea. Our heads were still spinning with the wonder of it all, as we said our good-byes and boarded the private bus that would take us back to the station. While on the journey I chatted with one of the other passengers, an actor by the name of Freddie Jones. 'What a day' and one that I will never forget and I still feel tremendously privileged to have had the opportunity of experiencing it all, thank-you again Ivor for making it all possible!

Now back to my work! My arrangement with Mr. Singh appeared to be working out fine. Once a week he would arrive to pick up all my stock and within three days I would receive payment in full. Because he was living in Manchester, he was not always able to get to Birmingham, so in order to maintain the supply I would send all the completed chokers to him by train, and he would then send the payment back three days later by courier. Then one day he telephoned me to tell me he'd received the largest order for chokers he'd ever got, so could I step up production and have as many chokers as possible ready for the next pick up. The following week he telephoned me again and told me that he couldn't make it down and to ship everything out by train as usual. Three days later, the courier didn't arrive with the money, so I telephoned his apartment several times to find out why, but each time to no avail. Things just didn't feel right, so I jumped in my car and sped off to Manchester.

Going directly to his apartment, I discovered it had been vacated, so I asked his neighbours if they knew where he was and they told he had moved out three days earlier, and no one knew where he had gone. "Jesus H. Christ." Everything I had was tied up in that sale. With my heart pounding in my chest I went to see the Police, who then pointed out a slight problem. Just in and around that area of England alone, there would have been approximately 1,000 Mr. Singh's and every one of them had a beard and wore a turban. "It would be like looking for a needle in a haystack," they said! Extremely shattered, I drove back home to lick my wounds and to figure out what to do next. I'd sent him every thing I had, over £1,000 worth, a lot of money back then. In fact it was half of all I had, and now I was left with £1,000 and a big decision. I decided to leave it to fate, and telling everyone of my dilemma, I left it up to them to tell me what they wanted!

Number 1, they could wait for their money, so that I could use what I had left to go back into production, that way they could carry on earning, or #2, they could take what they were owed, leaving me virtually broke and unable able to continue, and leaving them without further income. Human nature being what it is, 90% wanted the money. So be it! That's what I did; I was now as free as a bird again, but with little money left to fly. As for the chokers themselves? They went on to sweep the world, eventually to be copied by large fashion jewellery manufacturing groups in Countries like India and China. "Imitation is the most sincerest form of flattery," they say and even today when I see a choker on display somewhere, I look to see if it has springs at the ends and I think to myself "if they only knew!"

Oh-well, at least I still had one consolation from my business left, my Daimler Jaguar XJ6, (fig.7) having recently traded in my E-Type, to accommodate all of Samantha's paraphernalia, pram, carry cot, buggy etc. The only question now was, "What to do?"

I was living in England's second biggest city, which I knew like the back of my hand, so why not utilise this knowledge? After-all, it was the era of the minicab, where drivers were able to use their own cars as taxis, (using a two-way radio booking system that bypassed the licensed taxi by-laws) and I had a car, and I knew the city. So I enrolled myself with a local company and set out on my first nights work. You'd never believe the looks on peoples faces, when I turned up in a new Jaguar XJ6, something they had never seen used as a cab before. Boy it was fun.

Every-time I picked up a client they would take one look at the car and think it was some kind of 'Candid Camera' trick! The only way I could convince them I was the real thing, was to show them my two-way radio. But as fun as it was, the novelty soon wore off, and after a succession of late nights and one too many drunks, I decided it was time to find something else, though my taxi work would not be in vain. Once more fate played a hand. One of my pick-ups had been at the County Hotel in Walsall, and it was there and then that I wondered what it would be like to manage such a place as that. So be careful what you wish for; little did I know it then, but six years later I would become the General Manager of that very Hotel!

Chapter Three

The End of an Era

A successful marriage isn't finding the right person; it's being the right person!

The idea of running a hotel kept playing on my mind. I was sure that I'd be good at doing something like that. After all, it was in my blood. (Mom & dad met in the service industry). After consulting with Debbie to get her feedback, (OK) I began to make inquiries on how we could get started. Visiting various hotels and talking with their staff, I was advised to get a copy of a monthly magazine called the 'Hotel & Caterer' and check out the employment section, which I did. Inside the magazine I found dozens of jobs I liked, but neither Debbie nor I had the work experience required to get any of them. It appeared that the only way in was at the ground floor. Thumbing back through the vacancies, I found only one company advertising for management trainees, 'Chef & Brewer' (a hotel and pub chain) that luckily had their training centre in Studley, only 25 miles from Birmingham. To make a long story short, we applied, were accepted and given a date to start... With the job now secure our next step was to inform our family and friends of our decision, from which, I received an overwhelming vote of no confidence.

"You'll never do it," they said, "you've been your own boss for far too long." "You could never accept such a menial position!" Like waving a red flag in front of a bull, their comments only made me more determined to prove them all wrong. But first I had to convince my mother to move back in with us to look after Samantha. This was no problem as she hated living alone, and once we'd got her settled in, Debbie and I were ready to take the first step of our new career and we reported for work. The training centre turned out to be an extremely old flour mill, converted into a fully operational Inn and Restaurant called "The Old Washford Mill". So old, in fact, that it is recorded in the 'Dooms Day Book,' an ancient historical document that was actually a census manuscript of 1066 AD. Situated on the banks of the Arrow River, the Inn now housed a 100-seat restaurant, three bars and a snack buffet, all beautifully crafted around a giant waterwheel, encased by glass and the centrepiece of the building. Although the mill itself was long gone, the wheel was still turning, as a small lock system diverted some of the river's flow and sent it though the middle of the building. The entire complex was staffed by trainee couples, who depending on their abilities could work their way up, section by section, until they attained their ultimate goal of 'Assistant Managers' over the entire operation and eventually get promotion to one of the Company's Nationwide Hotels.

Against all odds: As we sat there at our introduction meeting, it appeared that the Inn's manager, was yet another person who had doubts that Debbie and I would make it'. After-all', as he said, "We didn't really have anything in common with the other couples." We didn't drink or smoke, we had a young baby and owned a car that even the Company's Directors would be envious of! Could we really do the 12-hour days that would be expected of us for the next two years? "Oh well, only time will tell," he said, and he was at least willing to give us a try. We were given a tour of the building and introduced to the other couples, after which he explained that we would be starting out as general help, to be used wherever needed until we'd mastered the basics. How fast we moved on was now up to us. All of the trainee couples lived on the premises, due to the low wage of just £25.00 ($50.00) per week each, except us.

We had chosen to drive the 25 miles home each night to be with our daughter. Our work hours were 9.am to 11.pm, with a two-hour break between 3.30 and 5.30.pm, five and a half days a week. This meant we got around 6 hours sleep per night when working. After one month we were given our own bar to run. Although the smallest, it was the one that housed the giant waterwheel, something that I alone would be expected to clean. What a job that was. It entailed damming the flow of water to stop the ten-foot high wheel and climbing onto it's dripping paddles to clean off all the slime. Once that was done I then had to polish its entire glass casing, inside and out. But wait, there's more! We were there in the middle of a very hot summer, so I had the added bonus of being accompanied by thousands of flies while I worked. Yuck! Another bonus of the summer season was doing the endless field trips around the grounds to collect all the empty glasses. This also entailed a little fishing, but not for sport; it was to retrieve the dozens of glasses that our "considerate customers" had thrown into the river.

Besides the fun of glass collecting and waterwheel washing, our typical day was as follows: Arriving at 9.am we would clean everything from the previous night and prepare the bar for opening: 10.am to 3.pm we were open for service. After another half an hour of washing glasses, we'd get a well-deserved break, usually spent sitting around trying to get cool. At 5.30.pm, we'd unlock the doors to let in the flood of customers that had been waiting patiently for us to open, and then it was service with a smile until 11.pm. (fig.8)

After counting the cash and praying it would balance, we did a quick tidy-up and then crawled to the car to head off on our journey home. We did get one and a half days a week off, but all too frequently they would disappear, taken up by various training seminars on beer making, health and safety rules etc., Plus I lost my afternoon break once a week, because all the guys had the arduous job of cleaning and sterilising all the draught beer lines. Altogether, taking into account the traveling time it averaged out to an 85-hour week, each! "Oh well! Welcome to the Hotel trade". During what little free time we did have, most of the couples would congregate together for a well-earned drink, smoke and chat, something that I frequently missed, though not through any rivalry. With no desire to drink or smoke, I'd leave Debbie to sit and chat while I kept myself busy rearranging our bar and making new displays, even to the extent of cutting up old wooden sherry and beer barrels to make unique arrangements. (Tip! Something that was duly noticed). Having survived the first three months, it was time for us to move on to our next assignment, 'the Snack Bar'.

I should have been really excited about the promotion, but it was the hottest summer in years and knowing that the snack bar's speciality was 'Chicken in-the Basket', I didn't relish the idea of cooking 50 chickens, dozens of burger's, hot dogs and thousands of french fries each day, all without any air-conditioning. (It might have spoiled the heritage) Luckily it was only for a month this time, as we were required to return there for another two months, later in our training. While Debbie did the serving, I did most of the cooking and instead of gaining weight around all that food - I lost 20 pounds. In fact most of our wages ended up going on deodorants and perfume, trying to mask the smell of all the grease that had become ingrained in our skin and clothing. 'Ugh!' After emptying enough buckets of chicken fat to fill a swimming pool and a succession of cleaning, cleaning and more cleaning our month was finally over. Both Debbie and I vowed never to eat chicken again, well for a few weeks anyway.

Our next challenge was to be 'the Saloon Bar', the Mill's biggest and so busy that we would need the help of part time staff. It didn't take long before Debbie and I discovered the true definition of the word 'panic'. On nights when an employee didn't turn up, which of course was always our busiest, the customers would just keep on coming as if drawn in by some invisible force. (How did they know?) Most of the time we had no idea of who it was we were serving, all we could see through the sweat streaming down over our eyes, was an endless stream of hands waiting to be filled! Handing over pint after pint of luke-warm beer and shots of liquor, our minds virtually exploded with calculations as we added up drink after drink, because sorry to say, there were no fancy cash registers for us to use back then! But amazingly we coped and as time went by, many of our customers commented to the manager on how well we ran the bar and the artful way I had of arranging the displays, so as you can guess, we moved on up in record time. 'Up' being the operative word, up to the 'Restaurant & Cocktail Bar' on the first floor. We should have been going back to the snack bar, but to our surprise we were moved upstairs instead.

Here we were, Debbie running the 'Cocktail Bar' and me assistant to the Chef. The Chef, like most artists was a little extroverted to say the least. The years of coping with endless trainees had taken it's toll and his bad temper was legendary. I think his first words to me were "If you think working in the snack bar was tough, it's a picnic compared to working with me." It didn't take me long to find out why. There was only one way of doing things, his way, and everything had to be perfect. Forget about answering him back, as he had a tendency of throwing his knives at people. True to his word he was a hard taskmaster, pushing me to the edge of breaking point. Many times I stormed out vowing never to return, but each time I'd end up going back, as I couldn't let him jeopardise my entire career. I was so relieved when the three-month training period with him was near its end, until I received the news, that Debbie and I were to stay where we were for another term, and that the other couples would be moved accordingly to accommodate us staying. WHY! Had my work been so bad that I'd have to repeat it all over again?

When the manager asked to see us, I was sure that we were in deep trouble. Instead of losing it, he explained that his daughter was getting married next month and the reception was to be at the Mill, which would entail a lot of work catering for the over 200 guests, especially for the Chef! The Chef however had agreed to do it, but on one condition, I had to stay with him for another period. The reason being, I was the best trainee he'd ever had and he knew that together we would be able to handle it. It seemed he had pushed me harder than anyone else, because he knew I could do it, (so that's why none of the other staff had felt like quitting). Just shows how wrong you can be. With renewed confidence the next few months were great and I learnt so much more from him, things that were to help me a great deal in the future and yes, the wedding was a great success. The extra restaurant period ended and again we were called into the office. This time the manager informed us that we had completed our training in record time, (having proved all his doubts wrong), also the company now had an opening for an assistant management couple at 'The Swan Hotel' in Bolton, and it was ours if we wanted it! We had 24 hours to think it over. If we accepted, the position would require us to live in at the Hotel and Bolton was a 2-hour drive from Birmingham. How would we visit mom and Samantha? Sam was now 23 months old. Personally we couldn't wait to get our own Hotel and this was just the next step toward that goal, an opportunity we couldn't refuse. We'd still be able to visit Samantha on our days off and she was getting on great with my mother, so I convinced Debbie to give it a try and we accepted the job!

Two weeks later we arrived in Bolton. The Swan Hotel was quite a formidable sight, a huge white heritage building adorned with black wooden beams. Debbie and I took a deep breath and went inside! We discovered that concealed within it's walls were, (are you ready?) 75 Bedrooms, 2 Restaurants, 3 Public Bars, 1 Cocktail Bar, 1 Cellar Bar, a Disco Club, a Snack Bar, a large Banqueting Hall and numerous meeting rooms. 'Oh', and a staff of over sixty full and part time employees, all of which we were there to run. "Help!" At least we'll have the Manager to help us, so we thought, until he informed us that he'd only been there two weeks himself and, having no previous Bar or Catering experience, was depending on us to give him guidance on what to do! A close friend had given him the job. 'Oh well, we're in at the deep-end again,' I thought,' But we'll soon get the hang of it and thing's couldn't be any harder than our training.' That was until I found out a whole new meaning to the word 'Breakfast!' Yes, breakfast, a seemingly ordinary word, but for me it meant my day would now begin at 6.am, as I was responsible to supervise the making and serving of up to 70 of the blooming things every day. Still, getting up early never killed anyone, right? Wrong! When 'breakfast' follows another little word called 'disco' it becomes a whole new ballgame.

Supervising the nightly disco meant I was kept busy until the early hours most days and was lucky if I got five hours sleep! But at least our wages had been increased, we now got £35.00 ($70.00) per week each, and all we had to do for this King's ransom was a mere 80 hours work each! Talk about your slave labour! Where was Abraham Lincoln when we needed him? "OK John, remember, one day you'll have a Hotel of your very own, so it's all worth it," and we do live in rent-free. As "Assistant Managers" we did get our own apartment... By-the-way, the apartment was a tiny section of the 200 year old attic, that had been converted into two tiny rooms, bedroom and living-room, {complete with ghost} sparsely furnished and gloomily decorated. We even had to share a bathroom with the hotel guests on the floor below. Not to worry though, the amount of hours we were working, we only ever got to use it for sleep.

After supervising the morning breakfasts, my next job was to restock all the bars ready for opening while Debbie helped the staff clean and prepare them. Most of Debbie's other duties were related to serving and reception, filling in wherever staff hadn't shown up. However, most of her evenings were spent back in her old position of running the Cocktail Bar. As for me, my days became an endless succession of problem solving. No matter what the situation, the assistant manager was called to the rescue, from irate customers whose bed was too soft, too hard, too small, or their room was too cold, too hot or too drafty. To my endless interventions of stopping the staff from killing each other over some work related disagreement. I was expected to have the answer to everything, from their working conditions, to their personal love life. On top of all this, one of my other duties was breaking up the inevitable bar fights that always took place at the weekends, though in most other pubs fights were a nightly event. Luckily for me, we were considered a Hotel of good standing and only had a few in comparison. As the months went on I soon realised that the saying 'one man's meat, is another man's poison' is only too true. The extreme diversity of the demands made by our customers, had me running round in circles, incessantly trying to please them and adhere to their every whim. I was often told, "the customer is always right", but they forgot to mention that some are also, stubborn, ill mannered, bad-tempered, greedy, arrogant and downright lazy as well. On the rare days when all the customers were happy, the staff would be at war with each other. One occasion I remember well, a waitress in our main restaurant was being harassed by one of the chefs, he continued on through the night until the poor girl could stand it no longer. She picked up a bowl of sherry trifle off the dessert trolley and plopped the whole thing, upside down, on the chef's head and stormed out! To make it more hilarious, it was an open plan grill area so the diners witnessed the whole thing. It's OK; I told them that there wouldn't be any extra charge for the cabaret.

On another night, one of our cocktail waitresses who had been drinking on the job was called upon to take a tray of drinks downstairs to some customers in the T/V lounge. After having 'one too many' she walked towards the circular stairway and tripped, falling over the banister and landing spread eagled on the floor below, surrounded by all the spilt drinks. She then got up, picked up her tray and proceeded back up the stairs to get another round, non-the worse for her ordeal. Don't worry, I sent her home in a taxi. Fun aside, life goes on and so did the day-to-day running of the Hotel, and with a few months behind us things had settled down into some kind of routine. Debbie's hours now averaged out to about 50+ a week, most of which were spent in the Cocktail Bar, but me, my hours were more like 90+ a week! Sorry to say just like when we had the shops, Debbie and I once again saw very little of each other and when we did, we were either sleeping or arguing, the long hours having taken their toll on our relationship.

We did still have our one and a half days off each week, but they were spent driving to and from Birmingham so that we could have a little time with Samantha. Emphasis on a little, by the time we got there, settled in and got a decent nights sleep, we'd get only a few hours with Sam, before it was time to journey back! We did get a nice surprise at Christmas, however, when the manager invited mom and Sam to stay at the Hotel over the holidays. Great for Debbie, but I saw very little of them, being extra busy with all the holiday festivities of 'Company Parties, Dinner Dances and Disco's', which were on top of all my usual duties. Plus I had even more drunks to deal with besides helping the staff with their love life problems. "Love Life!" What the hell was that? I began to wonder if I'd ever have one again, my whole life consisted of work, work and more work.

Don't get me wrong; I enjoyed my job very much, maybe too much. Debbie, on the other hand, did not. She missed the money and the fun we used to have running our own business, and she complained that I wasn't fun anymore, too serious and too busy all the time, striving to earn our own Hotel.

Our arguing got worse, then one morning in February, I woke up in an empty bed, Debbie was already up and gone! Gone was an understatement. She'd gone all right, not to work, but for good. Debbie had run away, but why? My first thought being that it was because she had crashed our car a few weeks earlier. I figured she felt guilty because we only had third party insurance and were unable to get our car repaired, but at least we could still drive it, so perhaps it was because of our frequent arguments? 'Boy' was I wrong. When I told the manager Debbie was missing, he told me to sit down as he had something to tell me. He explained that Debbie had been having a love affair with a Disc Jockey and that everyone knew about it except me! He was really hoping it would soon blow-over for both our sakes, because the Company was about to offer us our own Hotel. My dreams had come true, but all hope of it died, along with Debbie leaving. The job was for a 'Management Couple' only. Talk about having the rug pulled out from under you, all those months of long hours and hard work were now in vain, because with Debbie gone, I too had to leave... So leave I did...

Old memories of looking for Debbie flooded back as I drove back to Birmingham and Samantha. By the time I arrived home I was a wreck. A constant stream of; if only I'd done this or that, ran through my mind. Now 27, I felt more like 87, with a young child who's mother had left me and I knew this time she wasn't coming back. Of course I blamed myself for everything. I was a lousy husband and terrible father, and no one could ever love me again. I wasn't fit to live! My self-hate became so bad that I contemplated committing suicide. I couldn't eat, I couldn't sleep, and each night I lay awake crying in bed, with Samantha cuddled up at my side. It was having Samantha there with me, that gave me a reason to continue, and I finally realised that there were people who still loved and needed me, my daughter and my mother, although my mother had little sympathy for me. "So what if Debbie's gone, you have a little child to look after don't you, now grow up, and get out there and find yourself a job," she'd say and she was right. I had to carry on. Once more I had to decide what to do with my life, but this time I did have two years of catering experience behind me. I also knew that I'd have to go job searching and attend interviews, and my Jag wasn't looking too good after the crash.

Although it still drove OK, it couldn't be used at night because the lights on one side were wrecked but it was still a fairly new Daimler/Jag and had to be worth something. I set off to a local Car Dealer's to see what I could get. On the lot outside was a Vauxhall Ventura, the same car as the one I'd sold to raise the money for my business years earlier. "How ironic," I thought, though this was a later model and looked in extremely good condition, so in I went to see the salesman.

I looked him straight in the eye and said, "I'll do you a

straight swap, my damaged Jag, for the Ventura." Half an hour later I drove away, the deal done, saying good-bye to my car and the last remnant of my days in the Oasis. I was now ready to scan the newspapers for work and as I did I noticed that the 'Rover Car Company' needed a supervisor for their canteen outlets. I could do that, so I applied and was given an interview. At the interview they explained that the position would entail supervising the day-to-day running of four small canteens, [snack bars] which were spread out around the factory away from their large central canteen. No problem, and as this time I did have the experience, I got the job. All I had to do was supervise the staff and maintain stock control, easy-peasy compared to what I'd done at the 'Swan Hotel'. In fact it was too easy, all the staff were so experienced and reliable, I was left with virtually nothing to do.

I spent most of my time just walking around the vast area of the car plant going from one canteen to the next! This gave me too much time to think, and think I did, about Debbie and what, if anything, I could do to get her back. I knew that she was now living with her half sister in Sheffield, (another story) and also she had a new man in her life, Mr. X! I will call him Mr. X, from now on. I don't wish to use his real name as naming the creep breaks the law, as I shall explain later on. (Something that still hurts to this day.)

With Debbie rooted in my mind once more, I drove to Sheffield on the weekend with Samantha to talk with her and convince her to give our marriage one more try, but no luck. Of course she was upset, we both were, but she was now having so much fun and living it up, going out drinking and smoking, that she didn't want to settle down. That's why she wanted me to keep Samantha, she knew that I was stable and Sam would be better off staying with me. With the realisation that it was all over between us, I returned to Birmingham and my job at the Rover Car Company and what was to be an amazing turn of events. As most of you can appreciate a car assembly plant is enormous, with thousands of employees all controlled by powerful unions. It was because of this union involvement that my life was to change once more.

My day started out as normal, after doing the morning rounds I was busy helping one of the canteen's get ready for opening, when it happened. 'Ping!' A light bulb on one of the warming cabinets blew, just minutes before we opened. No problem, as there was some spare ones in the cupboard below, so I unscrewed the plastic cover around the lights and changed the spent bulb, then replaced the cover ready to open on time. "No big deal!" The next morning when I arrived, I was summoned to the office and informed that I was in big trouble. I had nearly caused a walkout, 'a strike!' How? By changing the light in the cabinet myself. I should have called a shop-fitter to unscrew the cover and then an electrician to change the bulb. Silly me, I had deprived two union employees of work, and now they wanted to know what was I going to do about it? I did something about it alright; I quit there and then! Whatever happened to common sense? I guess that I will never know who reported me, but if I ever find out.... I will buy them a drink! That burnt out light bulb incident was about to change everything in my life!

Out of work again I stopped on my way home to buy a newspaper and later, as I read it, I saw another advert that interested me. This time, "The Night-Out Theatre Restaurant" was looking for a 'Cellar Manager'. Now this was more like the work I knew and I had been trained in beers and wines, so with renewed confidence off I went to see them. So confident in fact, that I was given the job at the interview and told to start the next day. (Put that in your pipe and smoke it, Mr. Rover Canteen Manager.) The 'Night-Out' was impressive, one of the largest "Theatre Restaurants" in Europe, that dined up to 1,400 people nightly and employed 350 full and part time staff. 'Stars' like, Gene Pitney, Tom Jones, Lulu and The Three Degrees, to name a few, appeared there nightly. 'Wow.' The following morning, bright eyed and bushy tailed I arrived for work and I was given the usual guided tour - what a building!

You could easily park ten Jumbo Jets in the main theatre area alone, and around the enormous dining area were four concealed bars for 'waiter only' service, with a larger 'customer service' bar in the lobby. At the rear, behind all the seating, was a door that led into the wine distribution area, which also housed the Bar Managers office and behind that was the cellar, 'my department'. The cellar was also huge; so big, that most of the beer was stored in giant vats instead of barrels, the beer itself being delivered by tankers that pumped the beer in, similar to that of a gas station. Stored next to the beer vats were hundreds of bottles of white wine and thousands of soft drinks to keep cool. The hard liquor, red wine and champagne were kept in a separate locked room. I'd never seen so much stock, though I soon discovered that the monthly turnover of liquor at the Night-Out was equal to one year's turnover at the Swan Hotel. 'Gulp!' I did not have to sort and dispatch it all on my own; thankfully, I had a staff of 8 to assist me. Each day I would receive a stock list from each of the five bars. It was our job to replenish them ready for that evening's onslaught, which together with the multitude of daily deliveries took a whole day. Everything had to be finished by 6 p.m. ready for the deluge of evening staff, who were then responsible for preparing their own section ready for opening at 7p.m.

I'm happy to say that I always managed to get things done on time, not an easy task, considering that all the rehearsals were done during the day as well, and I was constantly having to drag my staff away from the lure of the 'Dancing Girls' or whatever 'Celebrity' was rehearsing at the time. As for me, I never had time to notice the beautiful, sexy, young, tall, slim, scantily clad dancers, that were continuously exercising and prancing all over the stage. After all, my heart still belonged to Debbie. Or did it? I was happy again and enjoying my work so much, that I rarely had time to think of her, except in the evenings at home. I was now working from 10 a.m. to 6 p.m., six days a week and I became so totally engrossed in my work and dedicated to making sure everything was done correctly, that it kept my mind busy. I rearranged the cellar to make it more efficient and everything was running smoothly. Although I'd only been there a couple of months, my efficiency had been duly noticed and this led to my next step. It seemed the Company was having a problem with stock shortages in the evenings and they called me to the General Managers office for a meeting. He explained to me that the problem had been going on for sometime and it had become so bad that there was now a £5,000.00 ($10,000) deficit in the liquor stocks, and something had to be done! Their suspicions were centred around the 'Bar Manager' and a few others who were drinking away the profits and allowing liquor to disappear from the bars for late night parties. Thus it was time to make some changes, and that's where I came in. (fig.9)

I was promoted immediately to 'Cellar & Bar Manager', they were so pleased by how much attention I'd paid to my work and noting the fact I didn't drink, they combined the two jobs into one, which meant that 'little old me' was to have total control of all beers, wines and spirits. "Stone the crows!" That meant everything was now my responsibility from 10 a.m. to 1 a.m. the next morning! Oh, and another thing, I now had to control a staff of over sixty, as the evening's entire bar and waiting personnel were also my responsibility! Long hours again, I thought, but least I was able to take time off when and where I could get it and I still had Sundays off.

Besides all the staff, I'd also inherited something else, the stock deficit of £5,000.00. An enormous sum of money when compared to my salary of £70.00 a week back then, and I had undertaken the responsibility of decreasing it. My first line of defence was to secure the large liquor room. There were four people that had keys to it: the general manager, the assistant manager, the head of security and me. So this is what I did. I installed a large steel locker, just outside the door of the liquor room. Inside it, I placed 6 bottles of each of our most used products, complete with a stock control sheet for recording what was taken, when, why and by whom. My next step was to go to the other three people and exchange their liquor room keys, for keys to the steel cabinet. This was not an easy task, but I refused to take 'no' for an answer! I then placed stock control sheets next to the wine and bottled beers and informed all staff that if anyone required anything during my absence, they were to use the liquor locker and fill in a requisition for any beers or white wine used, making sure that my cellar staff monitored all these things very closely.

With the cellar now secure, I turned my attention to the bars.

I knew that each night after we closed, some of the security staff and others would hang around to talk and play cards, having a drink or two with the local police. I also knew that it was at that time when my bars were their most vulnerable. I made it known that I was checking daily on bar inventory and all bar staff were to mark the level of all part used bottles every night, not a popular move. Over the next month as bar manager, I could feel the knives in my back and I became the recipient of many 'one finger salutes.' If looks could kill, I would never have survived the glares I got, especially from the late night security personnel. Security!!! To be fair, I did tell them that they could help themselves to the odd beer or two, 'nudge, nudge, wink, wink, say no more' as I could cover some loses by writing it off to spillage and wastage from cleaning the beer lines etc. ' Having no temptation myself, the poor guy's couldn't even persuade me to join them in their late night gatherings. 'What a party-pooper I was.' On the up side, I did aid them in other ways. One of the benefits from our vast liquor turnover, was that sales representatives would shower me with free samples, which I would pass on to the head of security, for him and his boy's. But drastic losses called for drastic actions and eventually, when the weekly stock-takes began to show vast reductions in the deficit, people began to appreciate what I was doing and things improved all-round...

One other thing I had to master in my new role was the art of purchasing supplies, 'and it was an art' because each celebrity attracted a different type of customer. Someone like Tom Jones would attract the ladies and we'd sell lots of wine, gin and white rum that week, but if a raunchy comedian like Billy Connolly was appearing we would sell mostly beer and whisky. It was important to have enough of the right supplies. During the day I was the 'Cellar Manager', doing paperwork and helping the lads move dozens of boxes, barrels and crates around, but at night I donned my formal tuxedo and transformed into the 'Bar Manager' over seeing the night's activities. Being a head of a department certainly had its perks.

I enjoyed a nice meal from that night's menu and was

able to sit at one of the management tables to eat it and watch some of the show. I also had my very own hospitality account and could invite family and friends for a complimentary evening. One regular recipient of such an invitation were Debbie's parents, (fig.10) as we still got on well together, especially with me having their granddaughter Samantha. Another of my other duties (perks) was to take hospitality drinks to the "Stars" dressing room, where I got to meet some amazing characters. One such person was comedian Dick Emery; remember him from Cranks in London? {This time I did get his autograph}. Another English comedian of great renown I met was Tommy Cooper, one of my favourites. Unfortunately, Tommy died on stage a few years later, right in the middle of his act at a Royal Variety Performance, in the presence of Her Majesty The Queen! "God-Bless him." That's one autograph I'll treasure forever.

The success I was having in my job gave me back my confidence, and I was able to face life again. A good thing too, as it was time to face facts. Debbie was happy with her new love, so we both agreed to sort out the divorce papers. The grounds for divorce would be adultery on her part and Debbie would not contest it, plus she was willing to give me full custody of Samantha. She still wanted her to stay with me, happy in the knowledge that my lifestyle and good job would be more beneficial to her future upbringing. In fact everything about the divorce was done in a cool, calm and civilised manner. We agreed on all things and parted good friends. The entire proceedings would last a year and end up costing just £200.00 ($400.00). The lawyers didn't get rich off us... But as one door closes another one opens and if you don't believe in love at first sight; you soon will!

At the end of each night as the bar staff collected and washed the hundreds of dirty glasses, my job was to go from bar to bar and take the readings from each cash register. Each of the four theatre bars had its own cashier, I would meet with them and total their till so that they could then take that night's money to the accounts department, in the hope that everything balanced. Every time I visited bar #4, I couldn't help but notice the cashier's beautiful hands. They were immaculate, tipped with polished long red nails.... In fact every inch of her was immaculate; her personality, face, figure, legs, and... But I'd had enough of women, so of course, I tried to put her out of my mind, however I knew her name was Mary. Like me, she also did two jobs, as she worked in the accounts office during the day and was a cashier at night. My loyal cellar staff, noting my interest, informed me that she was extremely shy and that many of the guys had asked her out, but all had been turned down flat! "But she's so perfect" I said, "No, no, no!" What was I thinking? I must concentrate on my work, and I continued on, though I must say I did seem to notice her a lot more during the day.

Then one night fate took a hand. Mary left to go home as usual, but her little Austin Mini refused to start and she came back inside to see if anyone could assist her, (don't forget it was 2 a.m. in the morning by then). I overheard her asking for help and offered to give her a lift home, so that she could attend to her car the next day. Though very shy, Mary accepted, probably because I was her boss. I don't know which of us was the most nervous as I proceeded to drive her home. Once there, we sat and talked for a while and then I wished her luck with her car and said goodnight. Her home was in fact 12 miles from the Night-Out, in the opposite direction to where I lived, so I now had a 39 mile trip home from there myself. 'Oh well,' it was nice to do a good deed and after all, she was very pretty. It seemed that Mary's car was quite sick and would take a few days to repair, so at the end of the following night, I offered to take her home again and she accepted. This time we sat and talked for an hour or so outside her house, followed by our first good-night kiss, then I drove home feeling ten feet tall, with a smile on my face as if I had a coat hanger stuck in my mouth. I prayed that night that her car would be still broken the next day, so that I could see her again. It was, and again we set off together. This time, we sat outside her house and kissed for two hours, and it was then that I asked her "Will You Marry Me?" And of course she said, "YES!"

We'd known each other for less than six hours, we'd never

been on a date or had a meal together, but to us, it felt like we had known each other all our life, or was it lives. Then as usual I sat and waited until she waved from her window, to let me know she was safely indoors and again set off home. I was as happy as a dog with two tails and I knew that I was in love, but this love felt different to the one I'd had for Debbie. I had feelings and emotions that I didn't even know existed, my heart was pounding in my chest and I was quivering with excitement. I wanted to climb the tallest building and declare my love for all to hear! As dawn broke, I arrived home and went to bed. Samantha was sound asleep and I cuddled up to her and said, "I've found your new mommy." I tried to sleep but the minutes passed like hours as I couldn't wait to see Mary again. Later that morning, I floated downstairs on a cloud of love, and then my mother served me breakfast, bacon, eggs and a slice of reality.

"What do you mean you're getting married?" "You're already married, and your divorce has only just started," - "you don't even know this girl," - "you're 27 and she's only 20, what are her parents going to say, you should know better" and so on and so on…

I left for work early that day and on my way in I stopped to buy Mary a 'red rose' to seal our pact. When I arrived my mind was racing with questions: what if she's changed her mind? What if she doesn't like Samantha? What if her parents don't like me? 'Oh, shut-up,' I love her and that's all that matters! I had to wait until lunchtime to see her again and once more I asked her if she would do me the honour of becoming my wife, and again without hesitation she agreed. We both knew there could be no other out-come; as if part of each of us had been missing all our lives. Like Anthony and Cleopatra and Kathy and Heathcliffe we were whole again. (I think I need a tissue.) News of our engagement spread quickly through the Night-Out and most were truly happy for us, though we could sense the odd whisper behind our backs. 'Mary's just infatuated and John's just on the rebound', that sort of thing. Other than that it was business as usual. But first, there was something that I had to do, and that was to ask her mother for Mary's hand.

Like me, Mary only had a mother as her father had died of cancer when she was 13. She also had two brothers: Peter (my age) and Francis, whom I already knew, since he was a waiter at the Night-Out. I took the bull by the horns and made arrangements to visit her mother during my afternoon break. How would she take the news, I wondered. Not only was I a total stranger, I was still technically married and had a 2½-year-old daughter. 'Oh my God' that not only makes Mary, Sam's mother, it makes Mary's mother an instant grandmother!

Feeling about as welcome as a fart in a spacesuit, I arrived at Mary's home and took a deep breath outside the front door, knowing that behind it lay a total stranger and Mary's giant 'German Shepherd' dog 'Oscar' who probably wanted to eat me! When the door opened and I was invited in, it didn't take me long to realise who Mary had inherited her personality from- her mother Dorothy, who instinctively knew that I was genuine. Because I was making her daughter happy, she gave us her blessing and Oscar even gave me a lick! (He liked me.)

The date set was June the fourth, ten days prior to my birthday and back at work I suggested to Mary that we combine it with a formal engagement party; that way all our family would be able to meet each other. Perfect. Mary and I booked that night off and I reserved two large tables at the Night-Out. That way the family could see where we worked and enjoy a show at the same time. Funny thing, here we were booking our engagement party and Mary hadn't even met Samantha, let alone my mother! So we arranged to do it on Sunday. (Our day off.) I met Mary downtown, and although she looked beautiful, underneath she was scared stiff and I didn't blame her. Regardless of meeting Sam, meeting my mother would put the fear of God into anyone. "Don't worry things will be fine" I said, (crossing my fingers) and off we went to find out... (fig.11)

Upon her arrival, Mary and Samantha eyed each other

warily. Sam wasn't used to anyone but my mother and Mary knew nothing of being around children, but they appeared to hit it off OK. My mother was a different story, she gave Mary a rather cold reception, but at least she was polite and managed to keep her objections to her self. Still, I knew that it would take a little time for them to adjust and so far so good! With that over, it was time to continue with the plans for our engagement. Coincidentally, my old partner, Jerry from the Oasis, was back in town and popped into work to see me. He was delighted by the news and of course offered to use his contacts to obtain for us a nice engagement ring at a good price, which we accepted.

The big night arrived, and what a night! The Bell family, my mother, my three brothers and their wives versus the vastly outnumbered Corfield family, Mary's mother and her two brothers- all meeting for the first time. You could have cut the air with a knife. Hardly a word was spoken, with the exception of David and Brenda, who genuinely wished us lots of luck, having been through a divorce themselves. My mother sat there with a face like a bag of spanners, and as for the rest of my family, I think the lights were on, but no one was home. 'Thank heavens,' Jerry was there to lighten things up a bit; still Mary and I were prepared to ride the waves, no matter what.

After the initial 'Shell Shock' of our engagement, life returned to normal. Well, with one exception. Mary, like a butterfly emerging from its cocoon, the shy young girl had transformed into a radiant young woman and became even more beautiful, if that was possible. My self-worth too had grown. Not only was I in love, but by then I'd managed to convert the huge stock deficit into a stock surplus, to the delight of the management who gave me a 10% pay rise. Everything was perfect and our adventures at the Night-Out continued. It was the peak of the 'Cabaret' era; a time when going out was a big deal and warranted getting dressed up in your finest clothes. Here at the Night-Out, strict rules of dress and etiquette applied; formal attire was enforced and if a gentleman didn't have a tie, he'd have to rent one or no entry!

Once inside, patrons could expect excellent service with good food and cold drinks, surpassed only by the fabulous entertainment. Over the next year Mary and I witnessed a cavalcade of top class entertainers. Each show was a delight to see, although there were the odd few that actually got booed off the stage, even to the extent of having food thrown at them, mostly un-funny comedians. They were the exception rather than the rule and 99% of the time everyone had a really good time.

On one memorable occasion, singer Gene Pitney was performing on stage when his trouser belt broke and Francis, Mary's brother, quickly came to his aid and lent him his, then after Gene had finished his performance, he autographed the belt to say thank you and handed it back to Francis. The only problem was, as soon as Gene left the stage, poor Francis was mobbed by dozens of crazed women, all frantically trying to steal the belt. Luckily for him, he still managed to hang onto the belt and keep his pants up.

Mary and I too had some memorable experiences meeting the various Stars, people like; Madeline Bell, Jack Jones, Rich Little and The Three Degrees, plus dozens of British Celebrities that are not internationally known, Morecombe & Wise, The Two Ronnie's, Mike & Bernie Winters, Jasper Carrott and the Black Abbots, to name just a few! (See the full list at the end of the book.) Whoop's, I forgot to mention that it was comedian Paul Melba who was on stage the night of our engagement. Tipped off by the staff, he got us up on stage to congratulate us and add yet another autograph to our ever growing book, an album that would quadruple in years to come.

It wasn't just meeting Celebrities that made the Night-Out a great place to work; it was also the staff of 350! What a fantastic bunch of people, characters from all walks of life and there was never a dull moment behind the scenes. As hysterical and chaotic it got at times, everyone got along, always pulling together whenever needed. One week in particular had a Spanish Theme and the drink of choice was Sangria; any of the staff that had any spare time, ended up in the wine cellar helping us peel the thousands of apples and oranges needed to mix with the wine. Gallons and gallons of the stuff was needed to supply the endless stream of waiting staff that kept running in to fill their jugs. By the end of each night, the whole cellar was awash with Sangria! (Enough to put me off it for life.)

There was one time though, when the staff wasn't so friendly and it escalated into a strike. A Trade Union was trying to muscle in, and they recruited some staff to picket around the Night-Out, in an attempt to stop the others from entering work. This made things difficult for everyone, and especially awkward for me, having to get all my liquor supplies into the building. The normal loading bay was surrounded by these pickets, which made it impossible for me to gain access through there, so I had to revert to other means, riding shotgun on the deliveries myself. I used a two-way radio system to call the security to open the stage doors, just seconds before we drove in, then we'd bounce up the ramp onto the stage at 30 mph, praying as we went, that we'd stop before shooting off into the stalls. When safely inside, the security together with my staff, would have to manhandle everything through the main theatre into the cellar. (That sucked, I can tell you.) Things got even worse at night, when the evening staff and customers had to run through a barrage of flying eggs and insults as they arrived. Throughout it all we still managed to conduct business as usual, and after two months the Union eventually gave up and things went back to normal, just in time for Christmas.

It was also when one of the Directors decided to leave, to take up a position within another Hotel chain. To our surprise, he asked Mary and I to join him, as they needed a Management Couple for 'The St. George & Dragon' one of their Inn/Restaurant's near Henley-on-Thames in Oxfordshire. "Wow" a place of my own at last. All those long hours paid off after all, though it ended up with Mary at my side, not Debbie, not quite what the family would of guessed three years earlier! Of course we agreed, and we were given our starting date, February the 15th, 1978. But first - we had to get through Christmas at the Night-Out. Want to know a good recipe to cure depression? Take 350 staff, add 1,400 customers, mix in an enormous dose of Christmas spirit, then wash it all down with lot's of alcohol, and it's guaranteed to cheer anyone up. In fact, if I could find a way to bottle an atmosphere like that, I'd make a fortune! Christmas at the Night-Out, was without a doubt one of the happiest I ever had, my only wish is that our present children could have been there to enjoy it with us, because it was more than a job, it was like being part of a huge family. It wasn't going to be easy to say good-bye to all our friends, but time and tide wait for no one, and all too soon Christmas was over. Before we knew what hit us, it was our last day. Holding back the tears, it was hugs all round, exchanging phone numbers with each other in the hope that we'd meet again.

Mary took it the hardest as she'd worked there twice as long as I had, and would miss all her old friends. In retrospect, it must have been pretty terrifying for her. She was leaving home for the first time in her life, to live with people she hardly knew, my mom and Sam, becoming a wife, a mother and hotel manageress, all at the same time, in a part of the country that she knew absolutely nothing about! (Moving to another part of England is like moving to a different country, my years in Nottingham can vouch for that.) If she did have any second thoughts, she certainly never showed them, and was 100% behind me. Personally, although excited about the prospect of running my own place, at the same time I felt sad. I would miss all the glitz and glamour, associated with the Night-Out. I loved every minute of my time there, but the era of the big clubs was coming to an end anyway, and as far as meeting the "Celebrities" was concerned, the best was yet to come!

Fate had far grander plans in store for us.

Chapter Four

Swan-Upmanship

The grass may be greener on the other side of the fence, but the water bill is higher!

Mary and I had bought ourselves a nice Christmas prezzy, a 1972 white MGB. I wanted Mary to experience the fun you can have with a convertible, not a lot of room for my mom though. (Hint, Hint.) Moving to our own hotel gave us mixed emotions and that's putting it mildly. On our last night at the Night-Out we were called up on stage during the cabaret, where I was presented with a clock and Mary received a giant bouquet of flowers. Everyone was in tears including us! At the end of the night we said our good-byes to all and left the world of Celebrities behind. Well, so we thought.

It was a wet and windy 15th February, when we made our way to the St. George & Dragon, a small hotel in the village of Wargrave-on-Thames, approximately three miles from Henley-on-Thames, famous for it's Royal Regatta. Wargrave itself seemed extremely small to us, its population was approximately 10,000 people, compared to Birmingham's population of 1.2 million. What it lacked in size it certainly made up in beauty. So did our little hotel. It was situated on the bank of the River Thames, adjacent to a boat rental operation and surrounded by acres of green fields. Built in 1780 AD, The St. George & Dragon is actually mentioned in a very famous English novel 'Three Men in a Boat' by Jerome K. Jerome. Once inside, we introduced ourselves to the staff as Mr. & Mrs. Bell and our daughter Samantha, plus Mrs. Bell senior. My mother would be living with us to help out with Sam, as the position was for a management couple. We then said good-bye to the exiting manager and commenced settling in.

The St. George was comprised of a large 150-seat restaurant, one large bar, a small function room, a very large kitchen and 9 bedrooms. Since it was no longer a hotel the first floor bedrooms had been converted into three staff bedrooms, an office and a self-contained three-bedroom manager's apartment. There was also a small cottage next to the hotel that housed the boiler room and three other staff bedrooms, plus another three-bedroom house in the village, that the Chef and one of the waitress's were living in. Besides the chef, we had five other full time employees that lived in and four part time staff that helped out at weekends. (fig.12)

Sorry to say, the St. George had seen a succession of past managers, each one staying about one and a half years and unfortunately the numerous turnover had taken its toll. Virtually all the interior was in need of some TLC (tender loving care) and some parts were downright dilapidated, so my 'Jack of all trades' experience would come in handy once again. Being a Gemini, I loved to do two things at once, so every minute that I wasn't needed to work, I spent painting and decorating. I stripped everything I could get my hands on, 'oop's sorry Mary', and refurbished it. Not all of it was fun mind you, I remember being up to my elbows in old sanitary towels, fixing a broken disposal unit in the ladies washroom. Now that's what I'd call 'dedication', wouldn't you? After three months I had to put the repairs aside and prepare for the up-coming summer season and the multitude of weddings that were about to descend on us.

Our picturesque location ensured that 'Wedding Receptions' were a weekly event and made up a considerable part of the restaurant's income. One up-coming wedding was very important indeed, reserved for the third of June. All it said in the reservation book was 'VIP Wedding', without giving any names and the staff had no idea who the lucky couple were, do you? Yes, it was ours! Just two weeks prior to the big day I called the staff together for a meeting. "Guess what", I said, "We aren't Mr. & Mrs. Bell; well not yet, but we will be on the 3rd of June..." I'm happy to say they took the news very well and became more excited about the wedding than ever. Meanwhile, there was one more thing needed to finish my divorce with Debbie and it entailed taking a trip to the Court House in Birmingham, to obtain my Degree of Absolution. With our wedding only a week away, Mary and I set off to Birmingham in our lovely MGB, with the top down and the wind in our hair. We were so happy that this day had finally arrived. We were three quarters of the way there, when 'bang' one of the piston rods went through the engine block and the car ground to a halt! Now, I know why the car was such a good deal.

"What the hell are we going to do now?" I asked. We had to be in court in just over an hour and we were still half an hour away! There was no way that we could be late, as it would postpone the completion of the divorce and we were getting married in a week! (Help.) We had rolled to a stop just as we'd entered a small village and just ahead was a small Service Station and car lot. We pushed our car there and asked for help.

"Sorry mate, the mechanic isn't here, I can't help you," he said,

"But we have to be in Birmingham in an hour, it's a life or death situation, can't you help us?"

"Sorry, but I'm on my own" he replied.

We were in a right mess and to make matters worse there wasn't a bus, train, or taxi available to get us to the court on time.

"Hang on a minute! I've got an idea," I said, as I scoured the used car lot, "what about them? I'll buy one of your cars!"

After all, an MGB even with a wrecked engine is still a sought-after car!" (Thoughts of my Jaguar flashed through my mind, funny how history repeats it's self.)

All he had in the price range of our sick MG was an old Simca sedan, but beggars can't be choosers, so after one of the fastest car deals in history, we were on our way once more. Like a bat out'a hell we set off to Birmingham with 30 minutes left to our court-hearing deadline. The air inside the car was no longer rushing through our hair, instead it was turning blue with my colourful language as I frantically tried to get a few miles an hour faster out of the old car. Debbie was anxiously waiting outside the Court House as we arrived, so we parked the car and all ran as fast as we could to see the Judge.

'We made it by the skin of our teeth' as they called our names just as we entered the room!

Everything went smoothly from then on and soon I was now a single man again, but not for long, Debbie and I said our last good-byes and she thanked me for being a good husband and wished us well for our up-coming wedding. I decided to take a different route back to Wargrave; I couldn't bear to see the MG lying dead on the garage forecourt. On our way we drove through the town of Leamington and something caught my eye. There on the front of a used car lot was the car of my dreams, a gold Jensen Interceptor.

"No way!" I thought, and turned the car around and went back to take a closer look. It was true! There it was, for sale at only £2,000.00. The lot was closed so I made a note of the 'phone number and we carried on home. The next morning I phoned the dealership to see if there was anyway we could get finance. Now £2,000.00 was the price of the average new car then and this car was 8 years old, though it was in the same league as Aston Martin and Lamborghini and well worth the money. So there I was, amidst all the wedding arrangements, trying to buy a car. Thank God Mary was very supportive and behind me all the way, she even asked her uncle if he would co-sign for us and he agreed! Three days before the wedding, the dealer delivered the Jensen to us. Talk about being on a roll, here I was with the car of my dreams, the job of my dreams and marrying the girl of my dreams! As for the old Simca, the dealer reluctantly took it away as our down payment. Funny, if it hadn't been for the MG breaking down, I never would have found the Jensen. It is amazing how many times in my life that something good has emerged from what appeared to be a disaster, a trait, as you will discover, that continues over and over again!

The Wedding

We were unable to get married in the historic local church, because I was divorced, but we were able to hold a service of blessing there instead. I really didn't want Mary to miss out on a traditional wedding so we made arrangements for all the guests to meet at the church, as they would usually do. We, however, planned to get married at the 'Registry Office' in Henley and after the ceremony Mary would go to a nearby hotel, where she would change into her wedding gown and I would return to the St. George and put on my top hat and tails, then both meet again at the church, like a traditional wedding. The night before the wedding Mary and her mother set off to the hotel in Henley as arranged, while Jerry (the best-man) and I dealt with any last minute details and helped the staff prepare the restaurant. 'Cockadoodle-doo.'

It was the 3rd of June, exactly one year to the day that I'd asked Mary to marry me, that night in the car. Everything was ready and the weather forecast was fantastic. Some of the guests arrived early at the St. George, taking the opportunity to freshen up after their long journey and maybe having a spot of breakfast in the bar, while Jerry and I with a few close family drove off to meet Mary and her mother at the registry office. Mary's uncle George also joined us there to give Mary away and to act as a witness. We were all dressed in Sunday best, Mary in a beautiful floral two-piece and I wore a grey velvet suit, saving the formal wear for the church.

At 10.am., the moment that we both had yearned for, we stood in front of the lady registrar, who to our amazement informed us that the last couple to be married there prior to us, were Olivia and George Harrison. 'Yes,' George Harrison of the Beatles! "Pretty awesome, hey!" (He also lived in Henley) Well now it was our turn. Married at last, legally anyway, we then made our way out of the building into the waiting cars and were whisked away to change into our wedding attire. Two hours later I arrived at the beautiful old church in Wargrave, 90% of the guests were already inside. The other 10% were the usual latecomers and the ones that couldn't wait to see Mary arrive. I can't blame them; she looked magnificent as she emerged from the car. This vision of loveliness was about to become my wife! I still go weak at the knees just thinking about it.

Now, together again, we walked down the aisle to the Altar. As we walked, the air around us seemed charged with a holy atmosphere of peace and tranquility. As if in slow motion, each step felt like we were being watched by the spirits of our fathers and other ghostly well wishers that may have inhabited the building from centuries past. The church itself dated back to 1100 AD. At the altar we exchanged our vows again this time while being blessed by the priest. During the last hymn, Samantha, who was then three, came running over and joined us. There we stood all holding hands as the priest gave us his final blessing. I think everyone had tears in their eyes, I know I did. (fig.13)

The ceremony over, it was now time for the mandatory photo session, and it was probably the first and only time in my life that I didn't mind having my photo taken. In fact, I enjoyed every minute, so proud to have Mary by my side. I thought, it must be nice to take photos of Brides and Grooms on their special day. (Remember: be careful what you wish for!) After the traditional family groups and a few romantic poses, it was time to be driven back to the St. George, in our new Jensen, of course, proudly driven by my eldest brother Ronnie. Everything at the restaurant was ready; our staff had done us proud. After greeting our guests one by one, it was time to feast. The meal, like everything else, was perfect; the toasts said and the cake cut, it was time to go outside and mingle. That's one of the nicest things about a wedding, the way it brings all the family and friends together at the same time, happy and in jovial moods, all enjoying themselves.

It was a beautiful hot sunny day, so everyone was down by the water taking advantage of the cool river breeze. Jerry had managed to borrow a row boat from the boathouse next door to take us for a ride along the Thames, so in we got to the sound of applause from all, including the many holiday makers vacationing on the river. It was so sweet! I remember being surrounded by Swans and Ducks, accompanied by hoards of baby chicks and across the river all the young calves had gathered together on the shore to watch us. It was like a scene from a Disney movie. All good things come to an end and it was time for us to go to the Airport, we had booked a little weekend package trip to Paris for our honeymoon. It was all we could afford and also the only time we were able to get off, as it was now the summer season.

We said farewell to our family and friends; leaving them to enjoy the evening's festivities, we didn't even have time for the first dance. 'Oh well' we were going to Paris. Again we set off in the Jensen with Ronnie at the wheel, this time to Heathrow Airport. We arrived at Charles DeGaulle Airport on the outskirts of Paris around 9.pm. They say that Paris is the City of Love, L'amour, but to Mary it became the city of tears. Yes, we were in Paris, but Mary's suitcase was still in London, complete with all her comfy shoes, clothes and new lingerie! She had to spend the entire weekend in the clothes she had on but her case did arrive at our hotel just one hour before we left to come home!

Still, we made the most of what little time we had, visiting the Eiffel Tower, the Louvre Museum, Notre Dame Cathedral and the Tomb of Napoleon, during which we realised that there was one other thing in Mary's suitcase, our pre-paid meal vouchers. With rumbling tummies, we soon found out how expensive Paris really was, heck, it would have been cheaper to eat the money… All we could do was gaze into restaurant windows in envy of those dining inside, the cost of a meal way above our budget. We used what little spending money we had to buy the odd burger and fries. We left Paris feeling, tired, hungry and disappointed. So much for our honeymoon- we were pleased to get home and back to work.

At home the tourist season was in full swing, thanks to the beautiful June weather. People appeared from everywhere and the demand for our boat mooring went wild. From the minute we opened to the minute we closed we were busy, busy, busy. Each morning there would be a line up of people at the door, many of them anxious to use our washroom facilities, having been moored at our jetty or camped in the grounds over night. Recollections of the Washford Mill came to mind, as again many hours were spent collecting the used glasses from the banks of the river, but this time we were unable to retrieve the ones in the river as it was too deep. If people only knew how many glasses riverside pubs go through each summer and the amount of money spent on replacements, perhaps they'd think twice before throwing them in. (Just venting.)

One nice thing about being on the river at night after we closed was how lovely it was to sit under the stars on the waters edge and relax, sometimes chatting with the families who were moored along the bank. Very pleasant as long as there weren't any drunken boaters around. As for regular drunks, they were few, but our worst problem was trying to stop the under age drinkers. There's not a lot to do in a small village after dark, so bored teenagers would try every trick in the book to get a drink. I constantly had to escort them out; unfortunately, they would vow revenge, which resulted in a great deal of vandalism. The gentleman's toilet was positioned just inside the front entrance and was out of staff view; subsequently it took the brunt of the damage. One sink in particular was constantly being ripped off the wall and the toilet seat was smashed frequently, roller towels were set on fire and the walls displayed some very informative graffiti! All too often, I would spend most of the day in the 'Gent's' toilet repairing all the damage. Mary would help by bringing me cups of tea and bacon sandwiches, much to my happiness.

Once I managed to purchase some old fashioned streetlights, which I eagerly installed on the bar patio and they looked great. That night I had to evict some sixteen year olds from the bar and the next morning I awoke to find the lights in ruins. Sob! When I wasn't fixing things, most of my time was spent doing bookwork, organising functions and (my personal favourite) working with the chef. Though the G & D was well known for it's traditional carvery of roast beef, pork or turkey, the Chef and I had added a full 'A La Carte' menu to the restaurants repertoire. We featured items like: Beef Wellington, Lemon Chicken, Steak Diane, Grilled Trout, Poached Salmon and Tornado Rossini, all to the delight of our customers. (I'm suddenly feeling hungry, how about you?)

Another addition that delighted the customers was the introduction of 'Theme Nights', the first one being a 'Medieval Banquet' we held on April 23rd., (St. George's Day) which became an annual event. Others themes included French, German, Spanish, Hawaiian, Moroccan and Jamaican nights, all with the appropriate food, drink and costumes. Entertainment at these events was provided by a wide variety of musicians, actors and comics, who were always accompanied by our regular troop of beautiful dancers. A local dance group called 'Cameo' became a regular feature at all our events over the next seven years. We always went a bit overboard on creating the right atmosphere, and a good chunk of the profit went to transforming the restaurant into our theme and renting great costumes. For our 'Medieval Banquets' I'd buy bales of hay and cover the entire restaurant floor; we'd be vacuuming it up for weeks after. But it was worth it, the banquets were great fun. (fig.14)

I constructed a set of Medieval stocks out of some driftwood and we'd put a basket of stale bread on every table for people to throw at who-so-ever was unfortunate enough to end up in them. The poor sod would end up being pelted with a variety of vegetables and chicken bones as well! Another great success was our Second World War, WW2 night. Guests arrived to the sound of air-raid sirens and bombing, then shown to their seats by beautiful young girls in Women's Royal Air Force, WRAF uniforms. They were then issued their ration book, from which they would have to take out a coupon to obtain each course of their meal. Mary's idea! Our comedian did a fantastic 'Charlie Chaplin' routine and the 'Vera Lynn' style singer initiated a traditional sing-a-long of all the old favourites, it was great! We all became one big happy family at the G & D, and I'm sure that my mother, who was then 70, acquired a whole new lease on life. She loved to help out where she could, something that was greatly appreciated by Peter Small, our kitchen porter/dishwasher, who had been there so long he'd become part of the fixtures. Peter was also in his 70's, and had not retired because, sorry to say, he had nowhere to go. He'd left his family years earlier after finding out his wife had been unfaithful with his best friend! This was something that destroyed him and he gave up his career and began drinking and all his wages were now spent on booze. He was rarely sober when not on duty. However, when my mother started to help him, she began washing his clothes and would nag at him if he didn't smarten himself up. They used to complain about each other all the time, but deep down they comforted each other and worked well together when things got busy.

One of our busiest days of the year was the local 'Wargrave Regatta,' an annual event that was held on the riverbanks outside the G & D. Fantastic for business, you may think, though you'd be wrong, because it was a bloody nightmare! Right from the very beginning at seven a.m., to 7 5

While on the subject of 'Regattas' it would be unforgivable of me not to mention the most famous one of them all! The Royal Henley Regatta was held annually three miles away from us in Henley-on-Thames. So close, in fact, that the Executives of Courage Brewery, (the buildings owners) would use our car park to store their cars, then take a boat down to their giant Marquee alongside the river in Henley. One of the perks from doing this was that Mary and I received an annual invitation to visit and partake of afternoon tea. One had to lean how to raise one's little finger first, don't you know. It wasn't really our cup of tea, though people would arrive early to get a good spot, most of whom wouldn't even step foot in the pub. It was also important that I made sure we kept enough room for the crowd of about two thousand that would gather throughout the day ready for the traditional fireworks display at the end. So many people, it was impossible for our little bar to keep up with the demand.

During opening times it was up to seven layers deep with people waiting to be served, jostling each other to be first. This meant that I had to employ a lot of extra staff and purchase hundreds of extra bar glasses, a lot of which ended up in the river. Then we'd get the complaints that the beer wasn't cold enough. "Excuse me," the bloody stuff wasn't in the pipes long enough to get cold! The poor coolers couldn't cope with drawing pint after pint, without stopping for a second. We were so busy that none of us had time to see any of the events, with the exception of the fireworks, and then everyone went outside. I must admit they did look nice; we always went out onto the restaurant roof to watch them.

There were boats moored everywhere, their lights reflecting in the river as did the bursts of fireworks. There were so many people outside we couldn't see any ground, just bodies jumping and dancing to the music, cheering every time there was a particularly nice display. Then, as the final sparks hit the ground, 'it was every man for himself' as the stampede of people began. Once the dust had cleared the entire grounds looked like a giant garbage war had been fought there; the wounded lay all around - dozens of broken plates, bottles and glasses. I think someone must have shouted, "Take no prisoners!" Inside the bar and restaurant it didn't look much better; all of us were exhausted and we still had the cleaning up to do and hundreds of glasses to wash, ready for opening the next morning, but not before we had a quick snack and a good gossip about some of the people we'd served that day.

While on the subject of 'Regattas' it would be unforgivable of me not to mention the most famous one of them all. The Royal Henley Regatta was held annually three miles away from us in Henley-on-Thames. So close, in fact, that the Executives of Courage Brewery (the building owners), would use our car park to store their cars, then take a boat down to their giant Marquee alongside the river in Henley. One of the perks from doing this was that Mary and I recieved an annual invitation to visit and partake in afternoon tea. One had to learn how to raise one's little finger first, don't you know. It wasn't really our cup of tea, though it was an amazing experience to say the least, like being a part of some bygone age, right out of the pages of history. From Vintage Punts and Steam Launches to the latest thing in River Craft, everything you'd expect. Champagne and cucumber sandwiches as far as the eye could see, plus all the pomp and circumstance to go with it!

Which brings me to my next story, about 'Swan Upping', this chapter's title, and believe it or not there is such a thing! The event takes place annually in the third week in July and is carried out by the Vintners Company, the Dyer's Company and the Monarch's Swan Marker, and dates from medieval times, when 'The Crown' claimed ownership of all mute swans, at a time when swans were considered a status symbol and an important food source for banquets. The Crown still retains the right to ownership of all unmarked Mute swans, but the Queen only exercises her ownership on certain stretches of the river Thames. This ownership is shared with the Vintners' and Dyers' Companies, who were both granted rights of ownership by the Crown in the 15th century. Nowadays, the swans are counted and marked, but rarely eaten. The Queen's swan marker, accompanied by the other Companies, use six traditional 'Thames rowing skiffs' during their five day journey upstream and still wear the traditional scarlet uniforms of the 'Queen's Swan-Uppers'. Each boat flies their appropriate flags and ornate pennants. One day a year these crafts can be found moored outside the St. George and Dragon restaurant, while the occupants visit us for lunch, all just part of the life and times of running a Country Pub.

Although at times the work was hard and the hours long, we all had a lot of fun and I enjoyed being part of the team. That's one of the great things about a small establishment, everyone pulls together, whether it was in the restaurant, bar or kitchen- if help was needed we all mucked in! I must admit, I had a good crew. Ena, my head waitress, knew her trade well and had even assisted at 'Royal Banquets'. She was a hard taskmaster and ran a tight ship making sure that everything was perfect. The bar staff, though good, changed frequently and most of Mary's time was taken up working there. My time, as I mentioned earlier, was divided between doing the bookwork, restocking and organising supplies, plus working in the kitchen, the part I liked the most. My chef training at the Washford Mill came in handy and Kevin, my chef, helped me continue in the art of cooking, enabling me to master our diverse menu and prepare meat for the Carvery. Mary had been up to a little cooking of her own and now had a bun in the oven. Everyone was overjoyed, it also meant that Samantha (who was 5) would be getting a baby sister (ultrasound) to play with, but before that, she would get something else to play with, that no-one would have ever imagined!

It was September and Samantha was eagerly looking forward to her sixth birthday in October, we were so happy with the news of the new baby that I promised her a special birthday present, whatever she wanted, and she wanted a chipmunk. Fair enough, now it was just a matter of finding one, chipmunk's are not natural to England and none of the local pet shops carried them, one of the staff suggested that I look in a weekly magazine called the 'Exchange and Mart' as sometimes they could be found in there. This I did, and there was an ad that read 'Chipmunk's for sale'. Great, but then something else caught my eye, an ad for something a little more unusual, 'Baby Leopard Cubs looking for a good home!' I could hardly believe my eyes.

"Hey Sam, how would you like a Leopard?" I asked. Me and my big mouth; one phone call later, the arrangements were made for us to pick one up in four weeks! Like us, everyone was excited and eagerly looking forward to our new arrival, with one exception- my mother. She was terrified.

"John! What on earth are you thinking?" she said and thought that I'd gone stark raving mad. She was convinced we were all going to be eaten alive! Mom was still trying to change my mind as Mary, Samantha and I got into the car to go and collect our cub, refusing to say good-bye and storming off in disgust! But nothing was going to deter us of our quest, and one and a half hours later we arrived at Southham Zoo Park, just outside Oxford, excited and looking forward to meeting Penny, as that's what we had decided to call her.

We drove into the compound past a group of ramshackle cages and made our way up to the main house. There, we were greeted by the owner, who had been as nervous about meeting us, as my mother had been about meeting the Leopard. He explained how he'd been looking for just the right people and although we sounded perfect on the phone, he now felt reassured that he'd made a good choice. The cubs' mother was their family pet, as had her mother, before her. This meant that the cubs were third generation tame and he did not want to cage them up or put them in a Zoo or Circus. He wanted them to go into a family environment where they could be loved and cared for, and he was pleased to see we fitted the bill.

While his wife prepared Penny to leave, he offered to give us a guided tour of his park so that we could meet some of his animal friends. As we walked he explained that most of his animals had been featured in many movie and television productions, his most famous being a tiger currently seen in the 'Esso advertisements' all over England. Next, we were face to face with the tiger, and the man went around the cage and in through a door to where the big cat was. The two began to romp and play with each other like big kids. We witnessed a similar display when we arrived at the lion compound where again he and a huge male played together. He sure loved and cared for them. In fact, all his animals looked happy and clean, which was more than I could say for their surroundings, a bit dilapidated to say the least, but still the animals looked content.

When our tour was over, it was time for us to meet Penny. We entered the room where she was and we couldn't believe our eyes. There to meet us was a cute little pussycat not much bigger than a regular six-week-old kitten. It seems that female leopards are not that big, about the size of the average dog when fully grown. The couple then introduced us to Penny's mother and gave us some valuable advice on food and how to care for this new member of our family. We had such a great time visiting all the animals and chatting that we forgot about the time and little did we know it, but my Mother was going nuts because we were late, again certain that we'd all been eaten. She was in quite a state by the time we eventually arrived home, running straight out to the car to mop up all the blood… I opened the car door and thrust Penny into her arms, and asked "Is this what you're scared of?" "What the heck is this?" she said. "It's the fierce 'Man Eater' that you've been so worried about," I told her, as Penny snuggled up to say hello. From that moment on they became best friends. Mom loved her as we all did- you couldn't help yourself.

Penny was just like the average kitten, playing with the staff and romping around the place, thoroughly enjoying herself. Just like with any pet, we had fun training her to use a litter box, and frequently we had to change our bedding, as during the night Mary and I would awake as the sensation of a warm liquid trickled its way along the sheets, Penny having had a little accident as she lay asleep between us. That sorts out the true animal lovers, I can tell you! We were careful not to let her roam about during opening hours though; I didn't want to scare the customers. Mind you - it worked wonders when I had to ask under aged drinkers to leave the bar. "Do as he say's or he'll set his Leopard on you" their friends would say. "Yeah right!" What's she gonna-do, lick em to death? I thought. Litter trained at last, Penny was as good as gold, though one of her favourite tricks was to steal a toilet roll from the bathroom and tear it to shreds, on our bed, then sit there as if to say "who could have done that?" (fig.15)

We knew, however, that her claws would not be there for much longer, as part of the legal requirements of having such an animal in our home was that it had to be declawed at six months old. I had made the arrangement for it to be done and we were just a few days away from the appointment. When I was working in the office and Penny, who was lying on the floor by the fire, started to spin round and around frantically on the floor. I jumped up and called to Mary. Mary came running in and picked her up. Penny's eyes looked weird and glaring so we decided to take her immediately to the vet's. Penny appeared to be in a coma by the time we arrived and the vet told us to leave her there and come back in an hour or two. Later, we went to pick Samantha up from school and then all headed back to the vet's. I went in on my own first to see if she was ready to come home, and came out a few minutes later carrying a large black plastic bag, with tears running down my checks. Penny was in the bag, dead! I explained to Mary and Sam what the vet had told me. Penny had contracted a disease called Parvo Virus, which happened to be rampant around the country at that time and extremely deadly to kittens and puppies. She had picked up the infection, probably from the grounds as many people walked their dogs there and, due to the fact that she had left her mother at only eight weeks old, she hadn't built up a strong enough immune system to fight it off. The vet also said the reason it had all happened so suddenly is that the infection had gone to her brain. It caused her to have a seizure and that's what had happened in the office, but by then it was too late to do anything about it.

Penny's death devastated us all; the fact she was a leopard made it even worse- we'd wanted so much to bond with her so that she wouldn't hurt anyone when she got older. Someone had been with her 24 hours a day over the last four months and now there was a huge gap in our lives. Her death hit Samantha and Mary the hardest, Ena said that I should be very concerned as Mary was then six months pregnant, the grief and constant crying could affect the baby! I had to do something and fast, I needed something to fill the gap and take their minds off Penny, but what? Somebody suggested I get them another pet, something they would have to look after and care for like a kitten.

I didn't think that there was a kitten in England that could replace Penny, but how about a puppy? I grabbed the local newspaper and scoured the pet section. Again one ad caught my eye, 'Old English Sheepdog puppies'. I called the number and found out that there were just two left, I jumped into the car and drove over to see them. One of the pups came bounding over to greet me and it was love at first sight. "I'll take this one," I said. I paid them the £100, and told them I'd pick up his papers in a few days, then left. I don't think they knew what hit them.

I arrived home, ran upstairs and plunked the puppy down between Mary and Samantha. "Here, he needs someone to love him," I said and waited to see their reaction. Neither of them showed the slightest interest and it took all their effort to manage a halfhearted stroke. It took a few hours but the little puppy started to win over Samantha and she started to play a little with him. He looked a little like a real life teddy bear, his black shiny nose protruding out from under all the white fur. How the heck could Mary still resist him? "Come on guy's, we've got to think of a name for him" I said! Ugh, three days later he still didn't have a name, Mary's grief was too great and she had barely looked at the dog. I couldn't stand it anymore, and I tried one more attempt. I took him over to Mary again and explained that we all missed Penny terribly and nothing would ever replace her, but this little puppy is entitled to a life too. He is one of our family now and his puppy hood will soon be gone, we need to share it with him and build up new memories together. He hasn't even got a name for crying out loud! "How about Paddington?" she said, and went on to explain how he did look like a little bear and Paddington Bear was one of Samantha's favourite TV programs. (fig.16) Well, Samantha liked it too, so Paddington it was and from that moment on we never looked back. Mary and Paddy soon became inseparable and loved to take long walks together, though our thoughts were still with Penny, who lay in one of our basement freezers, as we couldn't bare the idea of just disposing of her, and I had other plans in mind.

I'd telephoned some Natural History Museums, but they

weren't interested. One did want her skeleton, but I said, no! Then I remembered that when I lived in Nottingham, I used to love visiting Wollaton Hall, a large Elizabethan home that held Nottingham's Natural History collections and I wondered if they would be interested in her? I phoned them and it just so happened that they did have a Leopard display, containing a Male and Female and they had been hoping one day to find a cub. "Well this is that day," I said, and they couldn't have been more delighted. Mary, Sam and I took a day off and drove the two hours to Nottingham, with Penny well packed with ice in a large cooler. When we got there it was just as they said. Inside the main entrance was a large glass display and inside it were the mummy and daddy, as if waiting for their new adopted daughter. The curator introduced us to the head taxidermist who would be attending to Penny and had been eagerly awaiting her arrival, not only because of the display, but also because of her size. He wanted to take her with him on his regular visits to Schools and Children's Homes for the Blind. "Now the kids will get to stroke a real Leopard," he said. This was music to our ears. Not only was Penny to end up in a beautiful Stately Home set in 500 acres of the famous Sherwood Forest, she was also going to help future generations appreciate wildlife. I felt that her little life had not been in vain after all. Tears again filled our eyes as we said farewell to her for the last time.

Back home, Paddington went berserk when he saw us, probably wondering where we'd been, but he soon calmed down when Mary took him for their usual walk. He certainly loved his new mummy! Talking of new mummies, Mary was only a few weeks away from her due date and beginning to feel a bit apprehensive; it may have been fun getting a baby in there, but what was it going to be like getting one out! I guess all first time mothers must go through that.

The big day arrived March the 20th. 1981. Mary had chosen natural childbirth without an epidermal and managed to endure the seven hours of labour it took for Julie to make her entrance. I was there at her side and together we watched the dawn break, then at last baby Julie was presented to Mary, a sight I will never forget. Mary looked radiant as she lay there with Julie by her side; her smile said it all. Like all new fathers I felt proud, happy and relieved all at the same time, I raced home to tell everyone the good news, I telephoned Mary's mother and yelled out "Mary had a little lamb." Only joking! Well, though we didn't have a little lamb, we did now have two daughters and one son 'Paddy' and he was defiantly woolly enough to be a lamb. After all, he was a Sheep dog. All was not smooth sailing though. The following day the Doctor had asked to see Mary and I together, and when I arrived he told us that after doing the preliminary examination, they discovered that Julie had a murmur in her chest, probably due to a small hole in her heart. Hole in her heart! My heart felt like lead when he told us, but then he continued to explain that in time it should heal itself, it just meant they would have to keep her in hospital for a few extra days to monitor her condition. I think they were two of the longest days of our lives, Mary and I constantly reassuring each other that things would be fine, and 'Thank God' they were! At last Mary could bring baby Julie home, though she would have to return for regular check-ups over the next two years, but other than that everything was fine.

Happy to be home again, mother and baby were the centre of attention and Samantha too, was genuinely happy to greet her new sister. I had been a bit concerned in case she might be jealous. Our staff and us were now one big happy family and looking forward to the up-coming season together. Well, that's what we thought until we received an unexpected visit from the Company's area manager and he hadn't come just to see the new baby! There was an opening for a General Manager at one of their larger Hotels and he asked if I'd like the job.

Now this is where things get weird, because the hotel was 'The County Hotel' near Birmingham. It was the very one that I'd sat outside while doing the Taxi work six years earlier, the one that gave me the idea to go into the Hotel trade in the first place. Remember when I said, "be careful what you wish for." The coincidence alone blew me away, but also it meant that we would be working close to our families in Birmingham and as an added bonus Mary would not be required to work there, so she could devote her time to caring for Julie and Samantha. I agreed to take the job.

We had been at the St. George & Dragon for three years and had become extremely close to the staff; Ena and her family were like an extension of our own, it was very difficult to say farewell and leave it all behind. But life goes on and before we knew it we were moving in to the County Hotel. (fig.17)

The County was a large wood beamed period building that reminded me of the Swan Hotel in Bolton, though not quite as big, three bars, one large restaurant, one snack bar, various meeting rooms and of course seventy bedrooms. But unlike the Swan, I would not be expected to work 80 hours a week and here I had a staff of sixty to help me. We settled into the manager's apartment that had been constructed in the attic of the old part of the building. Its only access was a narrow winding staircase, that could be quite difficult when carrying a baby in a carrycot, but the apartment itself was great! Fully self contained with two bedrooms, a large lounge and a small kitchen, each room was adorned with four hundred year old wooded beams and sloping ceilings, and it felt like living in a piece of history. There was one sad thing though, because whilst in Wargrave Mary and I had built ourselves a magnificent 'four poster bed' and it was unable to fit in our new bedroom because of the low ceilings, so we decided to put it into one of the large guest bedrooms instead and call it the 'Bridal Suite'. It didn't take me long to establish myself, everything there had been a bit bland, to say the least, so I installed a tanning room for the guests and up-graded the bars, then changed the restaurant menu and livened things up more, by continuing the Theme Nights that were so popular at the St. George, complete with bringing our usual scantly clad dancers from Wargrave. The staff loved everything and again we all became the best of friends. There was just one problem though; once I had done the changes, there was nothing else for me to do, as the staff were all super efficient at what they did. I had a Head Chef, Head Waiter, Head House-keeper, and Head Receptionist. All I had to do was the bookwork, wages and budgeting, the rest of the time I was expected to just wander around dressed in a formal jacket and pin striped pants and mingle! Well, as you can probably guess, propping up the bar was not my idea of fun. I hated small-talk, I didn't drink, smoke or like sports; the only subject left that most men wanted to discuss was 'Sex' and I was 'extremely' happily married, so I wasn't into that talk either. Luckily, the wedding of Prince Charles to Lady Diana was at the same time and it gave me a good topic of conversation for awhile. I remember getting together with the staff to watch it on TV, but once it was over I was back to discussing the weather.

You can only talk about the weather for so long, I had to find something else to keep myself busy, so I spent the next four months renovating whatever I could find, painting and decorating all over the place. I totally rebuilt the reception and did a great job, though I say so myself. I think Mary too was finding things a little too quiet, I know she had the children to look after, but she missed working together and didn't really like the way the staff were always fussing over her as the Manager's wife. She had nothing against them, they were great, it's just she missed being one of them and wanted to help more. Secretly we both missed the St. George and this is where things get weird again.

Unknown to us the staff at the G & D had also been missing us, to the extent that they had all threatened to quit, if the Company didn't get rid of their new manager, but what they really wanted was for us to come back! To make matters worse it was coming up to Christmas, a busy time and the Company didn't want the G & D staff to walk-out on them, so again the area manager paid me a visit. Rather sheepishly he inquired if by any chance we would consider going back to the St. George and Dragon? Would we, you bet we would! So arrangements were made for us to move back in February. The news of our return was enough to appease the G & D staff, but all was not well, the staff at the County were now upset and they didn't want us to leave! Luckily their old Manager was not too happy where he was and he too was only too pleased to come back. This somewhat eased the situation with our staff but they still wished we'd stay. I explained how although I would miss them, running a smaller place I would be 'a more hands on' kind of manager, which is what I truly wanted. It was a good thing that it was the Christmas season because things became so busy no one had time to think much more about it. I loved Christmas and looked forward to putting up all the decorations and catering the office parties and other festive events. But one thing I didn't expect was to spend Christmas in agony.

It was in the second week of December and I had been having some trouble with constipation, which wasn't normal for me. It was while in the toilet and having so much trouble going that I split my back passage. 'By the Cringe' I'd never been in pain like it in my life! I ended up having to crawl around on my hands and knees for two weeks and each time I visited the bathroom, it was like being flayed alive. The Doctor told me that some of his women patients, who had gone through the same thing told him that they would rather give birth than go through that again! 'You'd better believe it.' I was too afraid to eat; my Christmas dinner ended up as a bowl of soup and a bit of custard. "Bah Humbug!" Between the painkillers and bathroom visits I did manage to enjoy the prezzy's and watch some good movies on TV. Work-wise, the staff were great and with Mary acting as liaison between us, everything got done and all the customers had a good time. My main concern then was to be well enough to attend the holiday's Grand Finale, our New Years Eve, Fancy Dress Ball! All the staff were looking forward to it so much and had spent hours making their costumes. The entertainment was booked and the dancers were coming from Wargrave. I prayed that I would be able to walk by then and thankfully I made it! Mary went as a Saloon Girl, "Woof" and I, was a Wild West Marshal, complete with a real Colt 45. Don't worry, it wasn't loaded and I did have a firearms license. The place was packed. News of our theme nights had spread, though there was also a lot of our own family members present. It was our last event and made a nice ending to our time there.

All too soon it was time to say good-bye to all at the county and perhaps my illness was meant to be after all, as I think it would have been a lot harder for us if we had gone through that

Christmas season together. When we arrived back at the St. George, everyone was there to greet us. It was hugs and kisses all-round, the staff eager to see how Julie and Sam had grown and I think a lot of them had missed Paddington too. It felt like being home, surrounded by our old staff again, though there was one person missing. Kevin, the Chef, had been unable to get along with the new manager and had left straight after Christmas.

"How are you doing the food?" I inquired. "Basically we just concentrate on the carvery," they said, so this was time for me to drop the pin stripes and don my Chef's hat once more, as I returned to a full menu. I was overjoyed to be back in the thick of things again, but I knew that with summer just around the corner I would need to find a replacement chef. The local newspaper was full of adverts for Chef's. Half the pubs and restaurants in the area seemed to need them, so I added mine to the list, but before I knew it summer had arrived and I still hadn't been able to find anyone. My budget wasn't up to the level that most applicants were asking and the ones that would take the wage weren't efficient enough to cope. I had but one other action open to me: hire one from a Chef Employment Agency, which I did. Within days a chef arrived; a German guy who really knew his trade. He was fantastic and could do anything, often spoiling Mary and me with his culinary specialities. Everyone liked him and nothing was too much trouble!

"Wow, this guy is to good to be true," I said, not knowing then how right I was. The Chef settled right in and after a couple of weeks with us he even bought himself an old boat, that he moored outside and worked on during his spare time. This made me feel as if he was going to stay around for a while, perfect! Then after only six weeks, he suddenly told us that he urgently needed to return to Germany due to a family emergency.

We were devastated, but knew his family must come first. It was then July and our busiest month, so once more I became the Chef.

When it rains it pours, and next my tea-total 'Bar Manager' turned out to be an ex-alcoholic. Thanks to some creep that slipped a gin into his orange juice, he'd now become a blithering idiot, and incapable of working, let alone run the bar... I also had to fire both cleaners and one of the summer staff for theft. What to do? I ended up persuading my brother Gordon to move his family down to Wargrave and take the job running the bar! My brother had been a labourer at a Coach Building factory and had never done bar work before, though I was sure that with his many years spent running grocery shops, he'd soon get the hang of things. I moved him and his family into the three-bedroom staff house that we had in the village. Once they were settled in, Gordon took over the bar and I decided to put his son Andrew through chef training school, so that he could help me in the kitchen. His other two children helped out part time when and where they were needed, and his wife did what she did best, nothing! What a comedy of errors this was to become. What on earth was I thinking? I should have learned from my experiences at the Oasis, that family and business don't mix!

Gordon took over the running of the bar OK! He ran it straight into the ground... The power went to his head. I don't know how one person could manage to upset so many others, in such a short time, and I was constantly called in to stop the arguing between Gordon and the rest of the staff.

If that wasn't bad enough, my luck went from bad to worse when I woke up one morning and walked into the office to bank the weekend's cash from the safe and noticed something strange, NO SAFE! Just a huge empty space where it used to be. I called to Mary, "Have you seen the safe?" Yeah right, like she'd put it in her underwear drawer for safekeeping. The thing was huge and must have weighed 400 pounds. On closer investigation, we noticed drag marks in the carpet along the floor and down the stairs leading to an emergency exit. I immediately called the Police. They arrived complete with a finger print expert and soon came to the conclusion that whoever took it, got in through the office window and dragged the safe down the stairs and by the sudden end to the scuff marks on the tarmac, they must have loaded the safe onto a waiting vehicle. Gulp! I now had to explain everything to our Head Office, and as you can imagine, they were not too pleased and I ended up to my neck in paperwork trying to figure out what was missing. The nasty thing was it left a horrible feeling between the company and us, even though we had nothing to do with what happened! From then on, it seemed just one thing after another: unhappy staff, low profits and large shortages in the bar stocks.

As the weeks passed I was constantly tied up with cooking, and having heard nothing from our German chef and guessed he must still be busy sorting things out at home. I wasn't too concerned, because he had left his boat at our mooring and I figured he'd have to come back for that. One morning I received a visit from two police detectives, who informed me that the German chef had been arrested.

"Arrested! What for?" I asked. "Armed robbery," they said. It appears that he and some friends had been caught knocking over an armoured car and that's not all, he was part of a criminal group that specialised in robbing restaurants and hotels. Their tactics being, the Chef would get a job somewhere to case the joint, then make an excuse to leave and a few weeks later he and his friends would return to rob it.

"Bloody Hell, it was a month after he left us that our safe disappeared," I said. That's exactly why the Police were there; they had been visiting all the places that the Chef had been sent to by the agency and had found the same scenario at many of the places he'd worked. The truth was that he'd never left the country at all, and had been working at another hotel just thirty miles away.

When I informed the detectives about his boat, they were extremely interested in it and for the next few days they were busy combing every inch of the craft. Their scrutiny paid off and they discovered a false floor had recently been built into it, probably to hide their ill-gotten gains or for smuggling. They confiscated it. Great. I was only too pleased to see it go, at least it was one less thing to worry about.

I was having enough trouble with the bar, the shortages were getting worse, I was getting nasty memos from Head Office and I desperately needed to sort things out. Stuck in the kitchen, I'd warned my brother over and over again that things must improve and he swore to me that he wasn't doing anything to cause them. Then I began to hear things on the grapevine, that he was giving some people free drinks and also complaining about his low wage, even to the extent of showing people his wage slip. What he didn't tell them however was that I was paying his wife the same wage and she didn't even work there. I did it to help him, so that he would not have to pay so much in tax! 'Why was he doing such a thing to me?' I genuinely wanted things to work out so that it would be like a family business, but it wasn't to be, the final straw came when Gordon started to tell Ena how to run her restaurant. She went wild and told me, "it was him or her, one had to go!" I was stumped. Gordon was my brother and Ena had been with me for years and so had most of her family, whom we loved and respected. When I received yet another memo from Head Office, telling me that the last stock report was the worst ever and that if I had one more like it, I would be looking for a new job, I made my decision.

I called Gordon into the office and told him that I had no alternative but to let him go, and when he walked out my office I think we both were in tears! I told him that he could stay in the house until he found work and somewhere else to live, and that his son Andrew was welcome to stay working with me. Mary then took over the bar and I don't wish to point the finger at anyone, but from then on the bar stocks were fine. As for my brother he moved to Blackpool, where he and his family found work and swore never to speak to us again and to this day he has never forgiven me for dismissing him. His son Andrew stayed with me for a few more months and then moved to Blackpool and became a Chef there, from which he did really well for himself. But sorry to say, his family now doesn't speak to him either.

Things finally returned to normal, and I continued to chef myself. Then one night Mary phoned me from the bar, saying that a man had one of the local lads by the throat and she thought there might be a fight. I stopped what I was doing and went to see what I could do. She was right, an enormous man that I had never seen before was virtually strangling the poor kid. I asked him to stop and leave the premises at once- big mistake! He dropped the lad and walked to the door, 'simple enough,' I thought and followed him to make sure that he left. As he went outside I stood in the doorway and suggested that he didn't come back, to which he responded by punching me in the chest. I fell backwards through the doorway, twisting as I fell and crashed to the ground. When I tried to get up I couldn't, as my knee had been dislocated. Ouch! I crawled to the bar and Mary came running out to help me while the customers stood there watching. One of the other bar staff called the Police and they called an ambulance. The next thing I knew, I was well and truly plastered, literally all down my left leg. The following day our local Bobby (Police-officer) paid us a visit to make a report. He knew the guy that did it and said that I'd gotten off lucky. The man was well known for his violent behaviour and had been released from prison only two days earlier, after serving a term for manslaughter! (A few years earlier he had killed one of the local garbage men who had told him off for using the dustbin as a toilet.) If my leg had not gone out I would probably have gone after him and ended up with an axe in my head, as he usually carried one with him! I was advised that it would be useless to press charges, but I'm pleased to say we never saw him again.

Like most small country villages, Wargrave had it's share of local characters and he was just one of the ones to stay clear of. We were the only Pub on the river and I think everyone in the village paid us a visit at one time or another over the years. Some of the more memorable were our local 'celebrity' neighbours, such as: Sir Robert Morley, Mary Hopkins, Dave Allan, Lonnie Donnagan, Joe Brown, George Cole, Roy Hudd, Kenny Lynch and Vince Hill (who became a close friend). All famous names, though mostly known only to people in the UK. One visitor of international fame was actor Jack Palance, who had lunch there one day. Boy, was he tall! One local person that never came to visit was our neighbour across the street, though most of his staff and some of his guests did. The reason being, the estate was owned by the Sultan of Oman, a good friend of Her Majesty the Queen and on a few occasions we saw her 'Black Rolls' make its way through his entrance gates. Oh, and she didn't visit us either, though we all believe that Lady Diana did once!

Not long after my brother had left I was speaking on the phone to my old assistant from the 'Night-Out,' John Bailey, a long time friend of mine and Mary's. He told me how he wasn't happy there anymore. It had changed and become more like an enormous 'Disco Bar'; all the stars had gone and so had half the staff. I invited him to visit us, which he did and ended up never going back. Instead he became my new assistant chef and started attending catering classes two days a week to get his city and guild's chef's diploma.

From then on things settled down, the stock shortages stopped and the staff were content. John soon mastered the cooking, which took a lot off my shoulders, giving Mary and I a chance to take a well-earned break. During my time at the St. George I had become good friends with the owner of a Rolls Royce dealership and used his mechanics whenever I needed work done to my own car, which was by then another Jaguar XJ6, having traded in the Jensen. It so happened that he was one of the few people in England to own a genuine 'American Winnebago Motorhome', a monster machine when compared to the British equivalent, and he was prepared to rent it to us for a vacation, something that I couldn't refuse.

We decided to make the most of it and go on a European Tour. The motor home was also left hand drive, which came in handy once we'd crossed the English Channel. Mary, Samantha, Julie and I were soon travelling to Paris, our first stop on the way to the south of France. With memories of Mary's suitcase disaster still in our mind, we decided not to stay there and continued on our journey, but every-time we arrived at the entranceway to the autoroute that leaves Paris, it was closed with a barrier across it and NO Detour sign!

"What the heck's going on and how do we get out of the City?" I said. We drove round and around trying frantically to find an alternate route, but again only to find them all barred. While parked looking at one of the barriers, a tiny Fiat car pulled up along side us; its driver had noticed the British registration plate and guessed that we were having trouble.

"All the entrances are closed," he yelled, "You have to get

on at the outskirts of town. Follow me and I'll lead you there."

"Thank-you," I replied, and then in a flash he sped off driving though the city at high speed. It was all I could do to keep up. Tearing around corners and through narrow streets coming within inches of passing cars, pots and pans (and children) sliding everywhere, but I was determined not to lose him. Then, at last, he squealed to a stop and shouted back, "Take this road it will lead you straight to the main highway through France." In the wink of an eye he was gone.

On the highway at last I could relax once more and clicked on the cruise control to enjoy the sights of our fourteen-hour journey to the Mediterranean coast. Upon our arrival at St.Tropez, I telephoned some old friends of mine, Les and Lesley, who I knew from working at the Oasis and had moved there a few years earlier. It was good to see them again and they were impressed with our hotel on wheels. After a couple of days sightseeing we were on our way to Nice and spent a day on the beach there. Mary and the kids had a great time swimming, while I just laid back and enjoyed the sights- and I don't just mean the topless women... Anyway, I was busy; Samantha had lost her sandals after burying them in the sand, and we never saw them again!

The next day we were off to Monte-Carlo, where we didn't spend a cent in the Casino's, but it was worth going for the view. To this day Mary gets the shivers just thinking about the mountain roads we drove, thousand foot sheer drops on her side of the road, and she hung on for dear life as we went round every bend! Samantha didn't help, shouting out every time she saw the wreckage of cars that had gone over the edge. Next, it was on to Turin, Italy, where we were astonished by the amount of bad driving we saw and felt so relieved when we finally arrived at the Mt. Blanc Tunnel! The longest tunnel in the world at that time, it is over eleven kilometers long and goes under the Alps, separating Italy and France. What an adventure, especially when you consider the millions of tons of mountain that's above you. We drove through in virtual darkness until we saw it... 'You know, the famous light at the end of the tunnel', the one everybody talks about. Slowly the light got bigger and bigger until we were back in daylight and in Chamonix. 'Phew.' What a change in weather and temperature, only hours before we were in ninety degrees lying on the beach, now it was freeeeezing cold! We found a nice location and parked for the night. Next morning after having breakfast, we all boarded a train for an excursion up the mountains to the Mer de Glass. (Sea of Ice) Now, there we all were, at the top of a mountain surrounded by snow, and Samantha went down with sunstroke! Probably due to spending too much time on the beach the day before. We cut short our visit and went back to the motorhome so that she could rest. Mary and I got quite concerned when she became a little delirious before she fell asleep, but with no need, as the next morning she woke up feeling fine. So it was on to Switzerland and Geneva.

We drove into the city alongside the famous high fountain, the city's landmark, and proceeded downtown to do a bit of shopping. A bit was right, the prices were way out of our budget, so we had to settle for window shopping instead. Geneva itself was beautiful, very clean and picturesque, though there was a strange feeling everywhere, probably emanating from all that money lying in the banks! On our way out of town we stopped at a play area and Julie nervously went down her very first slide. Thirty minutes later we had to carry her away from it, kicking and screaming for more. We were having a spot of tea in the Winnebago, when suddenly I realised that we had only eleven hours till our ferry reservation to cross the Channel back home. The only problem was the ferry was in Calais and we were still in Geneva, eleven hours away! Oops. Seconds later we were on our way to Dijon and the highway through France. Stopping only for gas, we arrived at the ferry just as it was loading, drove straight on board and within minutes we were sailing. Talk about by the skin of our teeth.

One and a half hours later we were back in England and made our way home to the St. George. After greeting everyone we cleaned the motorhome and returned it to our friends. "Thanks it was great". We'd been at the St. George and Dragon for seven years and because I had personally spent hundreds of hours fixing the place up, it had become more like our home than our job. What happened next really pulled the rug out from under our feet. (The old 'making ends meet' curse struck again!)

We were informed by the area manager that the lease on the property was to expire next year, but due to the large increase that Courage Brewery wanted and the fact our Company wished to concentrate on its larger locations, they were not going to renew it. One other thing, because of the downsizing there wasn't going to be a management position available for us, though they might be able to find us an assistant managers job somewhere. Assistant Manager! That meant we would have to move into a poxy little apartment or even worse squash all four of us (and the dog) into a couple of hotel rooms. No way, Jose! What were we to do now, and what about all our staff?

A cloud of doom and gloom settled over us and I think we all lost our enthusiasm to do any work. It was a year however until the lease ended and things had to continue on. I did what I always do when I'm upset, I traded in my car and we bought another Jensen; we'd both missed our old one so much. A few weeks later Ena went to see a Psychic, and was so amazed by what she'd been able to tell her, that she suggested Mary and I pay her a visit. Mary was extremely interested by this because she'd visited a Palmist, prior to meeting me, and the gentleman had told her that he saw her working in a *large building surrounded by figures.* She would meet an *older* man there, who would be of great significance in her life and his name would begin with the letter J.

She was working at the 'Night-Out' in the accounts department at the time, a large building surrounded by figures, and then four months later, we met and became engaged and guess what, I'm seven years older than her! That clinched it, we decided to go and see the lady ourselves.

A couple of days later we arrived at the home of Mrs. Becket, a lady in her late seventies. She invited us in and we were given tea and biscuits while we told her of our concern about our job. She told us to sit and relax and she would see what images came into her head as she looked at each of us in turn.

"I see you leaving the restaurant trade and doing something

totally different," she said, something I did not want to hear! She continued on discussing various things and one that was really strange was she saw us living in Canada, close to the U.S. Border in a large house on the side of a hill near a lake or a river. "Canada! In your dreams," I thought. Can't she get anything right, though she did know that both Mary and I had lost our fathers when we were young and she had described them both perfectly. She also went on to predict that we would have three other children, but one would not make it due to a miscarriage. One of the last things she said was that a man would visit us with some very bad news, but not to worry, as it would all work out fine in the end.

After she'd finished I asked how much we owed her and she said "Just a few coins, you will need all the money you can get very soon so this will be fine." Next she showed us around her beautiful garden and told us how the spirit of her mother had once saved her life, and then we thanked her once more for her kindness and said good-bye. As Mary and I drove home, our minds were racing as we tried to recall all the things she'd said. The part about me leaving the catering trade didn't make any sense to me at all, the last thing I wanted to do was throw away all my years of Hotel training. I didn't really pay any more attention to the other things she'd seen and got back to work as usual, unaware that the seeds of change had been planted weeks ago and our new path had already begun to take root.

Chapter Five

The Envy of all My Friends

The road to success always seems to be under construction!

For many years photography had been a hobby of mine and whether it was by fate or coincidence, I was attending weekly evening classes and had been for the previous six months. I'd set up a darkroom in one of the spare bedrooms so that I could practice my new developing and printing skills. Part of the course had been devoted to model and fashion photography and I'd persuaded Mary to do some posing for me, fully dressed, of course...

The photographs turned out great; so good in fact, that on our theme night, some of the dancers asked me to do promotion photography for them, which I was only to pleased to do. I used the restaurant and grounds as the location, something the local lads were only too pleased about, watching all the scantly clad young ladies running about the place. It was as good as putting on a daytime Cabaret! After printing the best shots, I went down to show the staff to get their opinion as usual. Everybody raved about them, including our new waitress, Ella, who had recently moved into the village.

Ella was not like the other girls and didn't fit the usual criteria I would have expected for a part time waitress. She had a certain poise about her, and I was not surprised when she told us that some of her previous work had been in the fashion modelling industry. When she said how impressed she was by my work, I was extremely flattered. This again is where fate stepped in. She said my work was so good, I should think about taking it up professionally.

At first I dismissed her comments, though I had to admit, 'John Bell, Professional Photographer' did have a good "ring" to it... Then the Dancers, who'd been so pleased with their photographs, began to show them to their friends, who in turn contacted me to do work for them. I soon found myself swamped with orders and I must say, I was enjoying every minute of it. I was always excited after printing my latest creation, again eager to show everyone to get their opinion. The more work I showed the staff, the more Ella insisted that she was serious about what she'd said, and that I should open my own studio!

"I wouldn't know where to start," I said, and was surprised when she offered to help me. Ella went on to explain it had always been her dream to open a Model and Promotions Agency and how she thought Henley-on-Thames would be a perfect place to do it.

"We could join forces," she said. "Combine the agency with a photographic studio." "My Gosh, I'd love to," I enthused, but how, where and when?

Over the next few days we began to talk more seriously about it and everything she said made such good sense. After all, I was going to be out of work in a few months anyway, what did I have to lose? "OK, let's do it".

Ella and her husband, along with Mary and I got together to plan things out. A month later, after visiting the bank, finding a location, doing the paperwork and buying the equipment, we were ready for business!

The grand opening day of 'Photogenic Modelling Agency and Photographic Studio,' arrived and everything was ready. Mary, Wendy, (Ella's new assistant) and I were there, anxiously awaiting the arrival of the local press, but someone was missing. Ella! Where on earth could she be? Then the phone rang. It was Ella's husband, and he told us Ella had been rushed into hospital with appendicitis. What a time for it to happen; we would have to carry on by ourselves. When the press arrived, we explained what had happened and did the best we could to promote the agency, but without Ella's expertise on the subject, I don't think we accomplished quite the impact we'd hoped for. Wendy agreed to hold the fort for Ella and I promised to drop in as much as I could as I was still running things at the St. George and Dragon. I had expected only to be at Photogenic whenever needed to do photography. 'Still,' I told myself, 'it's only until Ella gets well again.'

Three weeks later, Ella telephoned me. "Glad you're okay, when can you come in?" I asked. You could have seen the colour drain out of my face as I heard her tell me she was never coming in, that her husband had decided he didn't want her to go into business after all.

I don't think we ever saw her again after that. Her husband and I did the negotiating necessary to finish things and I agreed to repay them their half of the money it took to open. That was a big mistake I found out later; they were the ones that quit, so I should have been the one to lay down the terms. I then tried to figure out how on Earth I was going to run things alone. To make matters worse, Ella was the only householder, so the Bank cancelled our line of credit. Now I had my own business, but nothing to run it with.

Mary, as always, was a great support and helped out as much as she could. Everyday I would end up driving back and forth between the St. George and Photogenic, trying to keep things running. One person who encouraged me to continue was Wendy. She loved what we were doing and didn't want it to fail; she was sure that she could raise the money to run the agency herself and take over what Ella had started. 'It's just a matter of time,' I thought, but had other equally important things on my mind.

I had to find somewhere to live, because there were only a few months left before the lease ran out at the St. George and Dragon. I didn't have much money left, but what I did have was a great credit history and as far as any mortgage company was concerned, I also had a good job that I had been in for eight years as long as I didn't tell them about the lease expiring! We looked at a few houses and picked one we could afford, then contacted a broker and managed to obtain a mortgage with very little problem, and being first time buyers we only had to put the bare minimum down. I cashed in my life insurance policy and sold some jewellery to raise the cash and had just enough to get the house and keep Photogenic afloat. Things were settling down when suddenly, those bloody ends were moved again. We received a visit at the St. George from one of the 'Company Directors.'

Someone had told Head-office that I was running two businesses and now they were worried the St. George would suffer. "Suffer!" There were only a few months left before it closed… But that didn't make any difference and Mary and I were fired for breaking the terms of our employment and were given three days to move out. I personally think it was because they didn't have a job to give us, and also it meant that they were now off the hook, and wouldn't have to compensate us for the eight years we'd spent working there! Luckily only days before we'd already moved half of our furniture into the new house, so with the staff's help we moved out everything else and left. Not quite the way we'd expected to go and definitely an unhappy ending to our life at the St. George. On the positive side, I was now free to concentrate all my time on Photogenic.

Once more I threw myself into my work; I started taking more advanced photographic courses in the evenings, and as my confidence grew I began to do wedding photography. I soon found myself booked months in advance. The studio too was busy. During the day I did the photography and in the evenings I developed and printed all the black and white work myself, as I hadn't mastered doing colour yet. Things were also picking up in the agency and Wendy had been able to find work for some of her models doing product promotions and fashion shows. Neither of us was making much money, but we were able to pay ourselves enough to survive. By now the lease at the St. George and Dragon had ended, all the staff had been laid off, and the building had been sold to a large 'Steak-house' chain, which had closed it down completely for renovations.

Ena and her family ended up buying a small 'Bed and Breakfast Hotel' on the coast in Devon and John Bailey had gone back to Birmingham where he continued on as a Chef. As for Ella, I had no idea what she was doing and to tell the truth, "Frankly Scarlet, I didn't give a Damn", I was having enough trouble keeping up the repayments to them. Mary and I had nothing left for ourselves and had gone from eating in the restaurant to sharing a plate of 'Kraft Dinner,' between the four of us. Things were tight all-round, but at least we were working together and the children seemed happy enough. Samantha was also doing a bit of runway and photographic modelling. Slowly but surely we crawled our way back up and we even managed to put on our own 'Summer Fashion Show' in the centre of Henley, during that year's 'Regatta.'

Wendy had a friend at a local radio station that helped us compile the music for the show, and I managed to obtain a portable runway platform, which took hours to build but was worth it. Though I say it myself, we did a terrific job and the whole event was a great success. Wendy and I were given a standing ovation when it was over and we certainly made a great team! Sorry to say, the show was to be Wendy's 'Grand Finale.'

Not being able to raise the money she needed to take over the agency, she was finding it difficult to support herself and her two children on the pittance we were paying ourselves, so when a friend offered her a job at a much higher salary, she took it. I was on my own again, but not for long.

My accountant knew of a couple that wanted to invest in

my business. In fact, they wanted to go one step further and install a 'Mini Lab' there. You know, one of those 'One Hour Photo' set-ups. What a great idea, I thought; we could then do all our own film processing. Where do I sign? A deal was agreed upon and the lab was installed. This also meant we now had to take on more operating staff; it was a lot more complicated than it looked, and it looked bloody complicated. After a lot of trial and error, (and I mean error) we began to take in films and business began to pick up.

Things went great for six months, and then our new partners decided they wanted to pull out and take the 'Mini-Lab' with them! Why? I'll tell you why, it was because they also owned a large empty shop in the next town that had been for rent for the past year. They couldn't rent it so they wanted to move our lab there and reopen it as a 'One hour photo' and run it themselves. They may have wanted to keep the 'Photo-Lab', but they definitely wanted us out of the picture... For crying out loud what's up with this business, is it cursed or something? I should have let them take it, but I was too stubborn and anyway fate stepped in again, with yet another answer.

When I told my Landlord that I was going to have to leave he wanted to know all the details. He loved what we were doing and didn't want to see us close either, so he decided to buy out my partners and join forces with me himself! This time we 'pulled out all the stops'. He bought us a brand new van so that we could do a film pick up and delivery service in and around the local district. We also employed Jim, an experienced 'Photo Technician,' to manage the lab and we promoted Julie, one of our best models to run the agency, which left me free to concentrate on my photography. So with partner number three, things got back to normal again and, as the wedding season was in full swing, it didn't take long before we began to make a small profit.

Besides the weddings, I was doing the traditional portraits like families, children and pets, but of-course most of my time was spent doing test-shots for would-be models. The average test-shot session entailed photographing the subject in the three main poses, head shot (face), three quarter (fashion) and full length, (swimwear). These shots would be done in black and white only, after which I would print a contact sheet showing all 36 frames, so that Julie could pick one of each pose to be enlarged to 8x10. Then an appointment would be made with the guy or girl to see if they had any modelling potential, i.e.; Photographic, Fashion, Voice, Hair or Promotions.

There was one other outlet for work however. As most people know, Britain has three mainstream daily newspapers, The Sun, The Mirror and The Star, that are renowned for their depiction of topless young ladies, or as they were affectionately called, 'Page three girls'. Some of our girls would request a few topless shots done of them, without any coaxing from me, might I add. They could then send the best ones to all three newspapers to see if they could get chosen to be a 'page three' model. Their goal was to get the exposure, no pun intended! In other words their photo would be seen 'Nationwide', adding greatly to their portfolio. A model's portfolio was tremendously important and I discovered that it was a lot more complicated then just photographing the person in different clothing, or the lack of it. "A good portfolio" should show the versatility of the person and their ability to portray character and feeling!

I took this work seriously and spent a lot of time and effort combining the right outfit to the perfect location, even taking groups of beautiful girls to farms and building sites to achieve the effect I wanted. For some strange reason, no one ever objected to us using their premises, I wonder why? Taking photographs of beautiful half naked women all day long, was not an easy job, but someone had to do it... so it might as well be me. Not only did I have what most men would consider a 'dream job,' I also had a beautiful and understanding wife, two lovely daughters, a Jensen Interceptor, and an 'Old English' sheepdog. No wonder, I was the envy of all my friends!!! And if that wasn't enough to make them green with envy, I then took on another role, chauffeur/

bodyguard to the girls as we diversified and started doing 'Kiss - a- Grams.'

My job was to accompany the young lady to a venue (a party at a bar, restaurant or office) where I would then walk around picking up her clothes as she stripped down to her 'bra & panties', sometimes just the panties, after which she then smothered her victim with kisses, leaving them covered in red lipstick. Having received the payment before she did her act, I would then help her get dressed and we would both disappear out the door.

I frequently received quite a few choice comments from other guys in the room and dozens of requests for the girl's phone number. I just gave them our business card. I can honestly say without fear of contraception, I never strayed, but I can't say I never looked. As I said earlier, Mary was an understanding wife, who as often as possible would assist me when I did any topless sessions; this helped me and also made the model feel more comfortable and at ease.

Please don't think I spent all my time photographing beautiful girls, (fig.19) in fact, by then I was doing a considerable amount of commercial work. This often involved a lot of work on location and it was because of it I was considering taking on another photographer.

An American from Texas had become a customer at the photo lab, and he'd told the staff that he was an experienced fashion photographer and if we ever needed a hand to give him a call. So I did, and arranged to meet Tex, as I'm going to call him from now on. Tex didn't have a portfolio; he said it been stolen just after he arrived in the country. What he did have was an array of 'American' magazine adverts that he said were his work.

He did seem to know the business and, though he lacked the proof, he sure made up for it with his smooth style and a voice that just captivated the ladies. I think most of them would have paid for a photo session, just to be alone with him. He appeared to be just what we needed. But before I had chance to offer him the job, the rug was pulled out from under my feet again!

Jim, the mini-lab manager, didn't turn up for work for two days and no one knew where he was. I'd telephoned his home and his wife told me that he had stormed out of their house and disappeared after they'd had an argument. I was to find out why later. His absence continued for another two weeks during which I was doing both jobs. I spent my days doing the photography and my nights printing in the lab, grabbing just a few hours sleep on a sofa in the studio. I was just about at my wits end when Jim came in to see me. "Thank God, you're back" I said, but just like Ella he wasn't. He'd only popped in to tell me about what had happened! He'd discovered his wife was having an affair with his best friend and had run away contemplating suicide. The only thing that stopped him from doing it was the thought of what would happen to his three children if he did. With tears running down his face he apologised for letting me down and said that he was moving back north to be with the rest of his family, so I wished him well and he left.

The mini-lab was Jim's baby and he was the only one that really knew how it worked, I did what I could, but was lost when it came to all the technical stuff and it didn't take long before the colour settings went adrift and the more I tried to fix them the worse they got. Things got so bad we had to stop taking in films. I don't know whether it was due to the stress or just bad timing, but Julie and I had a big row and she too walked out! Once more everything was falling apart. Then, while I was sitting in the reception, Michael, one of our regular customers, walked in with a film.

"I'm sorry but we can't take it," I said and as I explained why, he sat down and listened to every detail. He then told me not to worry and that he had an idea and would be back the next day to talk to me about it. By now I was beginning to feel like Bill Murray from Groundhog Day. The same scenario was happening over and over again. Was I about to be saved again? The next day Michael returned and explained how he was the son of a wealthy Iranian who's main business was importing lamb into the Middle East from farms in New Zealand. Michael had told his father of our dilemma and asked if he could help me out by buying my business for himself as an investment. This would mean that my business could continue as it was, but I would be working for him! At least this way the last one and a half years wouldn't be wasted, and I agreed. It wasn't going to be quite so simple, as I had to explain everything to my Landlord, who was now also my partner.

The landlord wanted to use his building for something else, and agreed to sell his share to Michael on the condition we found another location and moved out. To make things a bit easier we decided to sell the mini-lab. I say sell, but really I just found someone to take it over and assume responsibility for the lease payments. Without the lab income, I would have to take on more photographic work to fill the void and so I asked Tex to meet with Michael and me to see if he would like to join us. This was my first mistake! Tex's charm soon won over Michael and we agreed that he should join us. Next, we found a great location that would be perfect for the agency and the studio, as we could drive into it; great for commercial work! Once more everything was signed and sealed and for the *fourth time* I got back to work. Tex's wife was to run the agency this time assisted by some of our models, while Tex and I did the photography and Mary was to assist us and do all the administration. It sounded great in theory, but in practice it turned out to be a whole new ballgame, right from the start.

When we moved in, Mary ended up helping me use a jackhammer to remove a concrete floor that blocked part of our entrance, since Tex kept on making excuses and disappearing to the local pub. He always managed to return just minutes before Michael walked in and then stand there talking to Michael, as if 'he'd' done all the hard work. "Oh well, perhaps he doesn't like getting his hands dirty," I thought. "Things will be better now the floor is done and at least he can help me build and paint the model's changing room." Wrong! Again he kept on making excuses. The way he did this was unbelievable, he would ask if he could help me by getting something that I needed (isn't that sweet) and off he would go to get it and he'd always be gone just long enough for me to have finished. Mary would end up running off to get whatever I needed, then when he returned he'd explain how he got sidetracked talking to a prospective client.

Every job we had to do, he would always find an excuse not to help, though he would always flatter me on what a good job I'd done and how pleased Michael would be when he saw it. Then, when Michael arrived, Tex would display my work and make out that we'd done it together, you know, as if I had helped a little. After we'd (I'd) finished building a darkroom we were ready to open.

A 'Celebrity' friend of mine, singer Vince Hill, (who was also my client) had agreed to be the 'Guest of Honor' and he did a great job impressing the local Press at this opening! With that out of the way it was back to the photography. This time, most of the models wanted Tex to take their test-shots. I wasn't too upset as I was up to my eyes with commercial work anyway. I had managed to get assignments from companies like Porsche, Ford and Hallmark Greeting Cards and was also doing the odd 'Magazine Cover'. The problem was that whenever I returned to the studio, there always seemed to be girls waiting to have their photo's taken. Tex had either wandered off or forgot that they were booked and gone home, or to the pub. I now had to do his work as well as my own.

I don't know whether it was by luck or some sixth sense, but Tex always arrived back minutes before his wife or Michael came in, and again he would make out that he had done everything himself. One thing that always amused me was the fact that his wife was a strict vegetarian, and she was convinced that Tex was too. Whenever she wasn't around, he would stuff himself with hamburgers and hot-dogs, and if she should suddenly walk in, he would make out that Mary and I had eaten them and left the wrappers lying around. I know this because I overheard him telling her once, while I was busy in the darkroom. Liar, liar pants on fire.

I didn't really want to say anything to upset Michael as I felt so indebted to him for saving the business, but when Mary and I arrived early one morning and discovered Tex opening my mail, we couldn't stand it anymore and told him that we were going to tell Michael all about him. Tex went into the studio and Mary and I made a pot of tea and sat there for a while to calm our nerves. A few minutes later, who should walk in but Michael. Tex had telephoned him from the studio, to complain that he was doing all the work and that Mary and I were doing nothing! Well, you can probably imagine the argument that ensued from that, but everything we accused Tex of doing, he turned it around and accused us of the same thing. Poor Michael didn't know what to believe and told us to sort ourselves out and left. The minute Michael had gone, Tex admitted to us that he did nothing, but if we ever tried to tell Michael again he would always accuse us of doing the same thing. He had a lot more practice at it than us and knew exactly how to manipulate people, so we may as well leave as he could always con someone else to do the work! How do you handle a situation like this? No Idea. Well we didn't know either.

What we did know was that we had to get away from him for a while, as we couldn't cope with the stress any longer. There just happened to be a two-day seminar on fashion and wedding photography coming up that next week and I really wanted to attend it. When I told Michael, he thought it was a good idea, and it might help things cool down a bit if Mary and I took a couple of days off and attended. To ease the heartache of working with this dork I'd changed my car again, and believe it or not, I now had a mint 1974 'American Ford Thunderbird.' Yep! Tex, the 'tough American' was driving around in our little company van and I, the 'English twit' was driving this huge 'American Monster.' The mind boggles to what he thought of that… Anyway, the trip also gave me the opportunity to test out my new car, so off we went. We arrived at the venue; a beautiful resort set in acres of woodland and immediately knew that the peace and quiet alone would do us good. I was eager and excited to get started, however two of the guest speakers were from America. You can imagine I was not too impressed about that, but we had paid to be there so we may as well hear and see it all. Wow, I couldn't have been more wrong, these guys were fantastic! They put on the best presentation I had ever seen. I loved every minute and spent all my time making notes. One man in particular, Ken Reidenbach, was one of the photographers for Vogue Magazine and he just blew me away with his presentation. He showed us all the most popular professional poses and how to create them, he taught us how to achieve great results whether people were short, tall, skinny, bald or overweight. Not meaning to offend anyone, but everyone wants to look their best when they are photographed, and here was the way to achieve it and make them happy!

During one of the breaks I dragged Mary over to meet him and we sat and talked. We hit it off immediately and at the end of the event he told us that if we should ever visit New York, we could stay with him and his family on Long Island. Yeah, in my dreams, I thought.

The event over, we were on our way back to Henley and Photogenic. On the good side I couldn't wait to practice what I'd learned, especially trying out the professional poses on the models! I couldn't help wondering why Tex, who was supposed to be an 'American Fashion Photographer' had never used any of the poses that the American guys from the seminar had shown us, funny that! The quality of my work went through the roof and I got even more clients, including one of the 'Benny Hill' dancers, you know, the famous 'Hills Angels.' I think Michael was pleased about that as they started going out together. Soon I was too busy to care about Tex, and concentrating on my work, I got my Master Photography Degree, LMPA.

Life was good and when the agency became involved in the local 'Beauty Queen Pageant', I managed to persuade another of the local 'Celebrities', comedian Kenny Lynch, to crown the winner. I was also extremely happy when I was offered the job as photographer at that year's Henley Regatta Festival. To think only a couple of years earlier I had been a visitor there as a Publican, and now here I was, 'The Official Photographer!' Only goes to prove, you never know what's round the corner. Both the organisers and I were happy with the results, and no wonder. Mary and I worked very hard to capture everything on film; we even climbed to the top of a Church steeple, lugging up all the equipment to take some aerial and panoramic views. Of all the shots, my favourites were images I took of the 'firework displays' and their reflections in the river. 'Magic! I also got an assignment from the 'BBC Radio' to photograph the pop group 'Madness' when they visited Henley. Mary and I made a great team and worked together on many assignments, both in photography and video. (fig.20) Throughout all my work I always felt extremely grateful to Michael for making it all possible, so when he asked me if I would do some photography for his father I was delighted to oblige.

His father had one of the largest collections of rare stamps in England, and he needed some of them photographed for a Philatelist Show. After meeting with his father I proceeded to do some tests, but found that the finished prints did not portray the stamp's true colours, some of the fine detail had been lost. Determined to get perfection, I contacted Kodak to see if they could help me. Kodak suggested that I try one of their speciality films and they sent me a sample. It worked, and from then on I achieved excellent results, to the delight of Michael's dad. In fact it was the best reproduction he'd ever seen, so then I began to spend a lot of time at his house cataloguing his collection on film.

Things between Tex and I had settled down, "so I thought." One day, Mary and I popped in to see our celebrity friend Vince Hill and his lovely wife Ann, just to let them know how well we were doing. Vince seemed a bit standoffish, so I inquired if he hadn't been happy with his last photo session, but he told me it was great and that's why he was very disappointed that I had refused to do his photo for the cover of 'TV Times', Britain's National Television Magazine. What cover photo? I knew nothing about it! He said that he'd specifically asked the publishers to let me take his photo, and that they'd called our studio and were told by a guy, with an American accent, that I was not interested in doing it and to find someone else! No wonder Vince seemed peeved; he thought I'd turned the job down and considering that he'd especially asked that they give it to me, I don't blame him! I went back to the studio and confronted Tex, who again denied everything saying they never phoned, but in that case, how did the TV people know that we had a man at our studio with an 'American accent!' "You F-ing Bastard. " For once I did swear, in fact I lost it completely and resigned, Mary and I then walked out! I was at home licking my wounds when Michael called, and I told him that I could never work with Tex again. Not only had he lost me a terrific job, I felt terrible for letting my friend Vince down! Michael again had no proof that Tex had done it so there was no way he could fire him. What could we do? When Michael told his father, he came up with an idea and Michael telephoned me again to ask if I had any experience in building models.

"Yes, when I was a kid, that's all I did" I said, "why?"

He asked me to go to their house and his dad would explain, so I did. When I got there his father showed me a secret entrance that led to the basement. At the bottom of the stairway was a very large room, half had been turned into a safe for his stamp collection and in the other half lay a partly constructed model train set-up that covered the entire room.

"I want someone to finish this," he said, "model trains are a passion of mine, I'll buy all the materials you need to complete it, if you take on the job." He then continued on to explain that I could also finish photographing the stamps while I'm doing it, and he would pay me the same wage that Mary and I had received working at Photogenic. How could I refuse? I could have hugged him! Again, Michael and his father had rescued me; I was now beginning my fifth chapter of the Photogenic saga and I was determined to do a good job and not let them down. So that's what I did, between building the train layout and photographing the stamps I also became his personal Chauffeur, taking him to and from Heathrow Airport and on business trips in London. While he was in meetings I would nip into the Harrods of London toy department to obtain any parts I needed for the model's construction. I soon became quite proficient with model train terminology, and his father and I would stand in front of the layout discussing what would go where. The layout was immense! Commencing with an Alpine village, the tracks wound their way along scenic mountains into a western desert and on through a series of tunnels into a traditional English town, complete with streets, houses, shops, factories and a beautiful cathedral, with chiming bell tower. What a masterpiece! A shame that hardly anyone would ever see it hidden down there, but at least Michael's father was happy.

The family also had an array of beautiful cars including a Ferrari and a Rolls Royce convertible and sometimes I'd end up taking one home at lunchtime. Across the road from where we lived was a young disabled boy who loved cars, and he would always come out to see me whenever I came home in something different. I told him that Michael had an Audi Quarto sports car and that if I could, I would bring it home to show him. One day I was taking the Audi into town to get petrol (gas) and I realised it was time for lunch. I then made one of the biggest mistakes of my life, something I regret to this day. I decided to go home in Michael's car so that the boy could have a look at it. When I got home I went over to the boy's house to get him, but no one was home, so I ate my food quickly and drove back to work. Michael was waiting for me and he went berserk, screaming and shouting at me for taking his car home without his permission. I didn't have the heart to tell him about the boy especially as he wasn't even there to see it. I felt terrible, the last thing I ever wanted to do was upset Michael, but I had, and Michael never forgave me for it. Things were never the same after that.

I continued with building the train set and concentrated on being of help to his father. I started taking on other jobs such as washing the cars and working in the garden. Mary began to help too and did some cleaning for them when their housekeeper was away on holiday, and also helped out whenever Michael's mother put on dinner parties and other events, to which one George Harrison and his wife were invited.

Although we were relatively happy, it had been two years since we'd had a vacation with the kids, and an opportunity came up that could solve that and help Mary's mother, Dorothy, at the same time. She had received news from Canada that her brother-in-law was ill with TB, and she wished that someone from England could visit him. She'd always hoped that one day it would be possible and now that he might be dying, she was even more concerned. Mary and I decided to be the ones to go and while there, we could take a drive down to visit Ken Reidenbach in New York, as it didn't look that far away from Montreal and that's where we were going. Luckily, we were now householders and we managed to get a loan from the Bank to pay for the trip, so off we went.

We arrived at Mirabel Airport just outside Montreal, and there to greet us were two of Mary's cousins Serge and Robert, both of them only spoke broken English as Francis (Mary's uncle) lived in Joliette, Quebec, and the whole family spoke French. No problem though, we had great fun trying to converse with each other. Soon we were on our way to Uncle Francis's home and forty-five minutes later we arrived. It seemed more like ten minutes, as we were so busy looking out of the car windows at all the sights. Everything seemed huge, the roads, the cars, the houses and the people! Once inside the house the emotions poured out as Mary and Francis finally met, Francis was the brother of Mary's dad and had been sent to Canada after they were orphaned during WW1. Mary's dad had been sent to a children's home in England. For fifty years he'd been waiting to see a family member from England, and now that day had arrived. Once the tears had subsided it was time to meet the rest of his family, and what a family. He and his wife Jeanne D'arc had ten children, and as they were both in their seventies, all their kid's were now adults with children of their own.

To make a long story short, we had the time of our lives and visited many sites, including Niagara Falls, from which we drove down to New York to take Ken up on his offer. After paying a hundred dollar fine for speeding, (speeding, I was doing 65 mph, which was crawling compared to driving in England) we arrived at Ken's Long Island home, having only got lost once. Ken and his wife Betty had two children and fourteen cats!

Heck, each morning at breakfast it was like a scene from the movie 'The Birds' as we sat there surrounded by felines, (on the cupboards, on the table, on the chairs and on us) all busy eating and preening themselves. Luckily we like cats! Ken and Betty were perfect hosts, they took us everywhere and it was hard to say good-bye, but time and tide wait for no man and our return flight to England was just two short days away! We drove back to Quebec, (this time ticket free) just in time to pack and say farewell to Mary's family and Uncle Francis, who we would never see again, as he died a few months later.

Mary and I had fallen in love with Canada and while we were there, I had visited a couple of photographers in Montreal and showed them my portfolio, which I'd brought with me to show Ken. Although I never expected anything to come of it, I would have loved to have found work in Montreal, though everyone told us that it was virtually impossible to get immigration. Nevertheless, for some strange reason I'd shown them my portfolio anyway. Back home again in England, things carried on as usual and I went back to building the train set, photographing stamps and working around the house. A few weeks later a letter arrived from Canada. One of the photographers I'd met was offering me a job! This was totally unexpected and I think it took a while to sink in... we couldn't just up roots and move to Canada, or could we? It would mean leaving all our family and friends!

Well, we didn't really have that many friends as we'd always been too busy to make any and as far as the family was concerned, as soon as we'd left the St. George they'd all stopped visiting us. In fact, none of my family had even seen our house. If it hadn't been for us going regularly to Birmingham to visit them, they may as well not exist, with the exception of Mary's family and my mother. We did feel at home in Canada and after giving it serious consideration we decided to leave it to fate. We would apply for emigration and if we got it, we'd move and vice versa. A few weeks later we received a letter from the Quebec Embassy in London requesting us to attend an interview and so we did. Everything went surprisingly smooth, though they did say that if I could show that

I had done something that required specialist knowledge it would make things a lot simpler. Well, just prior to leaving the studio we did photograph a 'Laser beam' for the front cover of 'Professional Photographer' magazine, which required using smoke to capture the image, and I had managed to reproduce the stamps to within 95% of their true colour, would that do? Now, the weird thing was, the Laser job was actually one of the few jobs that Tex had ever got for us and in doing so, was he about to help us get into Canada? Could it be that fate brought us together just so this could happen? God alone knows I suppose, but you'd never believe it, we were accepted into Quebec!

In truth, I don't think anyone expected us to make it, us included. Talk about shock! My Mother nearly died and cried her heart out. Mary's mom on the other hand was upset and pleased for us at the same time, but if it was what we really wanted she wouldn't stand in our way. The same applied to Mary's brothers, and as far as most of my family was concerned as long as it wasn't going to cost them anything, good luck. The only one that did seem to care was my brother David. Our last step was to pass our medical examination, which we all did, including Paddington Then we gave in our notice at work and tidied up all the loose ends.

Sadly, I had to sell my car, which by then I'd changed again to another Jaguar XJ6, though unfortunately for me the price of petrol had just doubled in the UK and the demand for gas guzzling cars had crashed. I got a fraction of what I'd paid for it even though it's last owner had been one of Britain's best-loved comedians, Bruce Forsyth. (Sob!)

Michael's father was the last person I would ever have expected to be the one that did not want us to go, to the extent that he offered Mary and I over five thousand pounds to stay! Now came the hardest decision of our lives, do we take the money or open the box, sorry I mean, do we go? By then, all our furniture had already gone to be shipped and even our flight was booked and paid for, so we had to make up our minds and fast. I loved working for Michael's dad and with that money we would be able to do so much, but if we turned down the opportunity of emigration to Canada we would probably never, ever get the chance again! Our sense for adventure and the fact that we would probably spend the rest of our lives wondering what it would have been like, made up our minds and we refused his kind offer.

On our last day at work, Mary and I accompanied by Samantha and Julie went down to the basement with Michael's family for a farewell ceremony. Michael's dad had placed nameplates on parts of the now finished giant layout, things like, Bell's Station, Mary Street, Samantha Drive and Julie Park. Other than still giving us the five grand, I couldn't think of a nicer gesture, though he also gave us a gift of a hundred dollars each. After an emotional good-bye, our time with them had come to an end. I had finally completed my last chapter of Photogenic; the saga was finally over once and for all!

fig 1: My brother Ronnie's wedding when I was five.

fig 2: Dad on stage
1955.

fig 3: The opening of the Oasis
with Pete Murr(a)y.

fig 4: Debbie and I at the
Sunday Market.

fig 5: The Oasis, still going
strong.

fig 6: Ivor outside 221B Baker St.,
on the set at Pinewood Film Studio.

fig 7. My first XJ6, and
Sam's first car.

fig 8: Ye Olde Washford Mill, Studley.

117

fig 9: The Night-Out Theatre.

fig 10: Debbie's family and I at the Night-Out.

fig 11: Mary and Sam's first meeting in 1977.

fig 12: The St George and Dragon, Wargrave.

fig 13: The Big Day! With Jerry and Sam, June 3rd, 1978.

fig 14: Medieval Banquet with JB and Ena.

fig 15: Penny playing with her toys.

fig 17: The Country Hotel, Walsall.

fig 16: Julie, Mary, Sam and Paddington, 1986.

fig 18: Photogenic and our 2nd Jensen.

fig 19: The Cameo dancers photo shoot.

fig 20: Mary video taping a 1960's event.

fig 21: Theme night at the St. George.

fig 22: All in a day's work

fig 24: Mary's extended family in Joliette, Quebec.

fig 23: Dubee

fig 25: Lynx Photo, Montreal

fig 26: My mother with Michael.

fig 28: Our house in Ottawa.

fig 29: Me in a 1928 Buick (wedding).

fig 27: Mary and family- Frank, Mom, Esme, Michael and Freya.

fig 30: The Pyramid vision/model.

fig 31: Yard sale before moving to B.C., Limousine not included!

Corporate Event.

fig 37: William and Leah.

fig 33: Lyndsay and Hammy.

fig 34: JB outside the 'Millennium Cafe'.

fig 32: Decrepidtruckasaurus, say no more!

fig 36: Flo and I with David Icke.

fig 35: Wes, Dawn, Mary, JB, and Dave.

fig 38: Meet the family: Julie, Michael, Me, Mary, Samantha and Lyndsay.

Dorothy, Mary's brother Peter, Lyndsay, Julie and Mike.

Chapter Six.

A War of Words

Standing in the middle of the road, you may get knocked down by traffic from both ways.

There's a lot more to emigrating than merely moving house. Everything had to go! Thirty-eight years of accumulated stuff up for grabs, as we could only afford to send a little furniture and our most treasured possessions. Everything else had to be sold, or should I say, given away! Gosh, when people know you have to sell things, the prices they offer you are a joke. We were lucky if we got more than 10% of an item's true value, a scenario that was to be repeated thirteen years later.

It's like dying and being reborn; first you close down your entire life in one country, only to reestablish everything again in the next. We ran here, there and everywhere cancelling everything: credit cards, bank accounts, power, newspapers, Doctors, Dentist and Milkman, list after list of things to be done and people to see. You'd think having all that to do would be enough to occupy my mind, but no, question after question kept popping in: would I like my new job, would the kids be happy, was I doing the right thing, will we miss our family, would we have to speak French and what about the 'lions and tigers and bears?' Oh my... Struth, your mind can be your worst enemy at times like these, I know mine was. Mary on the other hand was as calm as a cucumber, taking everything in her stride, and if she was having second thoughts at least she didn't show it, though I did enough pounding of the floor for both of us.

If all this wasn't enough to contend with, people kept telling us we wouldn't be able to stand the snow. "Montreal gets tons of the white stuff, thirteen months a year," they said, but it was 30 degrees when we were there, the winters can't be that bad! Shows what little we knew and little was an understatement! We knew nothing about Canada, it's climate, it's people or it's economy. The only thing we did know was that it wasn't all polar bears and igloos, thanks to our two weeks vacation, but then we were so busy having fun we didn't care about anything else. If we'd only known then that we would end up living there, perhaps we would have made more of an effort to find out things! There was one thing, though, that really helped ease my mind, and it kinda' reassured me that it was all meant to be.

Remember, two years earlier while we were still at the St. George, Mary and I visited Mrs. Becket, the psychic, who had foreseen us living in Canada? Well now she was being proved right, but how on earth could she have known back then? Something else that Mrs. Becket had been right about was that Mary would lose a baby, and I apologise for not mentioning this before. A month earlier it had been confirmed that Mary was ten weeks pregnant, but then a few days later she miscarried. Of course we were both upset, but relieved at the same time that Mary didn't suffer any complications, as that would have made things a lot more difficult for us at the time, so we put it down to fate and moved on. The accuracy of what Mrs. Becket had predicted had aroused our interest in spirituality and this was also supported by something that Peter Small (the kitchen porter from the St. George) had told us, just before he died! Peter had become ill and passed away in his sleep a few months prior to us being dismissed. This was probably a blessing in disguise, as he had nowhere to go when the place closed. I think he'd had enough trauma in his life and had decided to move onto a better place instead. I will explain about what he said later on, but now back to the move.

It was time to say good-bye! Our families had arranged a little get together in Birmingham, a little bit hectic on our schedule with only three days before our flight, but it did give us the opportunity to say farewell to everyone at the same time. Well, not quite everyone; my brother Gordon and his family never came, and whether it was through jealousy or bitterness, I'm not sure. My brother Ronnie wasn't there either; he was ill in hospital with 'cancer' and so we had to go and say good-bye to him there. This was not an easy thing to do after what happened to dad, and we never expected to ever see him again.

Among the people that did turn up was ex-wife Debbie, and Mary and I were truly pleased to see her and thanked her for signing the appropriate papers to let us take Samantha out of the country, one other thing we had to do. I can't say that the evening itself was much fun since everyone was upset about us leaving. My mom spent half the night crying and trying to convince us not to go, and for those that did break a smile, I think it had more to do with their intake of alcohol. Before leaving, it was arranged that my brother David would bring my mother to the airport to see us off and Mary's brother Peter would do the same for her mom. Then, holding back the tears, it was hugs and kisses all round and then we drove back to Henley to prepare for the big day. On the morning of our flight our good friends, Roger and Linda drove us to the airport, where we met up with the others, and again everyone appeared to be full of doom and gloom as we made our way to the check-in. Paddington was the only one that seemed excited and barked frantically as he was put into his crate and wheeled away. "See you in Canada," I said as he disappeared out of sight and that's when it hit me - what had we done!

Everyone was unhappy, and my heart sank as I looked at my sobbing mother who was crying so hard. This time, I thought, she was going to have a frigging heart attack. In fact, the only ones that weren't emotional were Samantha and Julie. Samantha thrived on adventure and couldn't wait to see what happened next. As for Julie, she was excited because it was her sixth birthday and flying to another country seemed like a great present- I hope she doesn't expect the same thing next year! Time for us to board the plane and, sorry to say, my mother was still bawling her heart out as we walked through the doorway and waved good-bye. Alone at last, Mary and I reassured ourselves one more time as we made our way along the ramp. Finally on the plane the adventure became more apparent. We'd arranged a little surprise for Julie, a birthday cake, to be given to her on the journey over. They did this halfway through the flight. The stewardess sang "Happy Birthday," and even took Julie and Samantha to meet the pilot in the cockpit, something they both enjoyed. Thankfully the event broke some of the heartache I was having, though I was in for a bit more anxiety once we landed.

When we stood in the line-up for the passport check, Mary said that she felt a bit weird, and then as we walked up to the official, she fainted! 'Out cold,' she fell into my arms as I tried to hand the passports to the airport security, "Passports, please," he said, as I tried frantically to stop Mary hitting the floor. "But my wife has fainted. Can you help me?" I said, to which he replied "Passports, please," without an ounce of compassion on his face! By this time Mary was on her knees, so I wrapped my legs around her and held onto her with one hand and managed to give him the passports with the other. Then Julie got upset and started to cry so Samantha tried to comfort her, no one was allowed to come anywhere near us until he'd finished examining our documents. "You will have to go over to immigration," he said, and at last he called for someone to bring over a wheelchair. So there I stood, Mary dead to the world in my arms, with a crying child and a group of frustrated passengers all glaring at me waiting for us to move... 'Welcome to Canada,' I thought.

A month later, 'well it may have been just five minutes,' a woman arrived with a luggage trolley and helped me put Mary onto it, and then off we went pushing Mary on the cart to see the immigration officer. Luckily, by the time we arrived at the office Mary had regained consciousness and with the help of a glass of water she was able to speak once more. Now, with our papers stamped we were permitted to get our luggage. As we entered the luggage area we were greeted by the sound of barking. Paddington was out of his crate and straining his leash to find us. His friendly face was just what I needed to see and, reunited again, we grabbed our bags and went out into the arrival lounge to see if we recognised anyone. We couldn't see any of Mary's family anywhere, and then a total stranger came over to us and asked if we were Mary and John.

"Yes" I said, "who are you?" He then introduced himself as Jean Paul, a cousin of Francis's daughter Nicole, who lived near the airport and had been asked to come on ahead to find us as Nicole and her husband had been delayed.

"How on earth did you know it was us?" I asked him.

He said that he'd been told to look out for an Old English Sheepdog and as Paddington was the only one there it wasn't too difficult. Jean Paul was then joined by his wife Jocelyn and his son Sabastien, who also spoke fluent English, as did his father. Together we made our way to the car just as Nicole and her husband Jean Guy arrived. After another bunch of hugs and kisses we were on our way once more to uncle Francis's house. It was on the journey there that Nicole explained about uncle Francis. Although he hadn't lived long enough to see us arrive, he did know that we were coming having got immigration, something that had pleased him immensely. Then when we reached the house the whole family was there to greet us, all ten children and their families. It was a welcoming party, and this time there wasn't a sign of doom and gloom anywhere! Just the opposite in fact, and we hadn't had so much fun since our holiday there 6 months earlier. The fun was even more intensified as we tried to communicate with each other, as only 10% of them could speak English and we could only speak about 10% French!

The family made us feel so welcome that our worries of doing the right thing began to fade. In fact, we then had more family and friends around us than ever, and everyone was genuinely eager to help us in anyway they could. Julie and Samantha never had so many pals and like all children the language barrier didn't seem to make any difference at all to them. Now in Canada, our first task was to rent a house, and although my work was in Montreal we rented one in Joliette so that we could be near the family. Denis, one of Mary's cousins, became a great help. Denis epitomised the traditional stereotype of a 'French Canadian Mountain Man', complete with handle-bar moustache and it was funny because everyone knew that he fancied Mary, but then I couldn't blame him, 'I did.' Anyway, he was one of the few who could speak English and he also helped me find a good car, an old Chevy. Not quite the Jaguar I was used too, but it was big and roomy and the suspension seemed out of this world, amazingly smooth in comparison to British cars, might I add.

After a couple of weeks settling in, it was time to start work and as my job was in Montreal, one hour away, it meant that I had to commute there every day. Being early summer the one-hour trip was quite enjoyable, but the family constantly reminded me that once winter set in, it would be a totally different story, and it would take me hours just to do one way! 'Again, this paranoia about snow?' I'd driven in snow before without any trouble, but the family was so persistent in their claim that we decided to heed to experience of others and move to Montreal, reluctantly though, since we were having so much fun with our new found family! Crikey, every weekend there was a gathering at one of the families' homes and everyone had such a great time, especially the children. Mary and I were always amazed by the amount of food that was consumed at these events.

No wonder the American visitors we had at the St. George

would look in amazement when we gave them one of our standard British sandwiches, two thin slices of bread and a tiny amount of filling. Over here, the filling itself is bigger than an entire English sandwich. The same could be said for the rest of the food. Restaurant portions are enormous compared to back home. Once, on a photo assignment I stopped into a store and asked for a slice of Pizza, and what they gave me filled a paper plate. Only having two dollars on me, I wondered how I was going to pay for this monster, but sure enough, it was one slice and cost me just $1.75. It's amazing what people in North America take for granted; everything was actually bigger and cheaper here.

I think it has something to do with the fact that Britain uses 240-volt power, which limits their choice of products when compared to the rest of the world, which use 120-volt. All those years spent growing up in England thinking as others do; that we did things right and the rest of the world was backwards. In fact, it's England that's out of step and its people are paying through the nose for being so different. Moving to Canada certainly broadened our minds, and our whole life style began to change. Instead of spending all our spare time in front of the TV, we were swimming, fishing, boating and cross country trailing on ATV's (all terrain vehicles), something we'd never done in England, and we were having the time of our lives! What could be better? "Wait till we pull out the skidoos," they'd say, "it's even more fun in the snow." There they go again, mentioning the snow, what's with them all? I know that it sounds naïve, but honestly we had no idea of what 'Canadian Winters' were like, so you can imagine it was quite a shock when our first one actually arrived that October.

For the first time in my life I had to buy a snow shovel, as I joined ranks with the millions of other Canadians who had to defend their driveway against a 'giant roaring beast' that would attack as soon as your back was turned, and cover your clean driveway with another two feet of snow! What an 'Evil Monster!' I can't tell you what I used to call it, but there were those who called it 'The Municipal Snowplow'... We were to see more snow that winter then we had ever seen in all our years in England combined. I'd always loved to get a 'White Christmas', but this one was frigging ridiculous.!

We were invited to spend Christmas Day with the family in Joliette, so early Christmas morning we set off; all wrapped up in warm clothing, snow tires on the car, bags of salt and sand in the trunk and a small snow shovel just in case. It was minus fifteen degrees Celsius as we made our way there for lunch. When we arrived I remember saying to one of the family, "Do you know it's -15 out there?" "Wow, that warm," he said. How on earth could -15 be 'that warm?' Don't worry I soon found out what he meant, because it was -30 with a wind chill of –45, when we next visited them on New Year's Eve. What's even more amazing is that we still went!

If anyone had ever told me that I would willingly go out in temperatures that cold, I would have wanted to know what they were smoking to even think such a thing. Yet, here I was with my family doing just that, and doing it over and over again. (fig.24)

Visiting the family in Joliette became a tradition of every festive occasion, something we all looked forward to, with the possible exception of winter indoor events. Only because everyone was gathered together in one house and all of the adults smoked, and since we didn't and never had, our eyes would become sore from the smoke as the evening progressed. It would get so bad that we could barely keep them open and we would end up having to leave early while I could still see well enough to drive home. Beside the cigarettes, the snow and the huge amounts of food there was another thing we hadn't expected, the language war!

Of course we knew that Quebec was predominantly French speaking, in fact, when we were on holiday it had been fun communicating with each other and we expected it to always be like that, but once again we hadn't done our homework, and had no idea of the battle that had been going on between the two languages for years. This conflict was about to take a turn for the worst and again our world was about to be turned upside down.

Personally, my work was going great, I was now in the big league working as a photographer for a large commercial and advertising studio. Our clients were the crème de la crème, Kraft, Pepsi, Coke, 3M and other large corporations. I had progressed from my 35mm and medium format equipment to 5x7 and 8x10 sheet film cameras, as the finished product could end up 8 feet high and 20 feet wide on billboards throughout Quebec. I really enjoyed my job and together Mary and I were making a pretty good living in Montreal, but that was about to change.

The Quebec Government introduced Bill 101 that outlawed all English signs, and as most of our work was for companies that advertised in English only, 90% of them ended up cancelling their commissions. If that wasn't bad enough, the rift between French speaking and English speaking grew once again. Most of the French Canadians that we knew spoke English refused to speak to us in English anymore. So after just seven months at my job I ended up being laid-off through lack of work. Well, at least Mary had her job I thought, even though she was three months pregnant at the time, but when I arrived home to tell her my news, she had some news for me!

She was having a problem with her pregnancy and was losing water; she'd seen a doctor and he'd told her that she had to quit her job at Canadian Tire, where she was lifting heavy boxes, or she could lose the baby. As neither of us wanted the risk of another miscarriage, quit she did. Now we were both out of work. Luckily we had a little money saved and we were sure it would be enough to tied us over until things picked up again, but what a 'bloody time' for all this to happen... Mary's mother Dorothy was arriving that weekend for her very first visit to Canada. 'Oh Hell!' We'd written so many times telling her what a great life we were having and now that she was actually coming to see us, our first news was to tell her that we were both out of work, and that Mary was having pregnancy problems again. Heck, things couldn't be worse.

And how many bleeding times have I said that before, and if by now you're ahead of me, you're right- they did get worse.

129

Dorothy arrived as scheduled and being the person she was, took our news in her stride, reassuring us that things would be fine. Mary had given a week's notice at her job and she was determined not to let them down, so while she was at work I decided to take Dorothy out for a ride. I had heard that a Fashion Studio was looking for a photographer and I'd arranged to see them for an interview. So Dorothy and I set off to the other side of town, and as we came to an intersection the traffic lights changed to green and we began to cross. The cross traffic stopped, as they should, but then a car came speeding up the inside lane and crashed right into the door where Dorothy was sitting. 'Crunch' The next thing she knew, she was lying in an Ambulance waiting to be taken to hospital. Not being hurt myself, I told her to go ahead and I would follow on later after talking to the police. When I arrived at the hospital I was informed that other than a small bump to her head she was fine, but as they had given her something to calm her down they asked if I could leave her there for a couple of hours, just to make sure that there were no complications. With two hours to kill I thought I might as well go and have my interview as arranged.

I was still able to drive my car as the impact had missed anything that could disable it, though it looked like Godzilla had taken a bite out of the passenger side. I arrived at the interview 20 minutes late, but when they saw my car in the car park they decided to still see me. I got on great with the owner of the studio and he was extremely impressed with my portfolio, I was just what he was looking for, and as far as he was concerned the job was mine. "Great!" There was just one little thing though; I had to meet the other staff photographers before it could be confirmed. When I entered the studio, as soon as I opened my mouth you could have cut the atmosphere with a knife!

"Do you speak French?" a voice asked. "A little" I said, and I was confronted by the person that said it. "We all speak French here," he continued. "Fine by me," I said and I explained that I was eager to learn the language better. The guy then grilled me for a while and left. After that I was a little surprised when the owner still gave me the job and I was told to be there the following Monday to start work.

With a renewed feeling of self-esteem I went off to pick up Mary's mom from the Hospital. When I got there, Dorothy was feeling fine and sitting in the back seat of the car, we returned home to give Mary the bad news and the good news! In just one week, I'd lost my job, Mary had to quit hers, our car had been destroyed, Dorothy had been in a car crash and Mary could lose her baby. Beat that if you can! Too late, I top even this in chapter ten.

Mary and I felt like the pioneers of the last century, arriving here only to lose everything and then having to claw our way back up again. At least we had our new family and it was Jean Paul that came to our aid. As he lived close to Montreal, he knew of a place that could repair our car. He was even nice enough to let me use one of his so that I could start my new job. That's right! I did have a new job and on the following Monday, I arrived at the studio 9 a.m sharp. I walked into the reception, where once more I could feel an atmosphere of tension in the air. Sheepishly, I was asked to go into the owner's office and take a seat, and a few minutes later he came in and by the look on his face I knew something was up. "I'm sorry but I dare not employ you, not with the current language situation," he said, and explained how he thought he could win over his other staff but he'd been wrong. He then slipped me a hundred dollar bill for my trouble and that was that!

They say history has a way of repeating itself, and just like when I left the Rover Company back in England, I stopped to pick up the daily newspaper on my way home and there inside it was my next job! A new Photographic store called Lynx was opening up just 2 miles from where we lived and they were looking for a Photographer. Here we go again! I telephoned them and the next day I was on my way to another interview, but this time I felt a little more confident as the store was situated right in the middle of the English speaking part of the Island. As soon as I saw the place I knew these people had style, the storefront was a giant

35.mm camera. 'Cool!'

I went inside. Wendy, the owner, had really gone to town. Everything was top of the line, including the studio, which had been installed with the latest front projection background system. Well, once they saw my portfolio, they had just one question, why would I want to work there as she could only pay me half of what I'd been earning at the commercial studio.

"I speak very little French," I said. "Well, that's not a problem here, 90% of our customers speak English and we can help you out with the other 10%," she said, and I got the Job!

What a relief that was! Now at least Dorothy can go home knowing that I was working again, though she'd enjoyed herself so much meeting her long lost family and sightseeing, my good news was just the icing on the cake. I'm happy to say that she didn't suffer any negative effects from the accident.

I wish I could say that from then on everything was a bed of roses, but I can't. Our income was now a third of what we had been getting and the language laws had gotten worse; everywhere we went everything English was being obliterated. Signs were taken down; any that were permanent were painted out or duct-taped over. I remember walking with Mary and the kids through the Mall and commenting on how the 'No Smoking' signs had been cut down the middle leaving only half the symbol and just the words in French. As you can imagine, living under this pressure there were days when we felt like outcasts and contemplated going back to England. One night in particular I was giving Paddington his walk and I was calling him to me when a man on the other side of the street started shouting, "Go home you English pig and take your filthy dog with you." Next, he started swearing and calling me other names, I just turned around and went home. I didn't even know the guy and we hadn't spoken to anyone on our street and neither had the children. Samantha and Julie were next to feel the sting; they were in a French-only school and were obviously finding things a bit difficult. No one there would speak to them in English, not even their teachers. I wrote notes to their school but every time, they would just send us a reply written in

French, which of course we couldn't read and I would have to take them to work to have them translated for us. Things really took a dive when we found out that one such note was warning us that unless our two daughters stopped speaking to each other in English during their break times, their grades would be reduced and they would be held back a year!

For heaven's sake, Julie was only seven and hadn't spoken French in her life, up till now. The poor kid was in a strange school with people that seemed to hate her. Speaking to her sister during the break was probably her only way of coping with things! Don't get me wrong, I guess the same things happen to French children in English speaking Canada, but two wrongs don't make a right. I know that Quebec was just protecting its heritage, but sometimes I think the pendulum can swing too far in the opposite direction. We loved this country and the lifestyle too much to leave and, if by now, you are wondering why we didn't just move into Ontario, we couldn't. One of the terms of our immigration was that we had to stay in Quebec for three years.

On the upside, we still had the family who were as nice to us as ever and I did enjoy my new job. Also, Mary was six months pregnant, and although her water was still unstable she seemed fine. In fact she looked great as the rest was doing her good. Mary and I loved each other very much and I know that this will sound soppy, but we were also best friends and didn't need much to make us happy. However, after saying that, we were about to meet a couple who would become very good friends indeed.

I was at work one day when I overheard a British gentleman talking to our lab assistant. He was a little upset about the colour of his prints; they weren't as accurate as they should have been. I couldn't resist his English accent and I went over to see if I could help. His name was Douglas Manning, an Artist, who after photographing some of his work, had been a little disappointed by the reproduction of the colours. This was right up my street as I remembered the trouble I'd had photographing the stamps. I introduced myself and explained how I understood his concern and agreed to help him by reprinting his work and told him about the special film I'd used back in England. He was delighted by the reprints and came over to the portrait studio a few days later to thank me. We conversed while I showed him around the studio and he was fascinated when I gave him a demonstration of the front projection system and it's ability to produce hundreds of different backgrounds. I explained how it used a variety of 35mm slide transparencies that were projected though an image splitter onto a special reflective screen, and I could literally reproduce any background people requested, even from their own slides. (fig.25)

Doug explained to me how he had worked as a special effects artist for 'Metro- Goldwyn-Meyer' in England and that after emigrating he'd worked for the National Film Board of Canada, so he could really appreciate the possibilities of such equipment. Another thing that interested him was what I had said about the film I had used in England. He explained that he had to photograph some of his art for reproduction onto plates and that the correct colour was critical, so I offered to find out from our Kodak representative if I could obtain the film for him here. On his next visit I had some good news for him, I'd found the film, though only in a professional size, but that was to be no problem as he had quite a wide variety of cameras himself and asked if I'd like to see them and view his art at the same time. "I'd love to," I said, and he invited Mary and the children along as well to meet his wife Coral.

When we arrived at their home, we discovered that Mr. Manning, like most great Artists was extremely modest. Mary and I couldn't believe our eyes, the whole house was magnificently decorated and his art was everywhere. To call it art didn't do justice, masterpieces would be a more accurate description. Doug was an artist and nature lover, a man of compassion for all humanity, with an immense affection for the 'Animal Kingdom' that he captured in his paintings. The quality of his work was rare and incredibly life like, capturing the very spirit of whatever animal he'd painted, Doug was equally adept in oils, water-colour and pastels, and everyone who sees his work compares it to Robert Bateman's. With no offence intended to Mr. Bateman, I personally think Doug's were far better. Though little known by the public, Doug's art is known internationally and hangs in many corporate and private collections including The Royal Bank of Canada and H.R.H. The Queen Mother, and he received the 'Pastel Silver Plate,' the Pastel Society of Canada's top award, presented to him in 1987.

Even with all his creative abilities things never went to Doug's head, and it never went to his bank balance either. Both he and Coral lived a modest life in the suburbs and were two of the nicest people you could ever wish to meet. They never had children and Coral had concentrated her attention on her garden. I wouldn't say she had green thumbs; what I would say is that she had green everything. They didn't have a garden, they had a floral paradise, and the aroma from all the flowers greeted everyone that walked up their driveway. Both in their sixties, Doug and Coral were as vibrant and energetic as people half their age, with a great outlook on life. Soon we realised that we had a lot of common interests and thus became close friends. As agreed, I began helping Doug to photograph his paintings that were to be used on the plates, which had to be done on 8"x10" transparencies, (sheet film) and the more I worked with him the more amazed I was that someone with all this talent was so little known.

After watching him at work I could really appreciate the frustration of Artists like him, that spend hundreds of hours creating a work of art that is full of spirit and feeling, only to have it sell for a few hundred dollars, while institutions like the National Gallery spend 1.7 million dollars on the atrocity called 'The Voice of Fire'. It was like the King wearing his invisible suit of clothes, that only the elite pretended to see, where in truth, to all us peasants, he was just a naked old codger with more money than sense! In the years to come I would discover a lot more about how the minds of our elite work!

Besides giving us a new interest in art, there was something else that Doug and his wife introduced us to, the world of the metaphysical and the spirituality of other cultures and religions, something we both found totally fascinating. One

135

day while at their house we met one of Coral's friends who was a clairvoyant. Obviously she could see that Mary was expecting and she told us that Mary would be having a beautiful baby boy with blue eyes and blonde hair, but that's not all she said, she also saw a similar little girl not far behind! "A boy's one thing and we could barely afford him, but as for there being another child, no way is that ever going to happen," I said to myself! Mary had been scheduled to have a Caesarean, as the baby had not turned, and on 24th May we checked her in at the Maternity Hospital in Pointe Claire in the West Island of Montreal. Coral was then looking after Samantha and Julie for me as I wanted to be present at the birth, though this time it would be a little different, I would be able to stay and comfort Mary as the operation was to be done by local anaesthetic. I held Mary's hand as she lay there on the operating table, her lower body covered by a screen, but things didn't go quite as they planned. Mary let out a small scream as the scalpel cut into her, and everything stopped as they realised that the anaesthetic hadn't worked. So I was asked to leave the room as they now needed to use normal operating procedure and Mary would be unconscious.

Waiting outside I was feeling a little concerned, but that soon vanished when the nurse came out of the room and she presented me with our new son. Poor Mary was still out coldl, so I was the first to greet him. He was perfect, blue eyes, blonde hair and everything else that should be there. After saying farewell to Michael, our son, it was off home to tell everyone the good news.

Samantha (14) and Julie (7) were overjoyed and couldn't wait to see their new brother. I told them as soon as mummy is able to receive guests we'd go straight over. Later that day I telephoned the Hospital to see how she was. Inquiring about Mary Bell I received quite a surprise when they said that there wasn't a Mary Bell in maternity. "But it's my wife, she's just had a baby," I said, then I remembered that in Quebec they always used the woman's maiden name, so I asked for them to look under Mary Corfield. "Sorry" they said "no Mary Corfield either!" For a split second I thought they'd kidnapped them both, then the receptionist said, "We do have a Dorothy Corfield, though." Mary's mother's name and her middle name. "That'll be her," I said, and we finally found out that we could visit. But as far as the Hospital records were concerned Michael had been born to Mary's mom.

We had a good laugh about that when I telephoned Dorothy in England. The girls and I set off to see Mary and Michael and I'll never forget it, Julie skipping her way into the ward and Samantha all excited about having a brother. As we entered the room Mary was already sitting up holding Michael, and she looked so radiant, you'd think she had just come from a beauty salon and spa instead of just giving birth. Once more her reassuring smile said it all and I fell in love with her all over again! "My God, I'm a lucky man" to have been blessed with such a fantastic wife and three wonderful healthy children. Oh and I mustn't forget Paddington. It's at times like these when I wish I could capture all the emotions and put them in a box and then the next time I feel depressed and fed up with life I can open it and immerse myself in a good dose of happiness and gratitude. Not to say that our lives weren't good at this time, they were, though there was one time that we nearly went insane!

When we moved into another house and noticed little black things jumping about in the sandy soil in the garden and I don't know whether it was that or from the kitten that one of Mary's cousins had given us, which they'd found outside under a pile of fire wood, but no-matter where they came from, our house became infested with fleas! They were everywhere: on the cat, on the dog and on us... Poor Paddington had never had fleas before and we had to bathe him every day, no easy task with a Sheepdog. We also had to bathe the cat. 'Ouch,' he didn't like that! Mary and I would use ourselves as bait and walk around the house in our bare feet so that we could catch any that jumped on us. 'Yuk!'

Mary had a lot on her plate with all the continuous cleaning, bathing of animals and looking after the girls and the new baby. Perhaps it was stage two of our pioneerism and our task now was to conquer the plague! What a nightmare! It took a month to rid the house and us of the pesky insects. As the house got back to normal, so did our life, though with only me working and after buying all that shampoo and pest control stuff, our savings had now disappeared. Although we didn't have much money, things kept falling into place for us. Whenever we needed something, it would literally appear and I'm not joking. It was if some unseen force was helping us. For instance: Mary would run out of diapers and we wouldn't have any money to buy them, then a few minutes later Coral would pay us a visit and in her arms would be packets of diapers. She'd been out shopping and by chance noticed that the store was having a special on diapers and thinking that we could always use them, she bought us a couple of bags as a gift. 'Alacazam! Problem solved.' Things like that happened now and then but our main source of supply will surprise you; it was what we found on the streets! In Montreal at that time the garbage collection trucks would take anything, even big things like refrigerators and stoves, and people would put everything they didn't want out for collection. For example, Mary said to me "we're going to need a buggy soon for Michael and I'd love one of those fold away ones." Not having the money to buy one I just agreed and thought nothing more about it, then a few days later I was driving home from work and as it was garbage day, along the side of the road was the usual items left out for pick-up. Suddenly, out the corner of my eye I spotted something that looked like a baby buggy amongst one of the piles. Stopping the car, I walked back to take a closer look and not only was it a buggy, it was the exact model that Mary had wanted, and in perfect condition! I put it in the trunk of the car and continued home. When Mary saw it, she was delighted and was then able to go for walks with Michael snug and warm inside.

That was just a fluke you might say and I would have agreed with you, but it kept happening over and over again, so I'm no longer as sure! On another occasion we had an old stove that didn't work too well and one day it stopped working altogether. I had seen used ones in the newspaper for $100 and I decided to look for one the next day, but that night when Mary took Paddington for his usual walk, she came back early. "Guess what," she said, "its garbage day tomorrow and someone's put out a stove for pick-up. Come and take a look." I grabbed my coat and went with her to see and sure enough, there it was and it looked in good condition too. How on earth are we going to move this, I thought to myself, and then I spied a kid's wooden trolley across the street sitting in a box also waiting for pick-up. I went and got it and Mary and I manoeuvred the stove onto the trolley, being careful to be quiet as it was 11.30 at night. We soon found out why the trolley had been dumped. One of the wheels was faulty and it squeaked like crazy, so there we were doing our best to be inconspicuous pushing, pulling and squeaking our cargo along the 'usually' quiet street. I'd never seen so many cars at that time of night! The two blocks seemed more like two miles! Eventually we got the stove home and the two of us carried it into the kitchen. Moving aside our old one, we plugged the 'new' one in and "hey presto" everything worked fine. The old owners must have been upgrading or redecorating, but whatever the reason, we now had a working stove again, and it even matched our décor. Just what we wanted when we needed it, spooky isn't it?

We soon got scavenging down to a fine art and would keep an eye open for tell tale signs such as garage sales, because afterwards everything that wasn't sold would just be piled at the bottom of the drive to await the next collection day. An even better sign was a removal truck, as again any surplus would end up left on the drive and would usually be good items. We found some great furniture, sofas and lamps from these events. Once we picked up a beautiful red velvet 'Lazy Boy' in mint condition. Again, it probably didn't match their new décor, so out it went, their loss our gain. I'm not saying that we took these things because we were poor, it's just that I was only earning minimum wage and with three children every penny went on buying food and paying the bills.

At least we still had a nice car and it looked great after being repaired. I'd had it back six months and was driving to Doug's, when a car cut a corner at in intersection and missed the front of mine by inches. "Wow, that was close. It nearly got wrecked again," I thought and continued around the corner. Half way along the next street, 'Crash!' A woman who had been pulling out of her garage had seen me and gone to put her foot on the brake, but instead, pressed the accelerator and sped straight into me. Where do you think she hit me? Correct, right in the passenger door! Whoever said lightning doesn't strike twice in the same place should have seen my car! Back to the repair shop it went and this time I had the colour changed, and that must have lifted the jinx because things were fine after that. I'm not saying that the driving was bad in Montreal, but I definitely saw more accidents in three years there, than I had seen in over twenty years of driving in England!

Talking of England, if you were wondering what happened to Photogenic studio and agency, it eventually closed down all together, three months after we left, plus there had been another significant event within the last year. Michael's father and mother had moved from England to Andorra, on the Spanish border, due to health reasons, and when I heard that news I couldn't help but wonder what would have happened to us if we'd stayed? Other than that, everything else was pretty well the same according to my mother, when she paid us a visit to see Michael. Even though mom was now eighty, she loved the journey and liked being in Canada. Her visits became an annual event and she too was adopted by the family in Joliette and even came to a couple of the families Christmas parties, but sorry to say the smoke got to her, too. (fig.26)

Our life was progressing nicely and I'd managed to get some good results at work using the projection system and bookings were up. I also started using some of my commercial expertise to do photography for local businesses. A good friend of my boss was the CEO of the 'Peerless Carpet Corporation' and a collector of fine art. He owned a multi-million dollar collection that he wanted photographed for a calendar. Wendy, my boss, asked if I would do some test samples to see if we could get the commission. Once more the film I'd used in England came in handy; they were so impressed by the accuracy of the colour, I was given the job. This was no ordinary assignment as some of the paintings were the size of the average house wall, so rather than move the paintings they flew me to Toronto to photograph them where they were on display in their Company Head Office. Every detail had to be perfect, so I rented a professional 8"x10" sheet film camera and took it with me.

Once there I had to take great care in handling the paintings as they were worth hundreds of thousands of dollars each! Amongst the works were several by the famous Canadian 'Group of Seven' and I am very pleased to say that they are all still in one piece and everything turned out great. They had enough material to make two calendars. I was delighted with the results and the job did help me a little financially. A little was right, as I was given a small bonus, ($200) a fraction of what I should have been paid for an assignment of that caliber, and I was none too happy when Wendy wouldn't let my name be put in the credits. All she wanted was, Photography by Lynx Studio, but I was their only photographer!

I think our relationship went down hill from then on, also I was finding the projection system a little restricting and I was unable to be as creative with our customers as I would have liked. I did have hundreds of backgrounds, but couldn't change my lighting to flatter my subject as it created flare on the projection screen if the lights were moved from their fixed position. So, when the Zeller's department store in Pointe Claire decided to open a new 'Photo Studio' and advertised for someone to manage it, I applied and got the job! Although I missed all the background capabilities, my creative juices were able to flow again and I loved being able to use the fashion and model posing techniques that I had learned from Ken Reidenbach in New York, who I'm sorry to say, had died earlier that year. The only thing that was to spoil things was the ongoing language trouble.

The 'Language Police' were enforcing the sign laws and anyone breaking them was fined. This was especially prevalent in the West Island, being predominately English. They also began changing all the English street names into French and the friction got worse. It even materialised in my customers, and the language issue got in the way, some people bluntly refused to be photographed by me, just because I had an English accent! Some French speaking parents that did let me photograph them would create so much tension in the studio that their children couldn't relax and wouldn't smile. This stopped me from obtaining the quality of work I wanted and would make me feel quite upset. I loved to capture the magic of a child's smile! I did some great work of our own children and used Samantha as a model for many of our advertising shots, still used in the studio to this day. Sam also ended up doing some modelling for the Zellers catalogues, nothing to do with me.

At home, Michael had just turned one and it was time for Mary's mother to visit and see him, but this time she was joined by Mary's brother Frank and his wife Esme, who by an amazing coincidence had given birth to a baby girl the very same day that Mary had Michael. It must be a genetic thing. It was great to see them again and it gave us the chance to meet Freya, our new niece. (fig.27) Once more our extended family in Joliette made them all welcome and we had a fantastic time and went camping with them for a few days. What fun that was, all nine of us in one car and we still weren't squashed! I do love these big American cars. We also took a trip into New York state and both Frank and Esme were amazed on how green and beautiful everything was. Most people in the UK think that America is nothing but endless cities and skyscrapers from coast to coast, and have no idea of the vastness and diversity of this country. Terrific weather complimented their entire vacation and the only bug was the odd mosquito. Even that was a new experience for them and they enjoyed every minute of their stay. All too soon it was over and Mary's family returned to England and for Mary and I it was back to business as usual, but not for long, as we would soon be preparing ourselves for yet another visitor!

A few months later Mary had some unexpected news for all of us, and you've probably guessed what it was, the psychic was right, she was expecting again. Sorry to say this was not what I wanted to hear and I'd loved to have gotten my hands on the stork that was bringing this little bundle, but 'C'est La Vie'. I'd put in for it, so to speak, all I could do now was to accept things and do the best I could to support Mary and the rest of my growing family. It's not that I didn't want the baby. I loved children, it was the lack of money to afford them that I didn't like. Mary could have gone back to work, but then we would end up paying for someone to look after Michael and Julie and who better to do that than their own mother. Then, if Mary stayed at home to do it, we wouldn't have enough money to make ends meet either! Talk about a catch 22 situation and one that a lot of families have to battle with I'm sure. As for us, we decided that it was better for the children if they were brought up by their mother, money or not!

After having an ultrasound, it again confirmed what the psychic had foreseen: Mary was having a little girl, so we needed to find her a name. A few days later, I was photographing a family whose daughter had a lovely smile and personality to match and her name was Lindsay. I thought, what a beautiful name and when I returned home and told Mary, she loved it too, so we changed the i into a y and Lyndsay it became. The next six months were pretty uneventful, unusual for us, then just prior to Lyndsay's birth things certainly made up for it!

The language war got worse and the Quebec separatists were gaining ground. There was talk of a referendum and separation from Canada. House prices crashed and many businesses were closing down and moving to Ontario. The owner of the company I worked for decided to join them, so the studio changed hands since it was not actually owned by Zellers, but a franchise. The new owners were a lot more aggressive and most of the staff left in protest. I tried to hang in there but the language once more became such an issue that I had no choice but to quit and took a job delivering pizza's! The talk of separation grew and we didn't want to end up isolated and unhappy in Quebec so we decided to join those that were leaving. At last our three years were up and now we could go wherever we pleased.

Ottawa was the closest English-speaking city and so we agreed to move there and took a day trip to find a house. We'd never been there before, but fell in love with the place immediately. We scoured the paper for rentals and found a house in an eastern suburb and went to see it. I don't know how we did it, but the landlord accepted us there and then, and the strange thing was he didn't even ask where I was working! I suppose he thought that if we were moving there from Montreal I must have a job to come to. Little did he know.

With a renewed spirit of adventure we made our way back to Montreal and in the nick of time, as the very next day Mary's water broke. Once again Mary went into the maternity hospital, but this time under her own name. Soon after arriving Lyndsay was born, naturally this time, and without complications, unusual after a prior caesarean. Mother and baby were fine and by now you guess the rest... We all visited, Mary smiled, and I wanted to put the emotions in a box!

As I held my new daughter for the first time the quandary I'd had of having another child disappeared and I felt proud to be her father. She was destined to be, and Michael and her would become each other's best friends! Within days of Mary and Lyndsay getting out of hospital it was time to pack up our possessions and get ready to move once more. This was my 24th time and I was beginning to feel more like what it was to be a gypsy.

Moving day came and it was time to say farewell to Quebec at last. Our only regret was moving away from the family in Joliette, but then Ottawa was only two hours further away so we would still be able to visit them occasionally. Jean Paul's family and Doug and Coral had offered to help us move, so together we soon loaded the truck and then with Lyndsay only two weeks old we said good-bye to Montreal and made our way west to Ontario and Ottawa.

Chapter Seven

Take Me Home James

"WARNING: Objects In Mirror Are Weirder Than They Appear"

A huge cheer rang out as we crossed the border into Ontario! What a feeling of relief- we could now speak English again without feeling like outcasts. I expect that the French speaking populace would have similar feelings driving into Quebec. We felt free again, no more French-only signs and language police. Sometimes I think it's good to lose something because you appreciate it so much more when you get it back. An hour later we arrived at the small suburb, Blackburn Hamlet, where we'd rented the house. It seemed a really nice area and just fifteen minutes from downtown; it didn't take us long to settle in, having had so much practice. My mission now was to find a job and fast, since we only had a few hundred dollars left after paying our rent.

My first attempt was to try and find work back in photography, but no luck. I was constantly told there were no openings, though I believe that after viewing my portfolio most photographers felt a little intimidated by what they saw. Oh well, perhaps it was time for a change! So what would I really like to do?

There was one thing that had always intrigued me, the stretch limousines that I'd seen travelling around Montreal. I always thought what a great job that would be and I did enjoy driving, especially prestige cars. There must be limousines in

Ottawa; after all, it was the nation's capital. The fact that I had driven Rolls Royce's and done chauffeuring in England should count for something and might help me get employment. It was definitely worth a try. I consulted the 'Yellow Pages' phone book and took down the names and addresses of some of the larger companies. Instead of telephoning, I decided to visit them in person. My first stop was the office of one of the largest, Culitons. I gathered up my courage and went inside, and after introducing myself to the receptionist she took me over to meet her boss Ester and left us to talk. Ester and I hit it off right away and I think my English accent helped clinch the deal as I was hired there and then and even assigned my first run, a wedding that coming Saturday. Employed again, I drove back home feeling excited and anxious to give everyone the good news.

The following Saturday morning after getting all prepped and putting on my black suit, Mary drove me to a car valeting station where I was to pick up my very first stretch limo. To ease me in gently, I had been given a white Cadillac formal, a basic Caddy slightly stretched to accommodate the two fold out seats.

It was all ready to go and on the passenger seat lay a piece of paper giving me the details of the pick up, plus a box of wedding decorations and a 'Just Married' sign for the car. After reading every detail of the instructions, I began to get acquainted with the car and also what was soon to become my new best friend, my Ottawa street map. Off I went to do my very first job. I arrived at the bride's home on time and eager to please. My knowledge of weddings as a photographer and restaurateur really came in handy, as I knew weddings like the back of my hand. I was able to do a lot more than the average limo driver by assisting them with other things throughout the day. My final task was to deliver the 'Bride & Groom' to their reception, where I congratulated the happy couple and collected the payment for our services. I also received something new to me, a tip! I think I'm going to like this job, I thought.

With a job well done, I returned to the office and to my surprise Ester asked if I was available to do another run, take a group of six to a Theatre Restaurant in Gatineau. Sure, I was available; so she told me to go to her house and change the car I had for a black Lincoln Super Stretch. I will never forget my first sight of that black Lincoln on her driveway, it seemed enormous. After parking the Cadillac I went to the front door of the house to exchange keys where I was greeted by Ester's daughter who gave me the keys to the car but left me to figure it out for myself. Filled with trepidation I opened the door and looked inside. 'Wow! I'd never seen anything so lavish in my life. Concealed behind its tinted windows was: a Television, VCR, Stereo, Bar, Glasses, Ice compartments, Glass divider, Privacy partition, Electric sunroof, Intercom and two Cellular Phones. Talk about being fully equipped. When I got in and turned the ignition key everything burst into life. "What the heck do I do now?" Above and around me lay an elaborate array of knob's and switches, but what worked what? Luckily I still had two hours before my pick-up so I decided to go home and get Mary's help to figure out what each switch did. I pulled out of the driveway and 'very carefully' drove the sleek black monster home. On arrival, the first thing I did, of course, was to run in and get Mary and the kids to come outside and see the car; then we all piled in for a quick ride around the block. To Julie, now 9, I had suddenly became the best daddy in the world, while Samantha 15, was more concerned with how cool it would be to visit her friends in one of these. Michael, only 2, was fascinated by the TV and three-week-old Lyndsay was completely oblivious to it all. On our return home it seemed like half the kids in the street came over to take a look. Our children had no trouble making new friends after that, I can tell you. Mary and I soon figured out what all the controls were and with renewed confidence I set off for my next adventure, which also went off without a hitch.

      There was no stopping me now and from then on I kept a car at home with me, as I was soon on-call 24 hrs a day, 7 days a week. Prior to each run I'd study my trusty map and write down the street names and any important landmarks onto a large piece of paper so that I could easily glance at it as I drove. This helped me so much in the beginning, if the job was for a 'VIP,' I would drive as much of the route as possible prior to starting to familiarize myself with everything, always making notes of main entrances and other important drop off points. Like most nation's capital cities, Ottawa was home to government, large corporations and scores of foreign embassies. This gave us an enormous diversity of clientele and as we were one of the city's largest limousine companies we got a big slice of the pie, often called upon to supply the transportation requirements for VIP's of all kinds. Movie Stars, Sports Celebrities, Television Personalities, Concert Performers, Government Ministers and Royalty- we drove them all. Once more the 'Rich & Famous' were to become an integral part of my life, but this time in a whole new way.

Again my courteous attitude and attention to detail paid off and people began to request me as their driver. Then, thanks to three VIP recommendations, I was about to get closer to celebrities than ever before. So close in fact, it would completely change my out-look on life! Neil Sedaka, Paul Simon and Rod Stewart were my first celebrity assignments and it seems that each of them had commented to their promoters on the extremely high standard of my service. This, of course, pleased the promoters, who in turn gave me a lot more work. Soon I was promoted to 'Fleet Manager' and my education of life took on a whole new direction. Within a few months I became personally responsible for the transportation requirements of 80% of Ottawa's celebrity events. Yes, little ol' me.

It was also around this time that I did my first run for a little known Quebec singer called Celine Dion, not knowing then that I was to become her Ottawa driver for the next eight years and would witness her progression to 'Super Star.' What a transition it was! From being a discreet passenger on a scheduled flight, she ended up having her own private jet complete with personal bodyguard. But I must add that Celine was one of the nicest celebrities that I met. She appeared to be genuinely friendly and caring to all, myself included. I was always taken good care of and had free range backstage, including eating my meal with her and her crew, who were also great.

I remember one guy in particular, Michele Dion, (a cousin, I think) who was the spitting image of Steve Martin and I was amazed how he always remembered my name and the name of my wife, Mary. By the way, Mary had driven them on a few occasions and she was allowed to join me to watch the show whenever she wanted. As most people probably know, Celine came from a large family and subsequently her extended family was vast, with a considerable amount of them living near Ottawa and I think all of them were invited to attend her concerts whenever she was in town. At each concert there were always dozens of family members and friends back stage, everyone enjoying a nice meal together as Celine mingled amongst them chatting and taking time to play with any children, as did her body guard who was a really nice guy. I always enjoyed the relaxed atmosphere of her concerts. It was a pleasant change compared to some; most others were carried out with military like precision!

Anyway, as you can see, my life had certainly changed. I was now playing in the big leagues, and besides the celebrities, I was in the world of the elite, corporate high rollers, diplomats and the super rich. What an eye opener.

Whatever you may have heard about the behavior of these people, in their stretch-limousines, believe it, it's true!!! I saw enough sex and debauchery to last a dozen lifetimes. Funny, years ago I saw a movie called, "Confessions of a Window Cleaner" but it was nothing compared to the real life "Confessions of a Limo Driver," and here I was in the starring role. Literally- well it may not have been a starring role, but I did actually get to be in a movie! It was called 'Random Factor' and stared Dennis Hayden, Andrew Divoff and the voice of Dan Ackroyd. A Sci-Fi drama filmed around Ottawa in 1996. The film company used some of our limousines and you can probably guess my role? I played the chauffeur to the American ambassador. Hint: it is available on video. I also appeared on TV on a few occasions and I can actually be seen opening the limo door for Hammy Hamster of YTV fame. Just one of my many talents...

Talking of talents, it's a good thing I was a Jack-of-all-trades, because all my varied skills came in handy as I realized that there was more to being a limousine chauffeur than just being able to handle a large car! Not only were you the Captain of the ship, you were also the Maitre-de, Waiter, Bodyguard, Housekeeper, Tour-guide and Errand-boy as well. I dread to think of all the hours I've spent washing and valeting cars and that's not counting the time spent preparing for a run, obtaining champagne, flowers, balloons and all the other items that may have been requested to be in the car. I've spent hours driving around Ottawa trying to find the specific brands of food, drink and cigars that had to be ready and waiting for that all important personality or rock band. It was also my job to make sure that everything I got was presented correctly, champagne and white wine on ice, red wine at room temperature, coffee hot, beer cold and all food prepared and ready to eat, making sure, of course, that there were plenty of cups, plates and clean glasses. Always having clean glasses was one thing that impressed many of my clients, and after leaving them at a venue I would always return with a tidy car and all soiled glasses washed; it's the little things that count.

I remember once spending hours trying to find something called starfruit and a special brand of water that had to be in the car for the arrival of a rock group, only to find it all untouched later; probably because they'd already had their fill of the stuff on their private jet, which had been also stocked to the hilt with all their favourite goodies. 'Talk about spoilt.'

On another occasion, a group wanted a certain meal for after the show and they couldn't get it in Ottawa so they sent their Jet to pick one up from another city, sending me to the airfield to pick it up when it arrived. Carefully, I loaded the precious cargo of take-out containers in the rear of the limousine and drove it back to the venue, where I'm pleased to say it was enjoyed by the band. I should hope so too, considering the whole trip would have cost them around $10,000! Still, it's their money, they can spend it on what they want, right? Sure, they can, but then, they could also have had a slap up meal from any of the hundreds of restaurants in Ottawa, and used the other $9,000 to stock a few food banks. That way they could have filled their souls and their bellies!

Is it just me or am I the only one that thinks spending $10,000 on a take-out is a little absofrigginglutely bloody ridiculous, when there's children out there working 15-hour days to afford a bowl of rice. Rock stars or not, what happened to their sense of value? Like the "Rap singer" who on the way to the venue was bragging to his friends about the $200,000 diamond watch he was wearing and the $170,000 white gold pendant he just had made. Strewth, if you also take into account the rings he was wearing, this 'brother' had on a cool million dollars worth of jewellery, all of which he'd earned from singing songs about the oppression and poverty of his own race! "Makes you think, doesn't it!" Don't even think that I'm racist, cause I'm not, I just think it's about time these dudes practiced what they preach, and I suppose the same could be said about most of the politicians I've driven.

I had a way of evening the score a little, and getting my own back at some of the other kind of VIP's (Vulgar Impatient Pigs), that I would have to drive around on occasions. For instance, after picking up such a party our first stop would usually be a liquor store. They would fill the car with expensive booze, and then we would spend the rest of the night cruising from bar to bar, always of course, pulling up as close to the entrance as possible to make sure that everyone saw them getting in and out of the car. This would then continue into the early hours of the next morning when the bars closed, then I'd have to go through the usual pantomime of trying to get them all in the car. I would frequently return with one only to find another one had gone missing. And people think they have it hard running a daycare. Well' I'd prefer the kids anytime, since I can assure you it's no picnic trying to control six or more drunks, being constantly on guard against those that had become moody instead of merry. After I'd managed to get everyone in the car I next had the task of getting them all out, even to the extent of literally carrying some of them indoors, and now the point of my story. Because they were all tucked up at home I'd be left with a disarrayed pile of unopened beers and half used bottles of wine and liquor strewn about the car. This was of no use to me of course, 'I didn't drink', though I would take some of the wine home for cooking, frequently using Dom-Perignon to cook with. It's what I did with the rest that's so funny. Since I knew where most of the city's vagrants hung out I would go with my hoard to find them. Pulling up alongside I would open the rear door and give them whatever had been left behind. As you can imagine they were always very pleased to see me and I would smile to myself as I drove away leaving them to enjoy their bounty. Again, it's the little things.

"It's nice to be Important, but it's more important to be nice" is a saying that many have heard before and it's also the reason why I enjoyed driving around regular folk, since 90% of them were so damn nice. They were always pleased to see me and some were even downright excited, especially if it was a surprise! Though the children were the best, their faces all lit up and eyes wide open as the car arrived, I loved showing them around the car and explaining how everything worked. They all paid so much attention to what I said and even used words like please and thank you, something seldom heard from the children of our elite. Sometimes when I arrived the parents weren't ready so to pass the time I would take their children for a quick ride around the block, even in their pajamas. It was great fun, and when it was the parents turn I'd open a bottle of complimentary champagne and serve it to them prior to leaving, making sure to pop the cork outside of the car, of course. After closing their door (and sometimes the privacy divider) we would glide on our way to a restaurant or the theatre for a special night out or maybe an anniversary. On occasions like these it's important to make the journey last as long as possible, so I always used a scenic route whenever possible even if it meant I had to go a bit out of my way to find one. This gave the passengers time to relax, talk and enjoy their champagne.

In a way these events always reminded me of my days at the 'Night-Out Theatre', with everyone dressed up in their finest and excited with anticipation. Seeing these emotions in people made the work a pleasure and I enjoyed doing all I could to make their evening a success, including taking that all important souvenir photo for them. There was just something about having a stretch limousine pick them up that made people feel special. Everyone was happy, though as with all things there were exceptions to the rule, such as a funeral or the occasional argument, but most of the time the arguments were due to an excess of alcohol! Sometimes at the beginning of the evening I would pick up a group of six or eight well mannered, well behaved, polite individuals and drop them off at a bar, and then when I arrived back in the early hours to take them home it would take me awhile to recognise any of them as their behaviour had totally changed. Back in the car they'd be shouting, swearing and falling around, spilling their drinks and trying to smoke and that was just the women.

As for the men, I would have to be on my guard again as one wrong word on my part could end up with one of them taking a swing at me. Luckily for me they always missed. Thank God, the ladies didn't do that, but even they could be a handful at times in an entirely different way! For some reason, the majority of women that did get drunk acted very predictably. First their language would become a lot more colourful, then the subject of sex would enter their conversations and finally, depending on the amount of alcohol consumed, off would come various items of clothing, usually to be followed by them standing through the sun-roof to present themselves for all to see! At this level I had to be on my guard again even with the women, as I had to be careful that I didn't get pulled into the back of the car, especially if it was a 'Hen Party'.

The way different people get drunk may vary, but what happens as they do rarely changes. I suppose that's one positive thing that can be said about alcohol, it certainly doesn't discriminate, because rich or poor, it was the same, Swearing, Sex and Gossip! Personally I'd rather people make 'Love not War' in the car and that's exactly what a lot of them did, and if you're wondering how many people had sex in the car while I was driving? The answer is, hundreds.

My first experience of it may interest you; believe it or not it was by one of Prime Minister Brian Mulroney's cabinet ministers. My instructions were to put a bottle of good champagne on ice and collect a plate of appetizers from a local restaurant, then pick up a beautiful young lady from a pre-arranged location and finally go to a city hotel and collect the Minister. As arranged, I was to take them to a 5 star restaurant in Montreal a two-hour drive away, which of course I did. After waiting for approximately two hours for them to finish their meal, I aided them back into the car and then went into the restaurant myself to pay their bill. I will explain why in a moment. As they closed the privacy partition I was instructed to drive back to Ottawa. That was short and sweet, I thought, since on my usual trips to Montreal I'd be lucky to get out of the city before 3 a.m. Turning on my radio, I relaxed back in my seat to enjoy the drive home. We were about half way back when suddenly the car started to behave in a weird way. Just my luck, I thought, here I am with an important government Minister and the car's going to break down. I was just about to call them on the intercom when I realized that the fault appeared to have a rhythm to it. "Can this be what I think it is?" and you better believe it, it was! A few 'minutes' later (sorry guys) the car returned to normal and we continued on our way. After dropping the Minister off at his Hotel, I was instructed to take the young lady home and that was that. If what I said about him having sex shocked you, you better be sitting down as I explain to you about the restaurant bill.

It appears that there was a reason why our company paid for the meal; it's the same reason why we paid for everything else he enjoyed that night. It's called a paper trail. By our company paying for everything, there was only one bill to be presented to the Government for payment. A thousand dollars for a Limousine rental in Ottawa, nothing out of the ordinary as far as the 'Canadian Tax-payer' was concerned anyway. What they don't know won't hurt them, they think. Well, I'll soon fix that in chapter eight.

People having sex in the car soon became just part of the job, but at least most of them had the discretion to close the divider first, although I had one gentleman client who liked to keep it open during his sexual exploits as he liked to shout out comments to me as I drove. It takes all sorts I suppose! As for me, I kept my eyes on the road and my thoughts to myself. I don't know whether it was due to the abundance of testosterone, but the majority of the men that I drove were sex mad and had virtually no conscience when it came to obtaining a little bit of 'slap and tickle,' and I'm sorry to admit it, but as the years progressed I began to be ashamed of my own species. Golly, I must have heard every chat-up line in the book, and at first I thought some of these guys were romantic. That was until I heard the same routine from them to different girls every week, but I must say they were pretty damn convincing especially on the fact that they weren't married. Strewth, even I'd have believed them, if it hadn't been for the fact that I'd probably just taken them out with their wife and kids a few days earlier.

I had one prominent 'CEO' that would go out with his family one night, his girlfriend on another night and then later he would be out again, but this time with his boyfriend... Bloody good-job I was open minded, at least they were consenting adults and responsible for their own actions, though there was one occasion that I had to ask the same guy to get out of the car when he tried something with a young boy. He did try to bribe me with a hundred bucks, but I soon told him where he could shove his money. The following week he called me again to take him and his family out, as if nothing had happened. (Talk about being thick skinned!)

Yep, they were all at it; Celebrities, Sports Stars, Government Officials, Foreign Diplomats, Corporate Executives and the Ordinary Guy in the street, and guess what? The average session was only 7 minutes! Again, sorry guys. 'Well' I had to do something to amuse myself while they went at it, and I'd set the clock on the car and time them; Oops! there goes another trade secret.

On the odd occasion though, it would be a Lady that instigated the proceedings, but I must admit it was always done with the utmost style, and here's an example of something that happened a few times. I believe they got the idea from a movie. It went as follows: I would be requested to pick-up the lady first, and she'd pay in advance, then drive to another location to collect her husband or boyfriend. Usually this would be a surprise for the partner and my instructions were to open the door to let him into the car, but not look inside myself. The divider was already closed, the reason being she was usually wearing a fur coat and very little else. I would then drive around for about 40 minutes before taking them to their final destination, where they would both emerge from the car fully dressed.

I always thought this kind of run was sweet and I must be an incurable romantic because I'd much rather people have sex in the car than get drunk. Drunks always ended up spilling their drinks and swearing or even worse throwing up, which of course Mary and I would have to clean up. There were, of course, lots of other memorable occasions that didn't involve sex.

One of the funnier ones was when I'd arranged to do an airport transfer for the 'Make A Wish Foundation,' which entailed picking up a mother and her child early in the morning and taking them to the airport to catch a flight to Disneyland. Nothing unusual, except on this occasion I had been driving Michael Bolton around for three days prior. At 1 a.m the same morning I'd dropped him off at his jet, and keeping the same car I went home to get some sleep before going to do the Wish Foundation pick up at 7 a.m. As usual, everyone was excited when I arrived and looking forward to their Disney adventure. When the mother and daughter got into the car, the little girl was immediately fascinated by the TV, on which I had a Disney movie already playing. As we drove to the Airport the mother called to me and said, "I see you had a blonde with long hair sitting here last night." Glancing in the rear view mirror to see where she was sitting, I then told her that the hair could only be from Michael Bolton as he was the one that sat there last. The next thing, the mother went wild and screamed out that she was one of his biggest fans, and although she hadn't been able to afford to go to his concert, here she was sitting in his seat and holding one of his hairs, which she carefully rolled up and placed in her compact for safe keeping. She made it her own personal souvenir of the trip. Perhaps she too had a wish granted that day.

As you can probably see by the books cover, I too was able to obtain the odd souvenir during my years of service, autographs, signed photographs and backstage passes mainly, but sometimes I'd find the odd discarded item left in the car once they had gone. Many of these things I gave away, as I was constantly bugged by fans and friends to get them something and I couldn't always guarantee getting everyone an autograph. Some things, however, I still have, like wrist supports worn by Phil Collins! During his visit it seemed that the drumming had taken its toll on his wrists and he wore the supports under white cotton wristbands while on stage.

On the final day after his last performance we left the arena and set off to the private airfield. On the way there, he took off the wristbands and left them on the floor of the Mini Van. 'Yes' I did say Mini Van, as that's what his management had requested along with three 15-passenger vans for the rest of his entourage. On the Journey, Phil asked me what a lad from Birmingham was doing driving limousines in Ottawa, and he was nice enough to sign a CD for me. Phil was what you might call 'a Real Gent' and so was his road manager who had allowed all my staff to watch the shows and even invite their wives or girlfriends to join them. Plus, we were all permitted to help ourselves to the 5 star cuisine that was served back stage and if all that wasn't enough, every one of us received a generous tip! Ta, very much.

Another souvenir I still have are two used towels from Rod Stewart. Hey, I wonder if I've got some of his DNA? There's a story to tell here too, as right from the beginning it was not his usual concert routine. Rod arrived very late at the airport and we just made it in time for him to go straight on stage, no sound check. As I had driven him numerous times before, I was happy to sit back stage and watch the show on the monitor. As I did so I couldn't help but notice that there were no close-up shots of him that night, the closest ones always being full length. "That's funny," I thought, then before he'd even finished his performance I was instructed to reverse the limousine through the stage doors to within five foot of the stage exit steps, no easy task I can tell you. His manager also told me to make sure the privacy divider was closed and that there was plenty of water, crushed ice and towels in the rear of the car. As soon as the show was over, Rod came down the steps and immediately got into the car followed by his make-up artist and manager, no encore or autographs. The stage doors then opened and the police escort was there ready to go, and like a bat out'a hell we left the stadium, back to the airport where I dropped them off right next to their jet's stairway. Within a flash they were gone, leaving the two make-up covered towels behind, 'short 'n' sweet', to say the least. Perhaps it was a bad hair day?

Besides the odd gift, there was another perk from driving around recording stars, as 99% of the time I was permitted to watch the show, though one that I didn't, was one of Reba MacIntire's. At the concert her security was on full alert due to a bomb scare, and I was given a seat outside her dressing room and told to sit there, as they needed to know where I was just in case we had to evacuate in a hurry. This could have been a boring three hours but, lucky for me, her scantily clad female dancers had also picked that spot to rehearse and warm up, be still my beating heart. Plus, they did let me have a break to visit the canteen and enjoy yet another great meal. The scare, by the way, turned out to be a hoax and everything was fine and over the years I did get to see her other shows. What shows they were! Though I am not a fan of country music, her concerts covered the whole spectrum of entertainment and are definitely worth seeing...

Going back to the meals for a moment, the food that was served back stage at all these events was fantastic, all professionally catered and always delicious. The full meal deal came with a choice of appetizer, main-course and dessert, all accompanied by a selection of coffee, tea, water and soft drinks from all corners of the world, something for everyone. Usually the star and their staff mingled together to eat, one big happy family who'd all worked hard to prepare everything for that evening's show and deserved a break and a good meal. I must admit everyone did work hard, and I was always impressed at how fast and efficiently the crew managed to assemble a full stage set in time, only to dismantle it all again after the show, load it on a truck, drive over night to another city and put it all up again ready for another show the next day. No wonder they ate well.

As for 'The Stars' themselves, they too worked pretty well non-stop, flying in early to do a sound check and then the show itself, after which they'd do a meet and greet to sign autographs before going to the hotel to grab some sleep, only to fly off in the morning to the next city to do it all over again.

"Phew!" Having to maintain such a tight schedule is why they needed us, it was our/my job to convey them around, from the airport to the venue, from the venue to the hotel and from the hotel back to the airport, and sometimes all in one day. If they were lucky enough to be in town for a few days, it could also entail us taking them to radio and television interviews, not to mention, or should I, all their private outings...

One of the things I really enjoyed though, was taking celebrities on sight seeing tours, especially when I got to accompany them as they walked around the city visiting shops and museums, which certainly creates quite a stir. While they're busy looking at the exhibits everyone else is looking at them, probably wondering who the heck I was, though I must say, 'it certainly does wonders for your ego being so close to a star.'

In 1992 I had the privilege of escorting Shirley Solomon (of the Shirley Show, CBC TV, Toronto) around the magnificent Museum of Civilization in Hull. It was great, just the two of us leisurely making our way through the exhibits, as people kept coming up to us to ask for her autograph. What a beautiful lady, with a pair of legs that would intimidate an ostrich. It felt so good to be the one accompanying her that I think I grew a couple of inches, in height - in height! Hey just because I'm not hungry, it doesn't mean I can't look at the menu... Anyway staying close at hand was an important part of all my Celebrity/VIP bookings, as they needed to know where I was at all times, and on the odd occasion that I was allowed to wander off, it was only on the condition that I had a cell-phone and a pager on me, though sometimes I'd be given a walkie-talkie as well, especially if I was working with or for the police.

Working with the RCMP and the OPP was another ego booster, especially when I had a police escort, "You know, for that all important 'Super Star' or Head of State!" One case in point was, Her Royal Highness, the Princess of Thailand.

What an experience! They required a limousine for her and her husband, a mini van for her doctor and personal staff, a 50-passenger bus for the rest of her staff and a 5-ton truck for all their luggage! We also had to blacken out all the windows of the limousine with cardboard to keep out any sunlight, as the Princess was an albino and susceptible to bright light. At each stop, large umbrellas had to be up and in place before we could open the car door to let her out. The mini van also had to be a specific type, a 1992 Pontiac Transport, because her husband was a pilot and he had heard that the interior windshield set-up of this van resembled the cockpit of an aircraft, which it does. He was also a keen model builder and I took him in the Pontiac on a shopping trip to one of Ottawa's model shops, where we filled the entire rear of the van with about $5,000.00 worth of model building kits. And no, I didn't get any commission. But I did get some great food back at the Ambassador of Thailand's mansion when we went there for lunch, though I did have to sit and eat it in the basement. My five days with them was the longest I ever went with a police escort. I must say the majority of celebrities don't even bother with police escorts but of course, there were a few that demanded one.

'Thank God' Ozzy Osbourne wasn't one of them, as I can just imagine the look on a cop's face if he'd had to protect him while he took a leak at the side of the road, next to a 'Canadian Tire' sign! 'Oh well,' at least I was able to add that spot to my sightseeing tours and it became a site of great interest, especially with graduations. In fact it was Ozzy's story and others like it, that helped me get through the yearly 'Graduation Season' pretty well unscathed, since most of the kids were so interested in hearing what I had to say they never had time to wreck my car. Thank you! Thank you.

Again, there were exceptions and sorry to say, it always seemed to be by those that came from the wealthiest homes! This one example epitomises the kind. I was booked to do the graduation for a daughter of one of Ottawa's ex-Mayors, (sorry your Worship.) and as I arrived at the house everything seemed normal. There, waiting for me were the usual group of beautifully dressed young ladies, all happy and excited about their big day. As his daughter and her friends got into the car, the father took her to one side and laid down a few ground rules. No hard liquor, no drugs, no boys and no going over to the bars in Hull. (Quebec) He then slipped her $50 and said this is a tip for the driver.

"This is going to be a great night," I thought to myself, but 'boy' was I wrong. Our first stop was at a liquor store where they proceeded to fill the car with hard liquor (strike one), then throughout the course of the evening they broke every rule her father had set and even a few more just for good measure. After leaving the bars in Hull at 3.30 a.m, it was time to thankfully drive them home. Once more I went through my usual procedure of helping them out of the car and into their house, and when I'd eventually dropped off the last one I took a deep breath and looked inside the car. What a frigging mess. It was enough to make a saint cry and I think I did, and to add insult to injury she didn't even give me my tip. What a rip-off.

I don't think there's a single limousine driver, that doesn't have similar horror stories to tell, and as far as I'm concerned, the whole grad season is a bleeding nightmare! For the whole month I was booked on the hour, every hour. This meant that I had only minutes to get from my drop-off to my next pick-up, the kids having timed the run to make sure they got every second. The only problem was, my next pick-up was usually on the other side of town, plus I had to wash the glasses, refill the ice trays and clean the entire car ready for the next group, all in about 5 minutes! Once someone phoned my boss and said, "I've just seen John in a super stretch going about a 130k through the centre of town." "It's all right he's doing graduations" my boss said, "Oh, well that explains it," they said and hung up. Meanwhile, in the car my brain was going faster than the car was, as I constantly ran through the list of excuses I could use to appease my next group, who were by now standing outside their house with a phone in one hand and a rope in the other. Heck,' I'd end up promising so many people that I'd make up for every minute they'd lost that I'd be out until 5 a.m the next morning still driving groups around. Thankfully there were the rare occasions when I was lucky enough to have a spare car, enabling Mary to meet me between runs so that we could change, she would then clean the one she had and then meet me later to swap again, and on and on it would go for the rest of the night.

In fact, Mary used to help keep me supplied with all kinds of things, bottles of champagne, extra glasses, ice and a variety of vehicles, because going from booking to booking as I did, I was constantly having to change my car to suit the clients. An array of vans, sedans and limousines of various shapes, size and colour, all to accommodate their individual needs, and I could drive up to six different vehicles in one day. Thank heavens for my cell-phone, because I would never have kept up the pace without it, this was one job in which they really were a necessity. I think some of my clients would have had a coronary if there hadn't been one in the car during their journey. You will discover more about the people I am referring to when, in the next chapter, we delve more into the realm of our so-called peers. Talking of other realms lets leave behind the chaos of the Grad session and enter the realm of 'magic' and David Copperfield.

Mr. Copperfield 'appeared' in Ottawa every two years or so to do his magic show at the National Arts Centre, and his requirements were always the same, a large black super stretch limousine equipped with tinted windows, privacy divider, air conditioning, stereo, bar, working intercom and mature male driver. Something else that never changed was his attitude. He was a man of few words, just looks 'and what looks.' It still gives me the shivers just thinking of them... His events were run with military like precision and his security people were everywhere, none of the local staff were allowed anywhere near back stage, thus ensuring the secret of how things were done. Fair enough! I, on the other hand, was permitted to go as far as his dressing room, oh, and the canteen, of course. Then at the end of each show I paid close attention for 'the look', the one that meant 'we're out of here' and after exiting the stage door and running the gauntlet of autograph hunters we would be on our way, our destination being whatever he desired, a restaurant, a bar or maybe just back to his hotel.

On one occasion, we went back to his hotel and I was told to wait. As usual, I parked the car within three feet of the main doorway for his security, which didn't please the doorman as it was a very busy night to have a 27 foot long car blocking the driveway, but he knew the procedure and we both had to just grin and bear it. Three hours later, I was still there, so I took the liberty of phoning his manager's room to find out why, and a few minutes later he called me back to inform me that David had gone to bed and forgot to dismiss me, I was free to go. I'll leave it to your imagination what the doorman said.

The next night after his show, David decided he wanted to visit the Byward Market, Ottawa's trendy bar area, and as we cruised around he was busy talking on his cell-phone when he suddenly dropped it on the seat and shouted, "Stop the car!" Immediately he got out and went over to a beautiful blonde that was standing on the sidewalk. He looked at me and said, "Follow us" and the two of them went off to explore the bars... So picture this. Saturday-night in the busiest part of the city, streets full of people and traffic and there I was driving a super stretch limousine at 3 miles an hour trying to follow a couple on the sidewalk! Well of course the inevitable happened, as I got stuck at a red light the two of them walked around a left hand corner and out of sight. "Gulp!" As soon as the lights changed, I turned left but they had gone. Seeing a small group of people standing there I asked if they knew who David Copperfield was and had they seen him because he'd just disappeared!

"Wow" they said, " so he really is a magician," but for once I didn't appreciate the joke. Luckily for me, he did 'reappear' five minutes later, out of a bar. Other exploits I experienced with him are better left unsaid, nudge, nudge, wink, wink, but to say the least I was not impressed and that also applies to a few other well known Cele-brat-ies, that I've driven, including, Vanilla Ice, 'Hulk' you know who, and the lead singer of Simply Red, to name a few, but of course, this is just my personal opinion. Although to be honest there were others that I expected might be trouble, when in fact they turned out to be super nice. People like Andrew Dice Clay, Neil Young, Metallica, Motley Crew and Def Leppard, the latter three being regulars to Ottawa and I drove them often. The band Def Leppard, as most of you will probably know, originates from Sheffield, England, and whenever they were in town my staff would have to rely on me to translate what they said into Canadian. Great fun, though personally it made me feel a little homesick, as did the guys themselves, as they were always fooling around and being sarcastic to each other in a way that only someone from Britain could appreciate, especially all the quip's about their one armed drummer, like how do you handcuff a one armed man- that sort of thing. You know, good harmless fun! Even the band's manager Malvin was quite a character; affectionately know as "Stumpus Maximus." This fiery Welshman could put the fear of God in anyone, but I'm happy to say that we got along okay and everything always went as planned. Though I'm not a fan of their music I always looked forward to their visits, which also delighted my future son-in-law Dave, a big fan who, on occasion I would get to help me drive them around. Family perks.

Luckily for me, all of my experiences with 'Rock Bands' turned out great, though I must admit in the beginning I was a little bit concerned, as I too had heard all the rumors of what happens when then get out of control. But other than a few eye openers of what the word groupie really means and the expected use of drugs, I must admit they were all a pretty well behaved bunch. Mind you, I think things had changed a lot since the seventies and eighties; gigs are taken a lot more seriously now with state of the art security. Every band had their own security team whose job it was to ID everyone that entered back stage. No one was ever allowed in unless they had a current back stage pass, and even then they were restricted to whatever access their pass allowed, hence the passes on the cover of my book. Another thing every band had was a 'Gofa.' You know, someone that always had to go for this and go for that, one group even had a gofa to get them girls from the audience, and at each venue he'd be given a list of what each member desired that night, such as a blonde, a brunette or maybe an Asian beauty. Certainly beats shopping for groceries, but at least the girls went willingly…

I don't really want to go into the nitty gritty details, but I will tell you that some of those that lived up to their name and reputation were The Eagles, Vanhalen, Aerosmith, INXS, Bon Jovie, Chris De Burgh and most 'Sports Celebrities'. But other than the occasional self-centred, egotistical, out for all they could get 'Would Be Super Star,' everyone else was just as you'd expect them to be… Nice.

Some of those were: Celine Dion, Desiree, Michelle Wright, B. B. King, Paul Simon, Marti Webb, Phil Collins, Peabo Bryson, Anne Murray, Neil Sedaka, Julio Iglesias, The Beach Boys, Martha Reeves, The Moody Blues and The Rankin Family, and the list goes on to include many stars of TV, Stage, Sports, and even Outer space (Astronauts). "Phew!"

"That's enough name dropping for now," at least now you can see for yourself that I've met a lot of interesting people, although believe or not, I haven't scratched the surface yet. The transportation of celebrities, though a lot of fun, was only a small percentage of my job. By far, the largest part of our VIP work was the transportation of 'Governmental Bureaucrats and Corporate Executives'.

Though on call 24 hours a day, most of the social bookings occurred during the evenings and at weekends, so the weekly eight hour routine of 9 to 5 was constantly occupied with the transportation requirements of business and corporate clients. Due to working for a highly respected company and having a well-known personal reputation, most of my time was spent driving 'the crème de la crème' of this corporate elite. Here again I found myself privy to events and conversations that the general public would never see or hear, and I soon discovered that there was a lot more money in the world than I thought and it wasn't all being wasted by our governments!

No wonder the products we buy cost so much. They must maintain a huge profit margin to pay for the extravagant life-styles that some of these 'Executives' lead… Initially, I used to feel embarrassed asking for payment at the end of some bookings because most of my time had been spent just sitting in the car, waiting for them during their meetings, often only driving a few miles each day. Then I realised that the hundreds of dollars they spend a day on limousine rental is nothing when you compare it to the money they spend on Private Jets, First Class Hotels, Golf Resorts and Entertainment. The funny thing was, most of my clientele, although upper management and business VIP's, were names rarely know to the public. On appearance, they appeared to be like everyone else, but that's where the similarity ends! Talk about 'living the life-of-Riley!' These people wanted for nothing. In fact, I have seen major celebrities spend considerably less on themselves. One group of four executives spent over $20,000.00 on dinner at a restaurant, virtually my yearly salary. You must have to sell a lot of 'widgets' to be able to afford that!

If you are wondering how a meal could be so expensive, it's easy when you consider they can spend over $10,000.00 on a bottle of wine. I never got any of that to cook with. Nothing but the best for these guys, though I must say they didn't always have to spend their own money as they were constantly being given freebies, or do you call them "incentives?" Anyway, whatever you call them, they were constantly being handed around things like: luxury vacations, expensive booze, the latest electronic gizmo and free tickets to concerts and sports events, which of course would be the best seats or a private box, not to mention the free courtesy bar. Oops! Yep' and thanks to all that free booze, a lot of them didn't come out of these events in the condition they went in, as one of my drivers found out!

His job was to pick up a group of four 'Hi-tech' executives from an Ottawa Senators hockey match at the Corel Centre, 25 minutes from downtown, and as usual he was requested to park outside just prior to the end of the game. This could also mean that he would have to sit and wait for an hour, which he did! Eventually three of them came out, none of them knowing where the fourth one had disappeared. "Forget him," they said "Take us to a downtown bar."

Off they went, the driver pulling onto the main highway

that would take them back to town, proceeding up to the speed limit of 100 kph. He checked in his rear view mirror to see how they were, but this time it was to no avail as they'd closed the privacy divider. No problem, he thought, they seem quiet enough. All went well until they were half way to town, and then suddenly a face appeared upside-down at the top of his windshield. "What the Bleep!" Still managing to keep his wits about him, the driver slowly maneuvered the car to the side of the highway and stopped. Getting out of the car, he discovered one of his passengers lying along the roof and the other two standing up through the sunroof holding his legs! Then, not knowing whether to laugh or cry the driver managed to get the man down and telephoned me to see what he should do next. 'Oh, Boy' I had a few choice words for them, I must say. I told the driver to carry on to town with the divider down and drop them off at their hotel, and for being naughty little boys there was to be no going to the bar for them.

Looking back on it now the whole event seems hilarious, but I dread to think what would have happened if the driver had panicked and stopped fast, probably a bloody mess. In saying that, I'm immediately reminded of a real bloody mess that happened to another one of my drivers, Tom. As you can probably guess by now it was with another group of so called 'Hi-Rollers' though this time Tom's job was to take them bar hopping in Kingston, one and a half hours away from Ottawa.

Everything on the trip went as planned and at the end of the night Tom was busy as usual trying to find everyone to get them in the car for the journey home. Having managed to get the last one in, Tom had just gotten into his seat when one of the gentlemen got back out again to talk to a girl, so feeling pretty annoyed, Tom got out of the car to put him back. It was then that he noticed the mans trousers were covered in blood! Unfortunately, just prior to leaving the bar the guy had slipped off a bar stool and fell onto his drink breaking the glass, but being so drunk he hadn't noticed that he'd cut himself. He continued outside and got in the limo, where he'd been sitting for the last 10 minutes, all the time losing blood from the wound.

The only thing Tom could do was rush him to the hospital, where the doctors discovered a large cut across his buttocks that took 32 stitches to seal. Eventually, he was released and the party continued on their journey home. This was one time that getting back out of the car saved a life, because without a doubt this guy would have bled to death during the one and a half hour journey home. Which definitely would have given a whole new meaning to the phrase 'dead drunk.' Thankfully he recovered, though the next day it wasn't much fun for me having to hose all that blood out of the seat! Oh well! You live and learn, or you're supposed too.

Personally, I think a lot of the weirdo's I drove were a sandwich short of a picnic! Imagine trying to drive a limousine around the streets of Montreal with a young lady sitting on your head! That's what I had to do once when a girl climbed feet first through the divider. Instead of sitting next to me, this one wanted to sit on me, just one of many 'Hen Night' pranks that I had to endure. I suppose it goes without saying that from time to time I was propositioned by women who'd had a few too many, (hey, they weren't all drunk) but still I can honestly say that I never succumbed! "It's the truth, Mary!"

In fact I was regularly offered drinks, drugs and women; sometimes as bribes, but mostly by drunks who were just trying to impress me. I always kept my dignity and managed to remain, what they call, squeaky clean. One spin-off of driving around so many drunken clients was that I got to overhear all their conversations! An asset that enabled me to understand a whole lot more about the people I drove and the things they got up to. They always talk extra loud so even with the divider closed I could hear every word, and even though I never asked for it, I became privy to lots of privileged information, not only about their personal life but the lives of their well known colleagues as well. Nothing was sacred. Sex, money, gossip and corporate secrets- from their business affairs to what goes on in the White House... I heard it all.

Sometimes, even the sober ones would like to talk. For instance, when I was there, the only international airport was two hours away and people had to pass the time somehow, and what a great opportunity to get things off their chest. If someone had been having a bad day they would vent all their pent up emotions on me. I think some felt very guilty about what their corporations were up too, or maybe it was just their conscience getting the better of them. Anyway, besides the venting and the juicy gossip I was also given the odd insider tip, but sorry to say I never had any money to do anything about them. I did on the other hand overhear a lot of people bragging how they were beating (or was it bleeding) the system, and the more work I did for these large corporations the more disgusted I became. I began to see how the general public had become just one large dollar sign to them and they would do anything to sell their products. And I mean ANYTHING!

During one run I was chatting with a top executive of a large pharmaceutical company, who I had driven on many occasions, and I mentioned to him that a Doctor had prescribed a well known stimulant for our 7-year-old son, Michael, and asked him for his opinion. Without hesitation, he recommended THAT WE DON'T give it to Michael! He further informed me about the many incentives being given to doctors to prescribe the stuff, from giant colour TV's to exotic holidays. The more they give the more they get! He also told me about other drugs, in particular, the anti-depressants that were being pushed for fat profits, all on the Q.T. of-course. The more I heard, the more my heart sank and I was outraged that once more the poor public were being used as pawns!

I also found out that price-fixing amongst these giants was just another fact of life. Sometimes we would transport people from rival companies to have meetings together, usually at 'out of the way' venues, where we were told to engage the utmost discretion and secrecy. Well sorry folks this guy has had enough, it's time to let people know the truth and if I have to take the flack, then so be it! Perhaps I'm just doing some venting of my own, but as you will discover when we move on to other areas, such as government, what I have told you so far is just the tip of the iceberg.

To lighten things up a little before we get there, here's a funny story that happened on another corporate outing that involved some real ice! One person that I did enjoy driving was the President and CEO of Lockheed Martin (Canada), Larry Ashley. I always found him very considerate and he always enjoyed a good joke, as some of his American guests also discovered one day! Larry had requested a large 15-passenger van to take him and some American visitors out for lunch and a spot of sightseeing. The plan was to take a trip to Chateau Montebello, a large 5 star resort in Quebec between Ottawa and Montreal. Our route there would take us across the Ottawa River via the bridge into Hull and then a leisurely drive along the Quebec side of the river to Montebello. Little did his guests know, but Larry and I had planned a little surprise for them on their journey home, as it happened to be the middle of winter and the Ottawa river was frozen over, something that had been noticed by his guests on the journey down. After an enjoyable lunch, we were on our way back to Ottawa when Larry explained to his guests how at this time of year it was possible to actually drive across the frozen river without having to use a bridge.

"Amazing," everyone said, and a lively conversation commenced. That was until Larry said, "Lets do it." Then there was nothing but silence! Next I turned off the main highway and headed for a nearby ferry point. With the ferry now in dry dock ahead of us lay a large pathway cut into the frozen ice, and I could feel the tension as we slowly drove onto it, especially as Larry was saying how a fully loaded 15-passenger van must be pretty heavy! The opposite river bank was approximately half a kilometer away but as far as my passengers were concerned, getting there felt like an eternity and their hands had become white knuckled as they gripped anxiously onto their seats. Halfway across, I stopped the van and asked if anyone would like to take any photographs. "NO! Keep going," came the reply, so we continued on our way. I don't think Larry was instilling any more confidence in them either as he kept saying, "Did you hear that, it sounds like ice cracking." Finally accompanied by huge sighs of relief I drove the van onto dry land once more, and as we continued our journey Larry and I smiled to ourselves, as we knew that even fully loaded logging trucks regularly used the same route...

Just for the record, Ottawa is the second coldest capital city in the world, with around five months of snow each year. (Ulaan Bator, Mongolia being the 1st.) So, as you can probably imagine, driving a 'Super Stretch Limousine' in snow is no easy task to say the least, and it can be quite stressful. Especially when you stop to consider that some of your passengers are the world's elite and their lives are in your hands! A full limousine is bad enough but when it's empty you can't relax for a second. If there's freezing rain on top of the snow, you'd be lucky if you could park without the car sliding away on it's own! Many times I have had to crawl out of the house on my hands and knees to get to the car because of freezing rain, as it was totally impossible to stand up and walk. Once in it, of course, I was expected to drive the thing! Life must go on no matter what the weather and winter storms were no exception. My stories of such events would probably fill a book by themselves, but here's one that you might find interesting.

I was called upon to take four government officials to Mirabel Airport (just outside Montreal) so they could catch a flight to Paris, and although there was a severe snowstorm raging it appeared that their flight was still going, so Off we went. When we reached the town of Hawkesbury, the halfway point, three hours later, (a journey that usually only took an hour), we pulled into a Tim Hortons coffee shop for some refreshment. 'Blimey' it was like a scene from one of those 'Disaster Movies'. The car park was a mess of vehicles all half buried in snow, and inside all the people were huddled-up trying to thaw out over hot cups of coffee. "Don't go on," they said, "The roads are a mess, you'll never make it."

I looked at my passengers and asked them what they

wanted me to do. After another phone call to the airport, we found out the flight had been delayed, but it would be definitely leaving later that day, so they decided to go on! As we made our way out of the restaurant everyone wished us well and slowly we made our way down the street. This time, I think I was the one that had white knuckles, as I gripped the wheel and tried to focus on the road as the endless hypnotic stream of falling snow hit my windshield. We'd been going for about 20 minutes when I spotted a family of four standing by the side of the road and behind them was their car half way down the embankment. I stopped to see if there was anything we could do. They asked if we could get them to the next town as they had relatives there who could help them. Sure, and in they got. My six-passenger car now held eight, but I think the extra weight helped me make it though to the town of Lachute. There we left our new friends and once again we headed to the airport. An hour later I pulled up outside of the departure terminal to the sound of applause from all inside and with only minutes to spare they made their flight. As for me? I stayed the night in a local motel and drove back to Ottawa the next day.

Trips like that one were a yearly experience; they were mostly for business executives who just had to make that all important flight or meeting, no matter what. Because the city of Montreal was just two hours away, many meetings were held there. During the winter the normal two-hour trip could take up to five hours, one-way, and on occasions I have had to make the trip 2 or 3 times in the same day. "Thank-God" I never fall asleep driving. And sometimes I wonder how I did it; it's astounding how I managed to get through my nine years of limousine driving without a single accident, as I must have driven over one million kilometers! A few of my drivers weren't so lucky, though I'm happy to say that no one was ever hurt.

"Always be prepared for every situation," was the motto I lived by, and although I was never a Boy Scout, perhaps that's what helped me get through. Heck, my briefcase felt like it weighed a ton, crammed with everything but the kitchen sink (the car already had one of those). Apart from the usual array of maps, pens and paper, it held various bottle openers, buttons, safety pins, glue, tape, nails, screws, scissors, pliers and etc., etc. Oh, and I mustn't forget the all-important pantyhose, yes pantyhose. Don't worry, they weren't for me, but having them on board saved the day for many a bride and bridesmaid, I can tell you! Which at last brings me to the part of the job I enjoyed the most, 'Weddings!'

Whether it was fate or just coincidence, weddings have played a big part in my life. I recently calculated that I must have been involved in over one and a half thousand of them, throughout all my various capacities as Restaurateur, Photographer and Chauffeur, plus getting married twice myself, don't forget.

By far the largest amount, a thousand, was during my years in the limousine business. In the summer, I could do up to four a week and at least one a week throughout the rest of the year. From the simple to the sublime, with as few as two guests to over two hundred I was there, feeling very privileged to be part of their very special day. Some were for only an hour, while others could take up a whole day, but for the most part they were around four hours.

Mary and I would start early on Saturday mornings. We'd gather up the kids and head over to the warehouse where the fleet was kept and there we would wash and prepare every car that was to be used for that day's weddings. Then, as each driver arrived, he would be assigned the appropriate vehicle and stock it with ice, champagne and the desired decorations. After a final check around the car by me, he'd be on his way. Whatever hours a driver could work determined which wedding he was given and of course the type of car he would use. This stopped a lot of in-house rivalry and as for me; I'd always take the last one, that way I could relax in the knowledge that everything else had been taken care of. This meant that I, too, had to take whatever car was assigned to it, and sometimes if would be our top of the line ten passenger limousine, a hundred thousand dollars of pure luxury. Other times, it would be our 'smoker's special' an old Cadillac that had definitely seen better days, although its original owner was the actor, Robin Williams. If only that car could talk.

Whatever car I ended up with, we became a team, and on the way to each pick-up I'd I have a little talk with it, telling it what a good reliable car it was and how together we were going to make everything perfect for our customers! Always look after the tools and they will look after you. Some people might think me nuts talking to a car, but I can honestly say, not a single car ever let me down during a run. On the odd occasion when something did go wrong, it would always happen before I started or after I'd finished, enabling me time to fix it or change vehicles. This doesn't mean, however, that we got away scot-free as our company certainly had it's share of mechanical breakdowns, although I must admit that 90% of the time they happened to those drivers that moaned and cursed at their cars, which certainly goes to prove the power of thought. What you think you'll get, "You Get!" You should try it, it works. Think negatively and you'll get a negative result, and vise-versa. The driver that went out swearing that his car would break-down, got exactly what his thoughts had predicted. The car broke-down, so really he was lucky; his thoughts had been granted! So be careful, the next time you think, "This always happens to me." Remember that your thoughts have power. Don't be surprised when things turn out poorly, because you're just getting what YOU asked for! In truth you were proved right, getting just what you expected, and that's why it happened to some of my drivers and not to me…

Anyway where was I? Oh I know, the car and I were on our way to collect the bride and her father, which was usually the first port of call, then together with the bridesmaids we'd all set off to the church. On the way there, I'd slip in my audiocassette of favourite wedding songs and within minutes everyone would be singing along with the music; it was great! When we arrived the photographer would be waiting for us, ready to capture the last pictures of the proud father and his soon-to-be married daughter as they entered the church. Once everyone had settled down inside, I could relax for a while before putting on the all-important 'Just Married' sign! Keeping an eye on the door and an ear out for church bells, I'd be ready and waiting with the champagne as the Bride and Groom exited the building, then after the usual mingling and pictures, it was time to take the happy couple on their first journey together as man and wife. Off we would go to take the photographs at whatever location the photographer or couple had chosen. Occasionally the couple was not able to afford the services of a professional photographer and had to rely on family and friends to take the pictures for them, and since most people didn't have a clue what to do, this is where my years as a photographer would come in handy. Heck, I was there anyway, so I might as well make myself useful. Having the responsibility to do the photography for such a special day can be a daunting experience for anyone, even for a professional, so to help out I'd offer my assistance in organising the groups and posing the couple in traditional and romantic ways. No one ever turned down my offer, and sometimes they would just hand me a camera and ask me to take the pictures for them. I didn't mind as I enjoyed every minute of it and I loved being able to use my past experience to capture the memories for them of that special day!

I remember one occasion, when we were hired to supply three cars for the wedding of one of Ottawa's concert promoters, a good friend of Celine Dion. A 'Photo Journalist' friend of the groom was doing the photography, and I stood together with Mary, who was driving one of the other limousines, and watched in horror as the poor guy got into all kinds of trouble trying to arrange things. Obviously he had never done a wedding before. This time I didn't know what to do. I didn't want to offend a fellow professional by offering my services, but then, I couldn't just stand there and do nothing. So gathering up my courage, I took the groom and his friend aside and asked if I could be of any assistance. "Would you, it would be most appreciated," the photographer said. "I'm a sports photographer and I've never done a wedding before." From then on I did the posing and his friend took the pictures. I never thought much more about it after that. A few weeks later while working at a concert, I noticed the promoter showing some of the wedding photos to his friends, and I went over to take a look. Ken immediately congratulated me on doing such a good job, since the photos had turned out great! Oh well, as the saying goes, "If you can help somebody as you go along, your living shall not be in vain…" But I digress; let's get back to the typical wedding routine…

Once the photography was over it was on to the reception, and this is where, most of the time, our involvement with it would finish. However, some parties would require us to return after the reception to take the couple home or to their hotel. Now when you consider that Saturday was also our busiest day for other social events, squeezing in this quick one-way transfer wasn't always as easy as it seemed, and often I would end up getting there late. Ninety-nine percent of the time no one ever noticed, as they were all busy having so much fun, but on this one occasion, someone did.

After leaving a couple at their reception it was arranged for me to pick them up again at 1 a.m and off I went to attend to the rest of that evening's bookings. As usual, I was busy doing other transfers to and from restaurants and bars, and my last booking, before returning for the couple, was for a group of drunken men who had no idea of where they were going and we ended up at a location miles from town, where I had the tremendously hard job of getting them out of the car. Sounds familiar! Finally I completed the task at 1 a.m, the very time for my next pick-up, which was also half an hour away. Even after driving the limo like a formula-one racing car I still arrived back at the reception twenty minutes late. There, waiting at the door for me, was the bride's father 'who was vewy, vewy drunk,' and as soon as I got out of the car he went ballistic, swinging his fists at me and chasing me down the hallway shouting out obscenities. Thankfully for me, the groom spotted us as we entered the room and just as the father was about to clobber me, he and some guests grabbed him and dragged him away. No way was I expecting that, and after changing my underwear (just kidding), we were on our way to the hotel as usual and as for the couple themselves, they hadn't even noticed the time, too busy enjoying themselves. They were nice enough to apologise for him and we all put it down to an excess of alcohol. I suppose I should have expected something like that to happen one day, going by all the weddings I've seen. I could pretty well guarantee there would always be someone who'd end up getting drunk. In fact, by then I could virtually predict the behaviour of the guests at most weddings!

No matter how big, small, rich or poor the event was, they were always there; the usual late comers, the show-offs, the macho men, the flirts, the eccentric uncle, the fussy aunt and the parents shouting at their children. There were also the smokers that would come out of the church during the service unable to wait till the end, lots of people dressed to the nines, while others looked like they didn't have a mirror in the house. Then there was the amateur photographer who would have more equipment than the professional and a mass of people with video cameras, all striving for the best position, and the list goes on. What an array of characters all playing their roles and all oblivious to me as I sat waiting in the car enjoying the performance...

Quite a spectacle you could say, but it was nothing compared to what I'd see from the next group of people I'm going to tell you about!

Chapter Eight

Politically Incorrect

*Politicians, like diapers, should be changed regularly,
often for the same reasons!*

By now you have surely gained an insight into my daily routine, realising the immense diversity and unpredictability of my clientele. It's my guess that some of you may have even suspected that I'd acquired quite a disdain for certain types of people. You'd be right. To say that I had a disdain for this next group of individuals though, would be just plain silly. In my opinion, this bunch is nothing short of disgusting, and as far as I'm concerned they're just a lot of greedy, inconsiderate, egotistical, power hungry, spoiled brats! Oh, and I forgot sex mad… I think you get my drift.

You've probably heard it said that the monkeys are running the zoo. Believe me, that's wrong; the monkeys just do the menial work for the wolves and the jackals, no disrespect to the animal kingdom intended. From the lowly bureaucrat to the top ministers, most of them appear to be bleeding the system dry, with little consideration for anyone but themselves. Believe me there's nothing I'd like better than to say everything you're about to read is just a figment of my imagination, but sorry I can't.

Personally, I became so disheartened by the things I saw and heard that I completely lost faith in governments and even gave up hope for humanity itself. I truly believed that it would be a matter of time before those in power destroyed this planet and us along with it. "Ridiculous," some of you may say, we live in a democracy and our leaders are voted in by the people, and I agree, we do have the right to vote, but do we have the right to choose? In essence we're just given a list of names we can pick from- most of which we don't like, and instead of voting for the one we like the most, we end up voting for the one we dislike the least!

Anyway, let's face it, if our system of voting could really make a difference, governments would have made it illegal... If we were truly in control, our government officials would have been more accountable years ago and poverty and hunger would be a thing of the past. Heck, at every election for the past hundred years, the public has voted for the politician who said he would fix everything, so how come we're still waiting? Nothing but empty words. That goes for their promises too; they'll agree to anything to get what they want, especially while the 'Media' is around. Once the public and the cameras have gone, it's a different story.

As I said in my introduction, it was like watching a Jeckll and Hyde transformation, with a Hyde personality that actually detests the general public and thinks we're just a necessary evil, a means to an end, so to speak. Don't get me wrong, I'm not saying that they're all corrupt; not every individual is like that. I have met ones that really did care and genuinely wanted to help their constituents. They were a precious few who rarely succeeded in their endeavors and most became so disheartened, they eventually gave up trying. Which brings me to my first story.

It was during the last year of Brian Mulroney's leadership and one of my regular clients, who was a member of the Liberal party, was hoping to become an MP in the upcoming elections. He was someone who really seemed to care and sometimes while journeying together he would ask me questions about my life and even seek out my opinion about current events. Full of vitality and confidence, he was convinced that once in parliament he would definitely be one of those who'd change things. I was convinced of that as well.

Just as he predicted, the Conservatives lost and he was successful in gaining a seat in the new government. I must say I was pleased for him, even though I knew it meant I would probably never drive him again as all ministers are allocated their own government driver. So it was for the next two years. One day his secretary telephoned me, to ask if I was available to take him to Montreal, as for some reason his own driver wasn't. That's nice of him to remember me, I thought, and off I went to pick him up, pulling up outside his office. I was eager to see him again, but when he came out I barely recognised the man. His hair had gone grey and he looked tired and dejected, though I am pleased to say that he still had his friendly disposition. He was happy to see me and inquired as to the health of my family. Then, just like old times we made our way to Montreal.

It soon became apparent during our conversation that all his dreams of making a difference had become just that, dreams!

"John," he said, "It's like an Old Boys Club in there. It's their way or the highway and don't even think about trying to change it."

Obviously he'd tried. All I could do was agree with him. But then I, too, had seen enough to know that what he was saying was true. I had heard comments of parliament being like an 'Old Boys Club' on many occasions, though personally I think 'Old Boys Kindergarten' would be more accurate. Just ask anyone who has watched our Government in action from the public gallery. Hour upon hour of childlike name-calling and snide remarks, accompanied by out-bursts from other naughty children banging on their desks. The more I saw the funnier it got, what a joke.! Well it would be, until you realise that all this fiasco is costing the Canadian taxpayer a bloody fortune! Can you imagine what it would be like if big corporations conducted their meetings like that? Not only would nothing get done, the executives would be fired for wasting valuable time and money.

When it comes down to wasting money, that's one area where our Government excels, and for this I award them an A+. The amount of money I've seen given out in ridiculous grants alone is unbelievable! Hundreds of thousands of dollars to find out the size of the average green pepper or examine the mating habits of the Bolivian pink eyed, three toed marsh rat. Like that's going to aid the economy. Don't get me wrong I'm not against this kind of research, but shouldn't we get our priorities right and put our own house in order first. From what I've seen and heard, most of these grants only serve as a make-work project for some government employee, or as a repayment for favours received. Our politicians appear to have no problem with using taxpayers' money to get what they want; in fact, they expect us to cater to their every need, 'No expense spared!'

You'd better believe it, only the best will do for this lot. First class meals, transportation and accommodation, five-star hotels, no problem! All on a "Canadian Express," Government Credit Card. Like little Princes and Princesses, they expect everything to be done for them, though I must admit I can see good reason why – a lot of them are literally incapable of doing anything for themselves, and couldn't fry an egg to save their life. I think they'd panic if they were asked to hammer a nail into a piece of wood.

That's probably why it costs the Government $300 for a hammer: $20 for the hammer and $280 for an instruction manual on how to use it! The manual itself compiled from yet another government grant.

Think I'm joking? Well, I'm not, and the above would definitely describe some of my clients that were members of "the Senate!" One Senator, in particular, wasn't able to find his way across the street unless he was driven, and once after a large winter storm I had to drop him 30 feet past the doorway of a restaurant, as snow had covered the entrance driveway.

The poor Senator stood there looking lost and deeply distressed, so I took his arm and led him back to the main entrance. Mind you, he often admitted that he could never find his way across the city, but after all, he'd only worked there for 30 years! Poor widdle chap, definitely not the brightest crayon in the box.

Don't you just love our Government officials? You do? Well, read on, I'll soon change your mind... As I mentioned earlier, a year after I commenced driving there was a change in Government, which as you can imagine involved various changes in governmental procedures. In Mulroney's reign, stretch limousines were permitted on Parliament Hill for the transportation of VIP's and for taking government employees to and from meetings, which were usually out of town resorts. This was one of the things that the Liberals changed; large stretch limousines were now banned. Well that's certainly going to save the taxpayer some money, you might think? Sorry, but you couldn't be more wrong. In fact, just the opposite. It ended up costing the taxpayer a heck of a lot more money.

For example, where before it required only one super stretch to take a group of four, six or eight people out to lunch; now, we had to supply two, three or four sedans to do the same job. Only two passengers were allocated to each car. Obviously, this would increase the cost but wait, there's more. One other thing that the limousine had to do was to arrive at least an hour prior to the departure, making sure it was nice and warm, or cool inside, depending on the weather. The car and driver would have to wait at the venue just in case someone had to leave suddenly, and you can add on another hour since they rarely came out on time! So instead of the Government paying for one super stretch limousine for three hours at $85 per hour, ($255+), they were now paying for three sedans for three hours at $65 per hour, per car, ($585+)! You don't have to be a mathematician to figure out it's more than double, but as far as "the public" were concerned it looked good not seeing stretch limousines anymore on Parliament

Hill.

Why on earth can't they just explain to us what they are doing, instead of trying to pull the wool over our eyes? I've said it before, 'You can't tell a book by its cover.' The new PM's car was another prime example. It was during a visit by the British Prime Minister, John Majors, that I became privy to this bit of juicy information.

I was employed to drive around Mr. Majors' press aides- what organised chaos that was! Anyway, as usual, most of my time was taken up sitting around and I was not alone, as my fellow RCMP drivers were also doing the same. They had it down to a fine art, even having pizza delivered to their cars. While we sat there eating the pizza I commented on the fact that Mr. Chretien was using a different car to Mr. Mulroney, a Buick Roadmaster instead of the usual Government Cadillac.

"Yes," said one of the officers, "our new PM is a 'man of the people' and the Cadillac was far too ostentatious for him." He then went on to explain that Mulroney's car was now mothballed in the RCMP garage. Oh, isn't that nice, I thought, he's saving us some money. "Wrong again!" Bullet proof Cadillac's are the car of choice for many of the world's VIP's and cost around $300,000 each. The Roadmaster, was a one-off and had to be specially built for our PM, at a cost of $450,000! That's an extra $150,000 to make him look like a man of the people. "Yea right." If he wants to be a man of the people, then try telling the people the truth. Does he really think we're so stupid we can't handle the truth? *Just try us!* I'm sure if he explained that by using Mulroney's car it would save taxpayers nearly half a million dollars, it would really prove he was one of us, and not one above us.

Incidentally, whilst on the subject of cars and drivers, I recently heard on the radio that some people are concerned about all the cars parked around Government buildings with their engines running, (sounds familiar) and why were people concerned? Because of the exhaust emissions, that's why, but what about the thousands of dollars in vehicle and driver hours that are also going up in smoke?

183

Believe me I know, I've been one of those cars, sitting there for hours waiting for officials, only to take them a couple of miles and then sit for another hour or more. We were always instructed to keep the engine running, as they never knew when they might come back. We had to keep the car warm for them in the winter and cool in summer. Blithering idiots, what's with them? Haven't they heard of the telephone? They all knew that I had a cellular phone, so why couldn't they just give me ten minutes notice? Too easy I suppose. Instead, I just had to sit there getting back and neck ache from constantly staring at the exit doors, too afraid to get out for a coffee or a pee. If I did, you could bet dollars to doughnuts that's when they'd come out!

One of the worst culprits of this routine was the Parti Quebecois. Their usual requirements were for a sedan and two passenger vans to pick them up from a small airfield in Gatineau, and then take them to the External Affairs building in Ottawa. Again, we would all sit and wait, sometimes for the entire day, just to take them back to the airport. The bill for this service could easily top $2000! And all they used us for, was two fifteen-minute transfers. Again it's only taxpayers' money so why bother sending the cars away and taking the trouble to call them back when they were needed? I bet it would be a totally different story if they had to pay the bill out of their own pocket! They'd soon make the effort to find a bloody phone then. No wonder Quebec needs extra federal funding with money wasting bureaucrats like that, paying for three vehicles and three drivers to sit and do nothing for seven hours. At least they gave us an hour off for lunch, which saved them an hour's charge.

Finding food to eat while waiting for clients was another problem, and most of the time I had to rely on fast food. Maneuvering a super stretch through the drive trough lane of burger joints is not an easy task, but it's something at which I became very proficient. Even when I was lucky enough to get home to eat, I've had to leave my meal to drive as fast as I could to parliament, after receiving a call from someone's secretary to get there 'ASAP' - only to then sit for an hour waiting for them to come out, probably busy finishing their lunch. Sob! Gee, what a bunch of money wasting pillocks! Still not convinced? Read on, I'm just getting started.

Once again we're back to the transition from the Conservatives to the Liberals. If you remember, the new Government informed the public that it was going to do some departmental down sizing. You know, all those golden handshakes of up to $200,000 each, that employees were offered to quit their jobs. Quit they did, quite a few of them and they left the Government for good! Well, that's what we were supposed to believe...

The truth is, a lot of them were back at their desks within weeks, only this time they were called contracted self-employed personnel. Although they were still being paid by the Government, as far as the public were concerned our leaders had kept their word; the list of Government employee's had decreased. In reality, it was more a case of sign here for your pot of gold.

I drove one man that actually bragged about how he'd managed to do it twice! First he took a $200,000 settlement, went on a dream vacation for six weeks and then went back to do his old job on a contracted out basis. Within a year, a different department offered him a job working as a salaried employee for the Government. Wow, he took all that money and was then back working for them again, tut, tut! It gets better, a year later he was offered a $180,000 buyout package to quit *this* government job, so there he was after yet another dream vacation, working back in his original job, again on a self employed basis. His pot of gold was worth $380,000.

At least he was working for his third of a million instead of it being given to those people on welfare. Though, at the amount a family of four gets, it would take them over 31 years to equal what he got.

Do you think there's something wrong here? Could it be: #1. *The Government for giving it to him,* #2. *Him for being greedy and taking it,* or #3. *Us for allowing it to happen in the first place.* Pick one, and then write your answer on a post card.

Then, like the rest of us, do absolutely nothing with it! Sorry for the sarcasm, but I haven't even got warmed up yet, there is so much more to tell... By now you will think that I'm anti Government, 'Bring on the revolution and all that,' but I'm not. I was just an ordinary guy making a living driving limousines, but everyday these absurdities were thrust in my face. I've written down so many complaints about the things I saw, that I'm now up to my neck in postcards! Perhaps it's time to post a few...

That's the uniqueness of being a limousine driver; unlike the police and government drivers I was never subject to any contracts of secrecy. Going by the amount of stuff I've seen, I dread to think what those who have been sworn to secrecy could tell us. One RCMP detective told me once, and I quote, "If the Canadian people really knew what went on behind the closed doors of our elite, they would never sleep at night." Makes you think doesn't it! I've always been led to believe that politicians started out as regular people, so how is it that they appear to lose all concept of a working class life?

I remember driving one lady Minister to the airport with one of her aides, and he was telling her about a field worker that had become so alcoholic she hadn't done her job properly for the last year.

"What shall we do about her?" he asked.

"What does she earn?" asked the Minister.

"Forty thousand a year," he said.

"In that case just leave her alone" she said and changed the conversation.

"My God," if a minister really thinks $40,000 a year is nothing, then why do they constantly complain when people try and raise the minimum wage from $8.00 an hour, which is less than $17,000 a year. Have you noticed not one of the people who are against raising the minimum wage, actually live on it. Do us a favour, try bringing up your family on eight bucks an hour first, and then maybe we'll listen. Even so, I suppose the wages we pay some of our government officials is nothing compared to what they would get in the private sector, and could that be one of the reasons why they appear to be on the take so much? OK, so pay them more!

We pay our Hockey players a fortune compared to what we pay our Prime Minister, so come on people "you get what you pay for." Is knocking a puck around an ice rink worth more than our Country? What's Canada worth? Most company CEO's earn a million dollars a year, so what should we pay someone who is expected to run the second largest Country in the world? If you pay peanuts, you'll probably end up with a monkey! Perhaps if we paid them what they're worth, we could then make them more accountable for their lavish expense accounts. Did you hear the one about the Ambassador that spent over $650,000 in just 10 months? Mind you, he was renting three houses at the same time, because he couldn't decide which one he liked the most.

If these idiots want to lead such flamboyant lifestyles, that's up to them, but why should we be expected to pay for it? And pay for it we do, over and over again. Did you know that your hard earned money is used to pay for hookers? Well it is! In one week our Government spent over $15,000 on girls for just one visiting diplomat! How do I know? I drove him! But that's nothing compared to other things I've seen... Millions of dollars spent maintaining opulent lifestyles that the average Canadian could only ever dream about. How many people can spend $27,000 on a table? That's what the Government spent on a table for our new Embassy in Japan, not to mention the hundreds of thousands of dollars they also spent on the Grand Opening Party! Were you invited? I drove a lot of people that were invited and some of them didn't even want to go. Of course they went anyway, all expenses paid, thanks again to the Canadian taxpayer! Well, its just part of their job. Maybe that's why the politicians don't ask for more money, because then they wouldn't have any excuse for these exorbitant expenses.

If what I've said about the hookers makes you feel sick to your stomach you'd better fetch a bucket, because I've yet to mention there are other perks! 'Perks', a seemingly insignificant word, and for most people it would mean getting a staff discount, the odd gift or even a free pizza, but as far as the government is concerned it takes on a whole new meaning... From floral arrangements to gold watches its take, take, take!

Take the average convention, for example; they usually consist of the following: beautiful floral displays and decorations to adorn the rooms, souvenir gifts for the attendees and lots and lots of quality food and drink, usually a buffet. Nothing out of the ordinary there you might say, and again I agree, but it's what happens when it's over that might interest you.

Usually I arrive at the end of such events to transport people back to Ottawa or to an airport. While I was standing there waiting for them, I'd get to watch the customary 'free for all,' as people ran frantically around the rooms trying to grab the biggest and best floral displays, plus any left over souvenirs and, of course, whatever food and drink was left over. At times the quantity was quite considerable, enough smoked salmon and chicken to last the average family months. Oh well, at least the $3,000 spent on the flowers wasn't wasted. Talk about filling your boots, and I've heard some of the organisers say that they haven't had to buy groceries for years!!! But don't lose your lunch just yet, as we are about to move on to even bigger and better things.

Some of you are probably old enough to remember an old World War saying, "Loose lips sink ships." I have had many a loose-lipped person in the back of my car, especially when drunk. Subsequently, I discovered other Government employee perks included things like furniture, fax-machines, computers, printers and even industrial photocopiers. Some even bragged that they had so many computers at home they didn't know what to do with them all. There was one for every member of the family, including the dog! Other perks are the ones given to the lucky employee who gets to escort a visiting delegation or diplomat around, since it's customary for the visitor to present their host with a little gift to say thank you. This 'little gift' could range anywhere from a case of vodka to a solid gold watch!

Astounding but true, on one occasion after driving an Ambassador from Brunei around for three days, it was time to drop him back to his private jet at Ottawa's military airport. We (the Ambassador, the tour guide and myself) pulled onto the tarmac and after saying goodbye it was time for the customary gift. The Ambassador then slipped me a nice new $100 bill, "thank you very much", then he presented the guide with a beautiful new gold watch! Probably worth over $5,000.00! But what makes this story so funny, if my memory serves me right, is that his guide was an employee of Revenue Canada, "I wonder if he declared that on his taxes", nudge, nudge, wink, wink, say no more! I bet not many Canadians knew about those kinds of perks.

Though obtaining news of what goes on in our nation's capital may differ depending on which part of the country you live in, a lot of the things I've told you were common knowledge in and around Ottawa, but the further away you go, the less people know! Hey that rhymes! A lot of people around the country know nothing about the 'Five Billion Dollar' renovation that was done to Parliament Hill, let alone the other bits of juicy information, like Ray Hnatyshyn's $275,000 holiday flight when he was Governor General; or how our Government spent millions for a select group of 25 people to tour the world in five star resorts, all in the name of multiculturalism.

In the early nineties there was a news article in the paper, about a tourist complaining that they had been mooned by someone through a window on Parliament Hill. It created quite a stir at the time, but eventually died down without the culprit being found. At first I thought is was a bit bizarre and then forgot about it altogether, until two years later. I picked up two rather inebriated bureaucrats and took them home after an office Christmas party. They were chatting merrily away when suddenly they started to talk of the mooning incident. Between the giggles one confessed that he knew who the culprit was and that it wasn't a mooning at all. Apparently it was a government official who was 'bonking his secretary' unaware that his bottom was in full view from the window! What an ass! Sorry, couldn't resist that. Whether it's true or not I'll leave it up to you to decide, but going by the other things I've seen, I wouldn't doubt it for a second.

Dealing with sexual situations was just another part of my job, and people are people, whether they work for the government or not. Sex is a fact of life, for crying out loud- it's just that the public/private sector doesn't expect the taxpayer to pay for it! Did you know that the largest section of the Ottawa 'Yellow Pages' when I was there, was the part devoted to 'Escort Agencies?' There's no smoke with out fire they say, and as far as I'm concerned they can screw each other as much as they like, just stop screwing the public at the same time.

Here's one government Minister that didn't use taxpayer's money; his little bit of hanky panky was paid for by one of the city's night club owners. My job was to go to a strip club and pick up two young 'ladies,' complete with bottles of champagne and then go to a hotel to pick up the Minister. My instructions were to drive around Gatineau Park for an hour and afterwards drop the Minister back at his hotel and the girls back at the Club. It seems it was a gift for the Minister's birthday. Of course, on no account did it have anything to do with the 'Bloody Great Government Grant' that the Club owner had just received to open another business! How could I ever think such a thing.

The more I saw, the more I began to realise there was one law for them and another for us. I think that, 'Do as we say, not as we do,' should be inscribed in Latin over the entrance to parliament, as most of them consider themselves above the Law. Don't bother taking any of them to court over it though, because a lot of Judges believe they are too!

For instance, I once drove seven Judges in a limousine that only held six in the rear, so one had to sit in the front passenger seat. On the journey they poured out seven glasses of twelve-year-old whisky and handed one over the divider to the Judge in the front seat.

"Excuse me your honour," I said, "You're not allowed to have liquor in the front of the car."

"What" he said, "There's not a cop in the country that

would dare to stop us!" and continued to, dare I say it, break the law! I won't bother to tell you about the rest of the evening, but I can say this, you can forget the saying, "Sober as a Judge."

There's been hundreds of times when I've sat in disbelief, watching drunken VIP's (pillars of society) stagger out of private clubs, only to get into their car and drive away, even in front of the police. I'd wonder to myself, 'What the hell am I doing here?' surrounded by such immoral and hypocritical individuals, preaching one thing and practising another. Perhaps I'm narrow-minded, though I always considered myself to be open-minded.

Whatever, things were beginning to take their toll on me. I'd compare myself to a nurse in a hospital for sick children, seeing their sickness on a daily basis, but unable to stop it. I couldn't get the things I saw out of my mind, even when not working. Poor Mary took the brunt of my complaining, as I vented my disgust of what I'd seen and the feelings of contempt I had for these men. It was mostly men who conducted themselves in such a manner, and the more money they had the worse they appeared to be. Government officials, corporate executives, and sports stars all appeared to be of the same opinion; money could buy anything and anyone.

In a restaurant one night, four gentlemen clients bet each other to see which one could get the waitress to have sex with him. They each gave me $500, and told me I was to give it to the winner. Believe it or not, one actually succeeded and later on the journey home he told the others how he did it. "Easy," he said, "I offered the girl $1000 and she accepted!" So not only did he have sex with the girl, he won all the money and made a $500, profit as well. I'll let you into a little secret here by telling you that they were N.H.L. hockey players for a well-known team. Don't worry, it wasn't Wayne Gretsky. Although I have driven him on numerous occasions and I must say his conduct was always impeccable, which is more than I can say for some of the players.

I drove another well-known player to a party where he was the guest of honour. I was told to sit and wait, just in case he needed me. Later that night, he and a female guest got into the car and I was instructed to take them for a ride around the Gatineau Hills. Here we go again. As usual the divider was closed but I could still hear every word. He told her that he'd never met anyone so beautiful before and that he was totally captivated by her and would like to see her every time that he was in town. He carried on showering her with so many compliments that the inevitable happened. Nine minutes later, I was told to take them back to the party. OK, not so bad, I thought, until I was driving him back to his hotel with a few of his friends, and he described their love making to the others in graphic detail. He also told them to make sure that she never got his phone number as he never wanted to see her again. I was flabbergasted! What about all those things he had said to her and with such conviction, that even I believed him. I felt as conned as the girl. Well at least the girl had consented of her own accord, which wasn't the case when a certain 'Super Star' attempted to rape a woman in the back of the car.

What a traumatic event that was. I didn't know what to do. Should I intervene and help the girl or do nothing and keep driving as I was told to do by the celebrity? I could feel my blood pressure rising and I was about to pull over when the internal phone rang and he instructed me to take him back to his hotel. What a relief! Upon our arrival he got out, slammed the door and instructed me to, and I quote, "Take the bitch home!" The young lady certainly had a few choice words to say about him on the journey, I must admit.

Who do these people think they are, or more to the point, what do they think we are? I sometimes wonder if they have to trade in their decency and compassion to gain power, or is it just that they never had any to start with.

I could go on and on with stories like these, but if I did we'd all have to take 'Prozac', but wouldn't they love it if we did, then the large corporations make even more money off us! So the next time you pay your taxes, buy tickets to a sports event or pay an extortionate price for a product, remember this, a lot of your hard earned money is going into maintaining a select group of people in lifestyles that you could only dream about! I suppose, though what we've never had we'll never miss. That's the way they'd like to keep it, but it doesn't hurt to remind these people that if it weren't for the general public supporting them and buying their merchandise, they wouldn't have all that power and wealth in the first place.

It's pointless sitting in a restaurant with a million dollars in your pocket if there's no one there to prepare and serve your food... I'm not saying that we shouldn't do the work; a lot of people enjoy doing what they do, but why should they have to scrimp and scrape to do it? I think the biggest oxymoron in the world is the saying "The working poor." Anyone who is prepared to work should never have to be poor!

Personally I think the world's gone crazy; everywhere people are struggling on minimum wage to make ends meet and yet say nothing when 'Sports Stars' are paid multi-million dollar salaries for doing what they enjoy... Well excuse me, if a club has that much money to spend, how about giving some of it back to the people who gave it to them in the first place, the fans! We pay some actors up to seventy million for one movie and treat them like royalty while they make it. At the same time, we pay our firemen, police and nurses a pittance for working 12-hour split shifts risking their lives!

What's the matter with us- don't we think we're worth it? Well, believe me we are! One thing I've learned from all my years dealing with these spoilt brats: "They need us, far more than we need them!"

Chapter Nine

My Reality cheque... Bounced!

Feed your faith and your doubts will starve to death...

I'd heard too many lies, seen too much corruption for one person to take. Now I was convinced our world was doomed, and it was just a matter of time before these egotistical greedy bastards ravaged the planet to the point of extinction, and us along with it.

Even the things I used to enjoy like the concerts, had lost their appeal. Now I couldn't wait for them to end so that I could get back home to Mary and the children, since I'd lost faith in pretty-well everyone else but them.

Eight years of being on call 24 hours a day, 7 days a week, had taken its toll on me. Everywhere I looked people seemed out of control, constantly pushing everything to the limit. Even the young people I drove seemed to have lost that sense of innocence associated with their youth; and they too wanted it all and wanted it now! Then again, how could I blame them? Going by the behavior I'd seen exhibited by their parents, a good role model was hard to find.

How the heck did our so-called "Peers" become so greedy and selfish and why on earth were "we the public" sitting back and allowing it to happen? Could it be my rich clients were right when they said "everything and everyone can be bought?" Why should they give a damn about our world and its future generations when the majority of us on the planet regard ourselves as worthless? Well, the majority certainly act like it, seemingly content to toil their way through life getting paid a pittance for what they do - making less in 5 years than this lot spend in a week.

Heck' did you know that 'Nike' pays Michael Jordan more per year for endorsing their products, than they pay all of the employees in their Malaysian factories combined, and that's just his part-time job.

In fact, two thirds of the world's working population spend their lives making things that they will never be able to afford. Think I'm exaggerating? Then consider this: one of the Directors of Wal-Mart gets paid over 30 million dollars a year, while in comparison an employee at one of their Chinese suppliers would have to work for 75 years just to equal what the Director gets for ONE HOUR! What an example of self-worthlessness that is. It wasn't that long ago that the pay ratio between an employee and their boss equaled about 20 or 30 to 1. Now it's common to see ratios of over 3,000 to 1, and that doesn't include the ratio of sports and media salaries that can easily exceed 50,000 to 1! Then again, I'm a fine one to talk. I certainly didn't set much of an example of self worth. For my $10.00 an hour, I was prepared to jump whenever asked to do so; being available 24 hours a day, 7 days a week, regardless of what my family and I might be doing at the time. It didn't matter where I went, I was always at their beck and call, whether on or off duty.

For eight years I never went anywhere without my cellphone and pager. In fact most of the time I felt more like a special agent on the 'X-Files' than a Limousine driver. Constantly on edge, I never knew when I'd be called away on my next mission, for Pete's sake! I may have been rubbing shoulders with the 'Worlds Elite' but it was certainly costing me my quality of life to do so.

195

It wasn't much better for Mary and the kids either, 'poor sods'. Every time I was called away they never knew if I'd be back in an hour or away for days. (Stupid thing was, neither did I.). This made it virtually impossible for us to plan outings together. Heck, I've lost count of the times I've had to leave them stranded somewhere, just because Steve, my boss, had called me away to do an all important job he said only I could do. He would then have to send one of our other drivers to rescue Mary and the kids and take them back home.

This scenario happened so often that everywhere I went I had to wear a suit; and I do mean everywhere, including at the park with the kids. Shucks' I've even slept in the bloody thing, waiting for a come-and-get-us call, from a more-often-than-not drunken client. (All the time praying that at least one of them would remain sober enough to remember my phone number.)

Sure… it all seems so funny now, but it certainly didn't feel like it at the time. Frequently having to work through the night I'd do my best to get at least some rest at home, even if only for an hour or so. If I didn't, I'd end up suffering from C W S, (cuddle withdrawal symptoms.) I'm positive that, if it hadn't been for love and support I got from Mary, I would have cracked under the strain many times. That's the beauty of having a strong relationship, and Mary was always there when I needed her. In fact, we'd been married then for over 15-years, and you could count the number of arguments we'd had on one hand. Even then, we'd never go to bed until we'd made up; although once we had to stay up for two weeks…only joking.

It was bad enough that we had to be separated from each other during the day. At night I'd constantly do my best to get back home. Even after a long run when clients offered to get me a room for the night, I'd always refuse. I'd be happy to grab a coffee and a sandwich and disappear into the night, knowing that with every mile I drove I'd be that much closer to Mary and the family. Stupid really, any other driver would have jumped at the chance to spend the night in the comfort and luxury of a fine hotel, but not me! All I could think of was getting back as soon as possible.

The only problem was, nine times out of ten, Steve would find out that I was back and give me another run. Something even more ridiculous was that I'd be stupid enough to accept. So why did I do it?

To tell the truth, I think it's because, deep down inside I knew that it was Steve's tremendous confidence in me that made him keep asking. So, not wanting to let him down, I kept accepting. Both of us were oblivious to the effect that all that stress was having on my mental and physical health.

Looking back now it's amazing that my clients never noticed. I'm sure once on duty, I became so immersed in what I was doing, I never let it show. I would keep it bottled up inside me until I returned home again, then I'd collapse in Mary's arms and cry like a baby, not knowing why or what to do... All that extra money meant that we didn't have to scrimp and scrape so much, and we were able to let the children have the occasional treat without having to say 'no' all the time. Yes, it made me happy to see Mary and the kids' enjoying themselves more, but to achieve it, I was making myself unhappy by taking on so much extra work. What a mess... "Well, that's what I thought."

In reality Mary and the children were happy regardless of the extra money, and always had been. All of them would have put my health above money any day. I was just too blind to see it! By constantly worrying about providing a good future for my family, I was depriving them of the quality of life that's important here and now! For once and for all why couldn't I get it through my thick skull? I would call myself a complete idiot if there weren't a few parts missing... One night driving back empty from Mirabel Airport, I began to get what I thought was a severe case of heartburn. I stopped to buy a packet of antacid and continued on my way, expecting it to pass. When I arrived home the pain was much worse. Actually, it was so bad I could hardly get my breath. My first thought was to take some stronger medicine and get Mary to pat my back, convinced that it was just gas and I'd soon be back to normal. Yeah right.

An hour later Mary was rushing me to the hospital. The next thing I remember was waking up with my chest bandaged and Mary sitting by my side. My gall bladder had been removed and Mary said that I should count myself lucky that it was her that greeted me and not an Angel. The Doctor had told her it was in such a deteriorated condition, it would only have been a matter of days before it would have poisoned my system and killed me. Serves me right, I suppose, for ignoring the pains I'd been having for months. I always shrugged them off as indigestion or at worst, an ulcer. What a nut! Did I actually think that drinking half a bottle of antacid a day was normal? Well, I certainly paid for that… I'd been so worried about missing a day's work that I ended up nearly killing myself and having to be off for two bloody months, without pay.

This is the part where my photography equipment and I part company, since our only way to survive was to sell it; the cameras, lighting and darkroom paraphernalia that had taken me years to accumulate and build a business. The funny thing was, at the time it didn't bother me one bit. I was so tremendously happy to be alive and there with my family, nothing else mattered. Even to this day Mary says it was the most carefree and contented she'd ever seen me, as if I'd found inner peace or something.

Don't get too excited, it didn't last long. Once the remnants of my days as a photographer were gone, it was back to work as usual. What else could I do? We had to pay the bills, pay the rent, clothe the kids and eat, and all that took money. Without the luxury of any savings to fall back on or any medical insurance there was no other option. Well, not any I knew about. Although this time I was determined to make sure I got at least one day a week to spend at home with the family.

Back on my feet again, I decided to put myself under the knife once more, when Mary and I agreed that four children were enough. With only one wage coming in, we knew it would make good sense financially not to have any more, so rather than Mary getting her tubes tied I offered to give Mary the ultimate gift a man can give to a woman, 'his manhood,' and I got a vasectomy! "Ouch" and you can say that again! Once the anesthetic wore off I hit the bloody roof. I bet you can still find my fingernail imprints in the ceiling. (Don't worry guy's it not always like that, it seems the clamps they put on me had been adjusted too tight. Our future son-in-law David had it done by the same doctor six years later with no trouble at all.) Though where I got the courage from to do it to myself, "I can't conceive." (Sorry folks limp humor, oop's I mean strong hard humor.)

With that behind me I felt a lot more secure financially and was happy that we were able to afford to let Mary stay at home. Mary and I had always agreed that her being there was important for the children's upbringing, even if it did make things a little tight. Mary, being at home, became an enormous asset to me and the other drivers since we could always count on her to assist us whenever needed. Don't worry ladies; I do believe that looking after a home and three children is, in itself, a full time job! In fact I think some of our politicians should try it. Perhaps then they'd find out what true budgeting really is.

Having two months off work did give me a well-earned rest, I suppose, but what a way to get it. Maybe it would have helped if we'd been able to take the odd vacation now and then, except time and finances were never on our side. We had managed to wangle only four weeks holiday in ten years. The main reason for that wasn't the fact of working 24/7, it was due to the frequent change of ownership of the business. Five times in all, (coincidently the same as Photogenic) and with every change, it was like going back to square one.

I always felt I had to prove myself over again to the new boss, and stopping to take a vacation would have only thrown everything off kilter. So, I'd put off any leisure time until things settled down, but, due to the constant change, they never did. Once I even tried to go it alone, but the Bank wouldn't loan me the money. They agreed I had an amazing list of clientele and numerous up-coming bookings, but because I was not a householder it meant I had nothing in the way of what they called 'security'. (What a shame, not a government grant in sight, when I needed one.)

Years ago my original boss, Ester, had to sell the company due to personal problems. When the second owner took over he didn't even have a garage for the cars. So, I ended up keeping some of them at home. Lucky for me we had a drive through garage that allowed me to keep one in the back garden, one in the garage, two on the driveway, and one on the street (fig.28). Whatever the neighbors thought of that I could only guess... You must have heard the saying "Five limousines outside and no carpet upstairs." Well, that about summed it up. The other drivers also kept a car each at their homes, but at least they also had a car of their own to use for other things. We didn't. My old wreck had died a year earlier, so we had to use a limousine for everything. The local supermarket nicknamed Mary the "Limo-Lady" and all the young grocery packers loved to help her out with her bags, just so they could have a good look at whatever car she was driving. She would take the kids to school each day in a stretch-limo. Funny really, because there were days when we were so broke we could barely afford to give them a packed lunch. Mind you - they certainly made up for it when it came to show and tell... sometimes I'd take a car. Each year on their birthdays we'd pick up their party friends in limousines. That certainly must have given the parents something to talk about. If they'd known, however, that we'd spent virtually every penny we had to provide the kids with food, they would have had even more to talk about. Which only goes to prove what I said earlier- you can't judge a book by its cover! The constant change of ownership had yet another pitfall, it meant that I never got around to asking for a rise. My wage remained at $10 an hour, for eight years. No King's ransom, I must say, especially when you take into account all the car cleaning and other work Mary and I did, all for free. It finally sunk in that, 'the man who works for nothing will be constantly employed.'

Yeah, busy but broke. Thank goodness for my tips, without them we never would have been able to make ends meet.

Okay, so there's more to life than money, and deep inside I knew it. Why else would have I continued working the way I did? Working all those extra hours ensured that things ran smoothly, and over the years Mary and I earned something that money can't buy... respect! Not only from my staff and clients, but from the other limousine companies in the city. Quite often we'd work together, me for them and them for me, as sometimes I've had bookings that required using in excess of 30 vehicles. One even required 60 sedans! It was through this constant working together that I eventually ended up working for Steve. We did hundreds of events together, from which he acquired an immense respect for me... and my client list, of course.

Steve had some of the nicest vehicles in the city, with an office in the prestigious Chateau Laurier Hotel. His clientele consisted mainly of boring government VIP's and corporate executives. I, on the other hand, may have had older cars, but my client list was to die for! It included 80% of all the celebrities that visited the city, a jewel that was sought after by many!

There was one more thing that Steve had that I didn't, and that was a great head for business. I was too soft hearted. Steve was not, although he did lack patience needed for the job and always had trouble keeping his drivers. On the other hand, I was renowned for my patience and always managed to keep a good rapport with my drivers. I guess it was just inevitable that we'd end up working together one day.

Within a year I was back burning the candle at both ends again. It still hadn't sunk in that I couldn't please all of the people all of the time. I just couldn't relax unless everyone was happy. Perhaps I was still trying to prove (mainly to myself) that I was worthy of being Fleet Manager. How could I let Steve down when he had so much confidence in me? In truth that was partly to blame... He had too much faith in me, and considered me a cross between a 'Super Chauffeur' and 'The Energizer Bunny!' Capable of handling anything, and the ability to keep going, going and going… That's why he gave me every VIP run we got, always squeezing in one after another wherever possible. I remember once when I was in Quebec City, I'd just dropped off a group of Lawyers when he telephoned me.

"I have a very important pick up for you at 10 pm," he said.

"What!" I replied, "It's 5 pm now and I'm 6-hours away from Ottawa. You've got to be joking."

"Go on, you can do it" he groveled…

From then on, he called me every half hour for an update of where I was. Once more I pushed the car and myself to the limit, eating while I drove and stopping only for gas and to 'point Percy at the porcelain'. British for 'use the washroom.' The closer I got, the more frequent the calls as he maneuvered the clients and me together. As soon as I arrived in Ottawa, I sped through the nearest car wash, cleaned the glasses and vacuumed the car. Arriving at the Chateau Laurier with just seconds my party came out. If only they knew!

There were times when I was so exhausted I just couldn't do another run. Steve and I would end up screaming at each other on the phone. Many is the time I've thrown my cellular across the car swearing that I'd never do another extra run again! Steve would then swear that this was the last time he'd ever ask. I think we both really meant it at the time, but neither of us ever followed up on our threats or promises…

In retrospect, I think Steve cared so much for his clients that he always wanted to give them the best. Even if that meant arguing with me to do it. 'The customer comes first,' was something we agreed upon and, as troublesome as it was behind the scenes, as far as our clients were concerned, it worked. Believe it or not, we made a great team. One complemented the other, and together we accomplished amazing feats of expertise. We were able to do the biggest events with phenomenal precision and not a single screw-up. If only I had been able to say "NO" occasionally, I probably wouldn't have ended up so stressed out and perhaps I would still be driving today.

It wasn't enough for me taking on most of the driving, oh no, not me! I had to do everything... and again I tried to do everything myself.

All my working life I've had a problem with delegating tasks to people. I never expected anyone to do anything I wouldn't, especially when it came to the menial and dirty jobs. I'd always have to do them myself. (There goes that low self-esteem again.) That's why I'd be found at the garage even when off duty, cleaning and fixing up everything in sight, back to my obsession to keep everyone happy. Keeping the expenses to a minimum for my boss, keeping the cars running well for the drivers and making sure everything inside worked and looked good for the customers. No frigging wonder I never socialized ... I never had the time! I'm positive if there'd been an association for workaholics I would have been nominated its President; but then again, I'd probably have been too busy to attend the meetings.

Maybe it's because I'm a Gemini, as they're renowned for doing two or three things at the same time. Though truthfully, I know it had more to do with my self-confidence, or lack thereof. I never considered myself worthy enough to take time off. (I hope all you other workaholics are taking note of this.) It's also the reason why I held so many management positions. I had to be at least the manager just to consider myself equal to the other employees!

They say, 'all work and no joy makes one a dull boy' and it's true! Most of the time I loved my job, but I did too much and in my exhausted state I let the negative aspects over power the positive ones. This manifested itself by me becoming dull, dismal and depressed. Once more I achieved this state of mind and everything appeared to get worse.

The drunks seemed to be more frequent, and dare I say it, even more obnoxious. My VIP clients had become greedier than ever and the graduations had become so bad, that companies were refusing to do them! Just when I thought things couldn't get any worse, we all began to have trouble with the Quebec Police.

Booking everyone on sight, they became relentless in their badgering of Ontario licensed limousines. In fact some were downright nasty! I remember going into Hull one night, to pick up a group of four that I'd dropped off at a bar earlier. Just for the record, I was a mile from the Houses of Parliament across the Ottawa River in Quebec. Knowing the current situation, I knew I had to be careful where I parked. On arrival I was very pleased to see my party standing outside the club ready to go. "Great," I thought, and pulled over to pick them up.

"Keep moving" a voice said. Turning my head I could see that it came from a Police Officer on the other side of the street.

"I'm just picking up my people," I replied.

"Keep moving," he yelled.

"But I'm just..."

"Keep moving you can't park there," he shouted.

"But I'm not parking, I just want to pickup my..."

"KEEP MOVING!" he boomed, as he walked over to the window of my car,

"But I'm," and before I could finish, he began to call me every f-ing name he could think of.

The guy was so angry he was literally frothing at the mouth, and even put his hand on his gun! Seeing my predicament, my passengers backed away and began walking down the street, not one of them daring to get in! Not wanting to be shot myself, I pulled the car forward and followed my passengers, who were then running as fast as they could. When out of sight of the cop I stopped the car, and everyone piled in on top of each other and away we went. I don't know whether the guy was just having a bad day or if it was connected with the other problems we were having with other police at Mirabel Airport!

Here they were on the warpath as well and refused to let Ontario licensed limousines pick up passengers. We were allowed to drop off customers, but only Quebec licensed cars were allowed to pick them up. This was something that caused the Ottawa companies considerable trouble, especially since most of their clients had paid in advance for a return trip. People arriving at the airport expected to be picked up by a driver they knew, and many had no idea of what was going on. This led to some quite irate phone calls, to say the least.

Things took a turn for the worse when the police began to seize the cars of Ontario companies that tried to pick up, charging them a hefty fine to get them back. Luckily, I wasn't one of them. We too had clients that required picking up, but I devised an ingenious plan on how to do it without getting caught: having an account with 'Budget Rent-a-Car.'

The first thing I did was drive across the river to their office in Hull and rent a sedan with Quebec plates. I'd drive to Mirabel, collect my passengers and transport them back to Ottawa. Afterward, I'd return the car back to Hull with nobody the wiser. Where there's a will there's a way, they say. On the down side, we probably lost money on the deal, but at least the customers were happy, although I must admit many of them weren't very impressed with the Quebec police's tactics. So much for Canada being one nation.

Oh well, C'est la vie. Three months later, the Airport decided to let us pick up our passengers as long as we could prove that we were the ones who had taken them there.

With this problem solved everyone got back to doing business as usual, but with one exception, ME! "I'd had enough." I was fed up with the bitterness I'd seen exhibited by people, all this greed over money and the dog eat dog mentality. The airport issue was just further proof of the nasty attitude people had for each other, at least when it came down to business. I never complained about Quebec companies picking up in Ottawa, we all have to make a living and that's my point. We all do, regardless of what province we happen to live in. Come on folks, isn't it time we showed each other a bit more compassion! Why can't we just all get along?

Perhaps if we stopped arguing so much with each other over petty issues, we'd have more time to notice the bigger picture of what some of these corrupt corporations are up to, and maybe even unite to stop it. The more we squabble among ourselves the better they like it; it takes attention off them and allows them to do what they want, when they want. Please don't think I'm trying to stir things up again, I'm not! The last thing I want is for you to think I've turned into some kind of radical 'conspiratorialist.' It's just that the amount of deceit and corruption I saw coming from our, "so-called," elite had virtually destroyed my outlook on reality. The intensity of their dastardly deeds was not only becoming more frequent they were also becoming a heck of a lot more vindictive.

Executives and bureaucrats alike seemed incessant in their contempt for the public. Some of the conversations I overheard were so unbelievably alarming I would never have believed them myself, if I hadn't actually been there.

Yep, I knew about the "Quebec sponsorship scandal," ten years ago, and overheard many people talking about how money was being channeled by the Government to a select group of people to pay for trumped up Government contracts and non-existent events.

One such example was how the Federal government paid over $300,000 in advance to a Quebec 'Rod and Gun' club for a booth to promote the Liberal party. If that alone seems excessive, wait 'till you hear the rest. When the club canceled the event, the government never bothered to ask them for a refund! Mind you, I suppose that's nothing when you compare it to the thirty million dollars they paid to Bombardier for Pilot training that they never even used!!! Can you imagine what you would do if you paid out that much money and never received anything for it? I can! Perhaps now you can understand why I was so pee'd off with things… If I'd said something at the time, I'm sure no one would have believed me!

Now as I sit here in 2005 proofing my work, I'm pleased to see that the whole patronage scandal has come to light, and don't be fooled by those who say they knew nothing about it. It was pretty well common knowledge among the government employees that I drove. In fact, I'll tell you something else you didn't know.

Canada Post once hosted an international convention and hid the entire thing from the public. Well, they did let us have some involvement; they put up the price of our stamps to cover cost.

By now you probably think I'm beginning to sound like a broken record, and you're right! But if you think reading about it is depressing, imagine what it must have been like for me to be surrounded by this crap every day!

Over the past nine years I heard so many negative things about people in power, I'd reached information overload. The thing that made matters worse was that I felt incapable of doing anything to stop it, and don't think I didn't try to tell people, I DID! But no one wanted to hear. After all, I was just a lowly limo driver. I really wish things would have been different, there's nothing I'd like better than to say it's all just a figment of an over-active imagination. But I can't. In fact, some of the things I saw are so unbelievable, if I told them to you, you'd probably throw the book out the window and walk away in disbelief... but what good would that do? It wouldn't change anything. Like the air we breathe, you might not be able to see it, but it's there!

Over the last nine years I'd logged up over a million kilometers and driven dozens of vehicles, cars of every shape, size, and colour. From a 1928 Buick, (fig.29) with wooden wheels to the latest Ultra Super Stretch. I'd also been responsible for the transportation of thousands of people, again of every shape, size and colour. And in weather conditions that sometimes had to be seen to be believed. I had done it all, seen it all and, sorry to say felt it all, and now it was time to give it all up.

Friends have advised me not to include this next section. They think it's too weird for most people to comprehend and, that by including it, people will think I'm some kind of nut. Dismissing all the other things I've said, they will end up throwing the baby out with the bathwater! But remember: each mighty oak tree started from just a little nut that stood its ground! So what if it's a bit strange? That's life and we've all done weird things at one time or another.

Exploring the world of the metaphysical was just my way of relaxing, and if I hadn't done something, I would have exploded years ago. Remember, I've never drank, smoked or took drugs, so please bear with me, and you will see there is a good reason for everything that I and my family did. If I didn't include this section I too would be guilty of censorship, and frankly I believe that the majority of people will be interested in what I have to say. So read on my friend, for the best is yet to come...

The seeds had taken root a few years earlier, when the organizers of a 'Whole Life Fair,' asked me to pick up one of their guest speakers, a psychic called Brenda, who was renowned for her weekly spot on a local radio station. Since all my previous encounters with psychics had been extremely interesting, I was eager to meet her. I pulled up outside her house just as she and her husband Ian were coming out.

"Pleased to meet you," she said, and asked if I'd mind if her husband took a souvenir photo of the two of us. Nothing unusual really since it happened all the time. The next thing she said seemed strange!

"I told Ian that I'd be meeting someone special today and that's why I want a photo." Duh, what the heck does she mean? I'm the one meeting someone special today, not her!

As we made our way to the venue, she told me that she could feel a lot of trauma in my life and how everything appeared to be centered on my work.

"Don't worry," she said, "There's a reason for everything and things will work out just fine."

I realized immediately what a compassionate lady she was. Later as I sat and watched her work, I was overwhelmed by the sincerity she had towards those who consulted her.

Although Mary and I were liked and respected by all, we still didn't have many close friends. We were both so happy just being in each other's company that neither of us socialized, and not since leaving Doug and Corel behind in Montreal had Mary and I met anyone we could really assimilate with. Meeting Brenda and Ian was just what we needed. Ian was an extremely compassionate person with a terrific personality, and considering that he was a detective in the RCMP, I personally found it very comforting to know that people of his calibre still existed in the police force.

I became so confident around them that I was able to share some of my experiences, taking some of the burden off Mary. Whenever I had a problem Brenda would take out her Tarot cards and consult them on why it was happening and how I could use the situation to aid my growth in a positive way.

I must add, though, that every time she'd insist that I was quite capable of finding things out for myself. All I needed to do was tap into the universal power that I and everyone else possessed, and just go within.

"No way," I'd say. "I'm no psychic!"

But as time passed, I began to think more about what she'd said and realized she might be right after all. Both Samantha and Mary did seem to have an uncanny ability to predict things, and I could always tell what sort of run I was going to have as soon as I laid eyes on my clients. Perhaps such ideas were not as farfetched, after all.

We decided to find out for ourselves and see if we did actually have what most people would call ESP. Off I went to get some books on how to start.

The first thing we tried were tarot cards, but the only one who seemed able to use them was Samantha. Determined not to give up we arranged that Samantha and her boyfriend Dave would get together with Mary and I on Sunday to hold a meditation session. Sunday was my quietest day and since Samantha was no longer living at home, we always made sure that the family got together for Sunday dinner. So later that evening when Michael, Lyndsay and Julie were in bed, the four of us got together in the living room and began. After lighting candles, we held hands and said the various prayers of protection we needed before we started, something I'd read to do. Then, using various mantras and relaxation techniques to enhance the mood, we sat in silence to see if anyone received any thoughts or feelings of communication.

Now before any of you dismiss this as a bunch of mumbo jumbo, please remember we were just four regular people sitting together in quiet meditation, and we weren't using alcohol or drugs to induce things. To us it was a great way to unwind and none of us took it too seriously.

Nothing much happened at our first session, though I must admit the guided relaxation technique definitely reduced my stress level. So we continued to do it on a regular basis, and after a few weeks of trying, our persistence paid off when Samantha and Mary began to receive images and messages in their minds. At first hardly anything made sense, but the more we did it the more proficient they became. Mary began to write down everything she received, a practice known as automatic writing, and it didn't take long before the messages became so fast and fluent she couldn't keep up with them.

To make things easier I took over the notation as Mary spoke out loud what came through. Mary described the sensation as if there were other voices talking inside her head and she always did her best to keep her own thoughts out of the way. Just like the rest of us, she too wanted to hear what was said. Everything that came through was tremendously sincere and loving, and said in such a beautiful way that we all felt privileged to be there. Sometimes Mary would receive images in her mind instead of words, and some were so magnificent, it could take her an hour just to describe them. One image in particular was repeated over and over again.

She'd be transported back in time to what appeared to be an Egyptian temple, where she would witness a ceremony involving the burial of an ancient scroll beneath the Sphinx. This apparition was so vivid she could describe every detail and could actually smell the incense in the air. Most of the other messages she received related to situations that each of us were going through at the time, and in no way were we ever asked to do anything that was detrimental to our well-being. It was as if someone or something was there to guide us and, to tell the truth, I've had that feeling most of my life.

Ever since the death of my father I've felt a presence

around me. Perhaps it was my father. I've lost count of the times that this sensation has saved me from harm, especially while driving. In fact, I bet there's many of you reading this book that have had similar occurrences yourself- that sudden impulse to turn and look in another direction, or a feeling not to do something or venture somewhere, as if someone was concerned for your safety.

As far as the automatic writing is concerned, that's been going on for thousands of years. Take the Bible, for instance. The New Testament itself was written by this method, hundreds of years after the death of Jesus, a process some call divine intuition, so why should it be any different today? There's no reason for it to stop 1600 years ago, and anyway didn't Jesus himself say that all he could do we could do and more? Don't knock it till you've tried it, and I suggest you read the book 'Conversations with God' by Neale Donald Walsch, and see for yourself. (Heck, I even channeled a lot of the same material myself, but that's another story…)

For now, let's get grounded back on earth and move forward to Samantha's Wedding. Dave and Sam had been inseparable since high school and although they were already living together, they decided at the age of 21 it was time to make their relationship official. Nothing too elaborate though, just a small gathering of family and friends, or should I say friends and family, since other than us, all the rest of ours were back in England. Well, with the exception of Debbie and my mother, who'd both come over for two weeks to attend. (Not together though, might I add.)

It was lovely to see Debbie again and Mary and I were determined to make sure she had the time of her life. After all, if she hadn't left me, we would never have met! Since we were so happy together we wanted to make her happy too. We decided to give her the royal treatment, including a champagne tour of Ottawa in our best limousine and a trip to Montreal, sightseeing together with Sam and Dave.

On the day of the wedding things couldn't have been better. Samantha had booked what was, without a doubt, the smallest church in Blackburn Hamlet. It was so tiny, that our little gathering of thirty guests completely filled it, or should I say, their wedding was so popular the church was filled to capacity- it sounds better! As for me, even though I got the day off work I still ended up as the limousine driver, father of the bride and the official photographer. It must be a Gemini thing! Everything was perfect, including the weather, and that evening at the reception, I could have cried when Samantha thanked Debbie for being her mother and Mary for being her mom. 'Good girl,' I couldn't have put it better myself. Debbie, Mary and I became closer then ever before during those two weeks, and on the day of her return we all hugged and kissed each other with tears in our eyes. Debbie was still crying as she went through to board the plane. What a wonderful thing to see her leave on such good terms and I think it was predestined for us to say good-bye this way. Because little did we know it then, but none of us would ever see Debbie again. She was to die unexpectedly a few years later.

Another thing we didn't know at the time was, that Debbie would never get to meet her first granddaughter. Leah, who by the way, arrived exactly as Samantha's guides had predicted, thirteen months later on the 20th of December 1996, making me a Granddad! Makes one feel old, but then again, they do say "a man's only as old as the woman that he feels" and since Mary's seven years younger than me, I'm OK with that...

Now before you all start wondering 'what the heck I was talking about' when I mentioned that Sam's guides had predicted Leah's birth, perhaps I should explain things in more detail.

One evening in the beginning of December 1995, the four of us got together for our regular Sunday meditation. Everyone was relaxed and happy and looking forward to Christmas. As usual, Mary and Samantha were the ones to be contacted. Suddenly, Samantha was blown away when she heard a little girl's voice in her head saying "Hello mummy." Not having a child and no current plans to have one, this voice didn't make any sense to her. The voice went on to explain that she was the spirit of the child Sam would have the following December, and that she was around her now to prepare herself for rebirth and had come through to ask if she could be named Leah!

As you can probably imagine this took everyone by surprise, especially Dave. We'd all heard about reincarnation, but it was something we knew very little about. Was it really possible for a spirit to visit its future parents, and if so was this the genuine article or just a figment of Sam's imagination?

A lot of people will probably believe that once this suggestion had been placed in Samantha's head, human nature would take it's course and that's why she gave birth to a baby girl a year later. Again, I would agree, but the fact Leah was conceived and born at the exact time predicted is amazing... it's not an easy thing to do, just ask any parents. Another thing of note was that Leah had said it was to be her rebirth and she'd picked Samantha and Dave because she already knew them from previous lifetimes, again the reference to reincarnation. I was determined to find out more about it.

I began by reading up on the subject and you'd be amazed just how much information there is out there. From recent happenings to incidents that go back thousands of years. Account after account of people's stories, some of which had been verified by experts. Take the story of 'Bridey Murphy' for example.

In fact the proof is all around us. Have you ever wondered why some people seem so addicted to past eras of history, wearing clothing and decorating their homes in styles from the past; Egyptian, Medieval, Spanish and Roman to name but a few? People crave food from other countries and continents, even though they have never been there in their lives. Mary and I love East Indian food, and could eat it every day, but neither of us has been anywhere near the Far East! And it's not due to our ancestry, that's Scottish, *and I dunna think they were too canny aboot a wee drop of curry, D'you?*

Our daughter Julie has acted like a 70's hippie ever since I can remember, but she only really found out about that period when she became a teenager in the 90's! We all think that she was probably a hippie that overdosed back then and has come back again, this time determined not to make the same mistake. One underlying theme I did find in my research was that most past life incidents had been recalled during hypnosis and once more I was intent on finding out for myself. I had never been hypnotized and didn't even think that I could be.

During one of my runs with Brenda, I heard about a woman hypnotist from America who specialized in the subject of reincarnation and she happened to be visiting Ottawa. My faith in men had been diminished to say the least and I didn't think that I could trust what a male hypnotist might tell me, but this was a woman, so I decided to make an appointment to see her.

When I arrived at her door I felt a bit apprehensive and nervous not knowing what to expect. When she opened the door and greeted me, saying "Hello Richard," I was even more perplexed. "It's John," I said, and went inside. I took a seat in the lounge and proceeded to tell her a little about myself, and the reason for my visit. Throughout our conversation, she continually referred to me as Richard. I'll explain why later. She took me into a small bedroom and asked me to lie on the bed and make myself comfortable, which I did.

It was nothing I'd expected, and she proceeded to talk me down by going through a succession of relaxation techniques. I remember thinking, 'this is boring,' but suddenly I found myself somewhere else. I was surrounded by smoke and there were people all around me. I was dressed in medieval clothing and one person in particular stood out from the crowd. He looked like a priest in a long red cloak and he was laughing at me… it was then that I realized that I was a woman and tied to a stake. I could see flames and smell the burning wood. I couldn't feel any pain, but what I did feel was rage. I was angry at the sight of this priest laughing at me and thoughts ran through my head, 'all I'm guilty of is trying to help people, so why is he doing this to me?' Gosh, the emotions were strong.

Then in a flash, I was standing on the deck of an old sailing ship. This time I felt like a young boy, hanging on for dear life, as the ship was thrown from side to side in a tremendous storm. I continued jumping from life to life, each one filled with tremendous emotions and yet I still didn't feel any pain or trauma from the experiences. It's as if I was watching a video playing in my head, observing everything with one huge difference- I was there...

What happened next was to change my life, well my name, anyway. I started shouting out loud, "My name is Saint John, my name is Saint John" over and over again. I then opened my eyes and was back lying on the bed with the woman sitting on a chair next to me.

"Wow, that felt so real," I said, "and what's with the name, Saint John?"

"I don't know. That's something for you to figure out" she replied, "I just help to take you back and what happens then depends on you and what you've carried over into this lifetime."

Regaining my composure I thanked her and left, and as I made my way back home I couldn't get the, 'my name is Saint John,' out of my mind.

When I arrived back home my mind was still drifting in and out of the past experiences. I remembered that I'd recognised some of the people I'd seen around me. They had looked different but I still knew them. I'd seen Mary, Julie, Samantha, Michael and my mother, but the most notable was Mary! She seemed to be with me in most of the lives I'd visited.

Everything began to make sense. How Mary and I had agreed to get married within hours of meeting and how we always seemed to know what the other was thinking. I also believe I had discovered the reason why I never wanted to be away from her for more than a day or two. Something connected with a life we had together during the Crusades, around 1180 AD. {A lifetime closely tied with my present existence, and also the reason that the hypnotist had kept calling me Richard.}

Anxious to tell Mary all about my experience, I made a pot of tea and we sat down to talk. To celebrate I had stopped on the way home to buy some of our favorite cakes.

Mary was as excited as I was and wanted to know every little detail. It was like reliving the whole experience all over again. Prior to going, one thing that had crossed both our minds was, what would happen if I saw myself getting hurt, would I feel it? Now I was able to explain how the hypnotist programs in the suggestion that you not feel pain or distress of any kind on any level into her method of talking you down.

"It was as if I was just observing things," I said, "There, but not there," if that makes any sense. After I'd told Mary all my experiences, I ended by describing how I came out of it shouting, "My name is Saint John," and sorry to say, it didn't mean anything to Mary either. So what did it mean?

Was I once called St. John? If so, when and where, and why does it feel important to me now? We decided to visit the local library to see what we could find about the name and see if anything would jog my memory. The name seemed to haunt me and I even evolved it into John St. John. The more I said it to myself, the more natural it felt.

The next day, Mary and I did research and found out there had been about a dozen people called 'Saint John.' They included the most famous, the disciple of Jesus, but I didn't think I'd been him! There was one though that did strike a nerve, 'St. John of the Cross,' a Carmelite priest, born 1542 AD, who became famous for his spiritual writings. However, to this day I'm still not sure why this name means so much to me.

One thing I did do though, was decide to change my name, and called a family meeting and told everyone of my decision. Mary didn't mind at all and Julie who was then 16 thought it would be great! She'd never liked her full name anyway, Julianna Bell, and wanted to use this opportunity to drop, the Anna part. Michael, then 10, wasn't bothered either way and Lyndsay loved the name St. John, so it was settled. Sam was married and already had a new name, Hamel.

Three hundred fifty dollars and a few months later, it

became official and the St. John family was born. (Well in name anyway!) We were all delighted, though I can't say the same for my family in England. Most of them were disgusted, and thought I'd wanted to distance myself from them even more... insulting the family name! How the heck, could I ever explain to them that it was because of a past life regression? They'd think I'd gone nuts. I've always been proud of my heritage, and the last thing I would do was insult it. I just believed that this name was important to 'who I am.' Every time a female in the family gets married they lose the name Bell anyway. I should have told them that I'd had a sex change and got remarried, perhaps then they wouldn't have been so upset.

It was also around this time that Mary's channeling became stronger, and just for the record she's not one for being in the spotlight. In fact, quite the opposite. She hates being the centre of attention, and doesn't even like speaking out loud. She's also extremely caring and compassionate, and incapable of lying to anyone. She hasn't got an evil thought in her head and would never swear. A real life Mary Poppins, so to speak.

One evening while in meditation, Mary said she could see beings all around me, and that there was a purple glow surrounding my body. I was quite taken back, nothing ever picked me before. Suddenly, a vision of a cross came into my mind, a cross in a shape I'd never seen before, with golden streaks of light emanating from it. Surrounded by golden letters, 'H.C.O.D.E.' The image was so vivid; I grabbed a pen and paper to draw it. This was totally new to me; I'd never seen anything before, not since my regression experience anyway. Later at our next gathering, Mary's guide told me that the cross I'd seen was, 'The Cross of Humanity,' and it symbolized the coming together of all religions. The letters refer to the 'Humanitarian Code,' something that was lost over twelve thousand years ago.

I know this sounds far fetched, but please don't quit on me now. I'm a tell-it-as-it-is kind of guy, and what I'm saying is exactly what happened. What you make of it is up to you, all I ask is for you to keep reading, because I'm not a fool and

I know it all sounds strange. If you had told me a few years earlier, that this would be happening to me, I would never have believed it either! But it did, and I do, so I'll continue... I was to have yet another visionary encounter, and this one would change our lives!

It happened in bed one night, Mary was asleep, and I was just lying there on the verge of sleep myself. The room began to radiate a purple glow, and everything in the room appeared to have an aura around it. I took my arm from under the blankets and raised it into the air. It too, was surrounded by this purple light.

"Wow, what's happening?" I thought, and nudged Mary to see if she could see it, but Mary continued sleeping, which was also strange. While still half awake an image appeared in front of my eyes. I don't know whether it was in my head or actually there in the room but whatever it was, I could see it for sure.

I saw what appeared to be groups of people standing and talking in a great hall, they were dressed in what looked like Greek togas. My attention focused on a group of four men. One of them turned to face me and he reached out his arm and handed me a scroll. Not a word was said. Then the room returned to normal; the image and the purple glow was gone. I lay there for a while feeling more than a bit astonished by what had just happened. Thinking it was over, I closed my eyes and tried to sleep.

Next, the image of a huge 'Golden Pyramid,' filled my mind and I began to be shown around it, room by room. Simultaneously, emotions of happiness and excitement filled my senses. When the images finally ceased, I got up and went downstairs to draw everything I'd seen, while it was still fresh in my mind. I couldn't wait until our next channeling session, to see what they were going to say about this.

I wasn't disappointed. After the usual greeting, they got straight to the point and told me I had been shown the concept of a Humanitarian Centre, constructed inside a full size pyramid. Inside was a spacious restaurant, dedicated to the finest dishes from around the world. Also a large stage/

theatre for shows and conventions, and on the same level there were meeting rooms for smaller gatherings, plus individual therapy rooms, a library, a relaxation area, and the ultimate children's activity play centre. Impressive? Just wait until you see what's on the upper level!

Here, people would enter into a great circular auditorium. Surrounding them as they walked down the corridor to the main arena was plush circular seating. A light of cosmic energy shines down from the top of the pyramid onto a large crystal, which hangs above a huge granite stone. This was surrounded by a ceremonial pool, encircled by earth and plants with four majestic candles burning at each corner. The top quarter of this great circle was occupied by individual spiritual altars dedicated to all the world's religions and native beliefs. Each constructed with the reverence and respect that they truly deserve. The reason for all this was to establish a centre that no one could have any excuse not to enter, since their beliefs, too, were represented inside. And if they didn't have any beliefs? Then this would be the perfect place to explore and find out which was the right path for them.

It's my impression that this building would be a step in helping people to understand each other's customs, while contributing to the preservation of our planet. Or, as one of Mary's guides put it, "You will never reach the sky by digging a hole in the ground, so how can you ever expect to get peace on earth when people feel so separated from each other?" Powerful stuff.

I was so impressed by what I'd heard, that I made a scale model of what the complex would look like, (fig.30) so that the others could see what I saw. I couldn't help wonder though, how, when and where such a place could be built.

Strangely, my vision appeared at the time when I was considering giving up my job. Maybe that's why it happened, you know… like the saying, "When one door closes another one opens." Perhaps this was a sign of things to come? All I know for certain is that it definitely woke me up, and I began to see everything in a different light. I began to feel more optimistic about things, and even the dark cloud over my head started to break apart. I'd never been what you'd call a deeply religious person, although I was the first person to be baptised at our local church centre when I was eleven. For me it wasn't a person's beliefs that were important, it's the person themselves. I don't care whether they worship Jesus, Buddha, Krishna or Mohammed, as long as they have compassion and love towards others. Personally, I think a man should be judged by his actions, not his beliefs. There's good and bad people the world over and it's only by their misjudgments that we can appreciate our wise ones.

If everything in the world were white, you wouldn't be able to read these words. We need the opposite to understand things more clearly. Just imagine what your garden would look like if there were only one kind of flower, or what the planet would look like if there were only one kind of terrain. It would be pointless taking a vacation if everywhere you went looked the same. Its great to have a choice; that's what humanity is all about, "choices". Every time something happens in your life you have a choice whether to accept it or react to it, but the decision is yours to make.

That's it- it wasn't the job I hated or the people, it was what they did that upset me. Instead of getting angry, I should have appreciated them for showing me how inconsiderate some people can be, and then thanked my lucky stars that I wasn't like that. At last things began to make sense. I felt free and invigorated once more.

This time I didn't go out and buy myself a car, instead I called the family together and told them that I felt it was time for us to leave Ottawa. Every one of them agreed, but where do we go? We put a map of Canada on the table in the lounge and then one at a time, while the others waited in the kitchen; we lay our hands slightly over it to see what area we were drawn too. I know this sounds hard to believe, but everyone of us picked the same area. A little triangle in the southern interior of British Columbia.

Considering that none of us had ever been further west than Toronto, it was quite a shock to us all. Once we'd made up our minds there' was no stopping us! Looking more closely at the map we decided to move to Kelowna, the biggest city inside the area we had all chosen. The next day I went to the library and looked up the names of rental agencies there, from which we managed to reserve a house for us to live in. Next, Samantha and Dave gave their notice at work, and I left Steve and worked part time for Fred, another friend of mine, while we sorted out the final details of how to move.

We couldn't afford to hire a removal company and even 'U-haul' was way above our budget, so my next task was to buy a cheap truck that we could use, and then sell once we were in BC. Every time I found a truck I liked, someone managed to beat me to it.

With time running out and only three days to go, I managed to find an old farm truck. It was a 27-year-old Dodge, complete with what they called 'suicide tires.' You'll find out why later. But the price was right, although it did need to be safety checked to get a highway permit. After I got the truck home, the whole family stayed up all night fixing it, ready for its test the next morning, and with only two days left to go, it had to pass…it failed!

They said it needed two new tires and some rear axle work. I re-booked for the next day and took the truck to a garage to have the axle work done, while I went out to find the tires. They had to be used ones, because that kind of tire wasn't made anymore, and after a few phone calls I was off into the countryside to get them. I got them alright, but no one would fit them for me. I tried garage after garage.

"No way, they're suicide rims," I was told. "You need a special steel cage to put them on." The steel rims were known to fly off during inflation and had taken many a guy's head off in the process. Hence the name, suicide.

After many frustrating attempts, I managed to find a station that still had a cage. My next job was to persuade someone to do it and again they said 'NO.' That was until I gave the guy an extra $20 and offered to help him fit them. With my tires now fitted to the wheels I made it back to the repair shop just before they closed. Good job too, as they couldn't take the truck off the ramp until I brought its wheels back! The next morning I took it for the re-test and it passed. At last we were able to start loading the thing, with only 24 hours left before the new people arrived to move into our house. If you think we were pushing our luck, wait till you hear the rest!

My mother was now living with us, as she had emigrated from England a year earlier. She'd had a small stroke three days earlier and was now in the hospital. Her doctor said that is wasn't too serious and that she'd be able to come home on the 31st of July, the very day we were leaving.

Like ants in a colony, we worked until 4 a.m packing and loading everything in sight. We had only a 2-ton truck so I had to make sure that every little gap was filled. The sad part was, all our lovely furniture would have taken up too much space, so we had to sell everything. (fig.31).

Again, as in England, people took advantage of us. Knowing we were short of time and that it all had to go, our $3,000 dining room set went for $400.00. A mahogany hutch unit went for $200, and our white leather sofa and chair went for $100.00! I could have cried; it had taken us years to acquire it all, and now it was being scattered to the four winds. I had some serious second thoughts, I can tell you.

We'd gone too far to turn back. So after three hours sleep, (on the floor) we were at it again. This time while the others stacked everything in the front garden, I frantically tried to make it all fit in the truck. It felt like being on a game show, trying to cram a ten ton house into a two ton truck, while someone watched over us ready to bang a gong and shout, "Times up!"

The new people arrived and we still hadn't finished. Mary was busy cleaning every square inch of the empty house, so I continued to load as by then everything was stacked in the garden. I ran around picking things out that would fill any and every little crevice. When the truck was full, and I mean 'FULL,' there were still dozens of things on the garden! So we packed what little we could into the trunk of Dave's car and piled up everything else at the end of the drive, next to a big sign, 'Free to a good home.' The new people weren't too pleased about that, but there was nothing else we could do. We had nowhere to take it and nothing to take it in, even if we did. It's not like we could nip back later to pick it up, not from British Columbia. Due to lack of transport and space, Samantha, Dave and Leah arranged to stay with friends for a week and then to fly to Kelowna and meet us when we arrived. I would drive the truck and squeezed next to me, on top of boxes, would be Michael and Lyndsay.

Mary was to drive Dave's car, an old four cylinder Chevy that was also loaded to the max. As well as Mary and everything needed for the seven-day journey, there was my mother, Tracy our Old English sheep dog, six houseplants, three cats and a hamster! I'll leave you with that thought as we end this chapter.

Chapter Ten

Canada's First Balti House

A skeptic is a person who sees the writing on the wall, then claims it's a forgery.

Here we go, emigrating again… we may as well be, considering that Kelowna is virtually the same distance from Ottawa as England. Only this time, we had no idea of what the place was like, and no one there to greet us!

The hardest part about leaving was saying good-bye to our daughter Julie. She had decided to stay in Ottawa, at least for awhile longer, not a problem as far as she was concerned. She was now 16, and capable of looking after herself. Well, in her opinion anyway. I must admit though, it did help matters a little since there wasn't any room in either of the vehicles, and it would give us chance to settle in before she joined us. At least we were able to rent an apartment for her and her friend Chantal, and furnish it for them before we left.

The time had come to say good-bye, (for now) and it was hugs and kisses all-round. Pulling away slowly, we made a final good-bye wave to the house we'd lived in for the past eight years, the longest we'd ever stayed in one place. Then slowly but surely we made our way to the hospital to pick up my mother.

I led the way just in case anything fell off, and I'm not joking! We even had things hanging on the outside, including a couple of spare tires. What a sight for sore eyes we must have been, as we pulled up outside the hospital.

Though the old truck was now mechanically sound, it definitely needed a paint job. What a mess. The 27-year-old relic, (fig.32) looked more like a prehistoric fat Dinosaur, and drove like one too! Parking in the driveway I went inside to find mom, who I'm pleased to say was now fully recovered and back to her old feisty self. Right! Full of hiss and vinegar.

Upon exiting the building she took one look at the truck and proceeded to vent her usual opinion of no confidence.

"We'll be lucky if we make it out of the city," she said.

To make matters worse, it was the 1st of August; the temperature outside was a humid 34 degrees and she detested driving in the summer heat- neither the car nor the truck had air-conditioning.

"Oh well, at least you have a seat to yourself," I said, "which is a heck of a lot more than I can say for the three of us in the truck."

"Don't worry, things will be fine with the windows open," I told her, and finally we were on our way.

Everything went fine for the first hour. 'And yes, I did say hour.' Then the 'Decrepidtruckasaurus,' decided to stop, right in the middle of a line-up due to road works. With my mothers negative predictions still bellowing through my mind, I got out and opened the hood. Going over to Mary's car to explain what happened, I braced myself for an 'I told you so,' from mother.

As I approached the car, I couldn't help notice that Mary's hair and clothing were covered in tiny pieces of wood and sawdust. In fact, the entire interior of the car was covered in the stuff, including mom.

"This is what happens when you combine a hamster

cage with an open window," Mary exclaimed, "it was far too hot to close them, so we both had to just grin and bear it." As for my mother, she didn't have to say a word; the look on her face said it all! Mary got out to wave on the traffic, while I returned to the truck to find out what was wrong.

Before I had chance to do anything, a car pulled up in front of me and a man jumped out.

"Having trouble?" He asked, "I used to have an old truck like this, let me take a look." An offer I couldn't refuse. He then proceeded to take off the air filter and poke a screwdriver into the carburetor intake. "Try it now," he said. So I did and it started! He then explained to me how these particular engines didn't like the heat, and suggested I turn the heater on in the cab. It would help keep it running if we had to stop in traffic again. Wishing us well, he jumped back into his car and sped off into the sunset, and just like the 'Lone Ranger' he was gone.

"Gee, who was that unmasked man?" I thought to myself.

I climbed back into the cab and, following his advice, proceeded to turn on the heater, which soon turned the already sweltering cab into a kind of mobile sauna unit.

"Oh well, as least we're moving," I said to the kids and continued on for another four hours, before pulling into our first motel for some well-earned sleep.

After obtaining a room, our first job was to feed and walk the animals, a task much harder than you'd think. Tracey, the dog was easy enough, but trying to control three paranoid cats was a nightmare! Claws and fur went everywhere, as did the cats! Thank heavens that Hammy had his own cage! He was content with his wheel, although he did require some extra sawdust. (fig.33)

With all the chores done we settled in for the night. What a weird feeling it was, to know that everything we owned in the world was parked outside; and for once I was glad that the old truck looked such a wreck. No one in their right mind would ever think of stealing a heap of junk like that... reassuring in one way, but creepy in another, especially when considering how far we still had to go.

The good news, day one was over: the bad news, we'd only managed to pass Toronto! Flat out, all I could manage was a top speed of 75 kph, and whether it was because the truck was too old or just too full, I really don't know. The person I felt most sorry for was Mary. She was the one that had to creep behind me for the next seven days, and all she had to look at was my backside; an eight foot high six foot wide grey metal door that constantly kicked up muck onto her windshield.

Well, I do recall our marriage vows mentioning something about 'for better or for worse'!

On the road again, I'd been chugging along happily for a couple of hours when Mary passed and flagged me to stop.

"One of the tires looks strange," she said, so I went to check it, and sure enough she was right. We had a flat. Luckily for us we had double wheels at the back that had stopped us from tipping over. However, it now meant all that weight was sitting on one wheel, so we had to get it fixed and fast! Unfortunately, it was Sunday and there weren't many places open, but thankfully we found a small service station with a repair bay that was open. Pulling in, I showed the mechanic our dead tire and asked if he could help us.

"They're suicide rims," he said. "I'm not licensed to do them."

'Oh-heck here we go again,' I thought.

"But hang-on a minute, what if I change the tire and you just fix the inner-tube," I said, and to that he agreed.

Problem solved, or so I thought. Then, as the guy was taking off the wheel he noticed there was something wrong with the axle bearings.

"I'm sorry, but you've got a bigger problem here," and pointed out the loose assembly.

He wasn't joking! It appears that the guys who'd done the safety check hadn't reattached the axle correctly and everything was about to come flying off. 'Holy Cow!'

It means if we hadn't got the flat tire and stopped, a few miles further down the road, the whole wheel assembly would have come loose and the truck would have definitely tipped over and us with it!

Once more, fate or something supernatural appeared to be looking over us, and if you think I'm joking, wait till you see what happened next.

The mechanic said he was unable to fix it, since it required a licensed truck mechanic and specialized tools. As we stood there looking perplexed, a man pulled in to pick up his tire that had been repaired the previous day. The mechanic knew him and said, "Hey Phil, take a look at this."

Phil just happened to be a licensed truck mechanic for a local logging company. After we'd explained our predicament, Phil replied, "I've got my tools in the car, so you two change the tire and I'll fix the axle." And that's exactly what we did.

When he'd finished, Phil wished us well on our journey and left without accepting any payment for his trouble. By this time the mechanic had fixed the tube, and I'd managed to change the tire without losing my head. So we paid for the repair and were on our way once more. Now figure that one out!

Continuing on until dark, we found another motel and went through the usual animal ritual before retiring to bed. Both Mary and I counted our blessings that night, I can tell you! The next morning I was beginning to wonder if we'd never make it out of Ontario. Here we were- day three, and we still hadn't left the province. It was endless.

Continuing on, we were just 50 miles from Kenora (the last city) when Mary passed me once again, and guess what? We had another flat tire. If that itself wasn't bad enough, this time we were smack in the middle of nowhere.

"For crying out loud, what do we do now?" I said. I knew that we'd probably have to reach Kenora before we'd be able to get it fixed, and that was another 50 miles away.

This meant driving with all that weight on one tire again, but this time there was nothing else we could do. 'By-the-cringe,' I don't think I've ever prayed so much in my life, because I knew that if the other tire blew, over we would go and that would be the end of our journey, and possibly our lives.

Mary was of similar mind. Following me as usual she gathered up all the willpower she could muster and projected it on to the good tire. If all that pressure wasn't enough, the temperature was in the high thirties, whilst the truck, of course, still had it's heater blasting on us, as we slowly made our way along the winding roads. Once more the image of pioneers came to mind. Looking up to the heavens I said out loud, "Oh God, please let this be our final test."

I could feel the pressure on my heart subside as we entered the city of Kenora, and I gave an overwhelming sigh of relief as we drove into town. Expecting to find help, I was surprised to see every repair shop and garage closed. "But it's Monday," I said.

The only problem was, it was also the first Monday in August, and a ruddy civic holiday.

Getting more than a little exasperated, I spotted a Tim Horton's coffee shop and pulled in to get us a cool drink while we figured out what to do. When I got out of the truck to talk to Mary, I was astonished to see her in tears.

"What's wrong?" I asked, and Michael and Lyndsay, joined me to find out what was happening.

"Hammy's dead" Mary sobbed, "He must have succumbed to the heat."

That's just what we bloody needed... now both Mary and Lyndsay were crying.

Feeling totally frustrated, I told everyone to wait by the truck, while I took the car to find somewhere nice to spend the night, 'and what a joke that turned out to be.' Forget the pioneers, I now felt more like Joseph and Mary in Bethlehem!

There wasn't a single room in the place, everything was full... everyone and their brother was in town for a giant Fireworks Display that was being held there that very night. "What the heck happened to our Guardian Angels?"

Without any accommodation or hope of getting our tire repaired, I went back to tell Mary and the family the bad news. Oh ye of little faith! When I pulled into the parking lot I saw a man standing with them and I wondered who he was.

"This is Nick," Mary said, "He saw us crying and came over to see if he could help, and when I told him what had happened, he said he had a lot of tools at his home and if we took our truck over there he would take a look at it for us. What do you think?"

"Blimey, what have we got to lose?" I said, and off we went following a total stranger to his home. Just like the star to the manger, you might say.

Arriving at Nick's house, he told me to park the truck on the front garden, and asked everyone to go inside out of the heat. Once inside, I looked around, and when he'd said he had some tools at home, he wasn't joking. There were tool chests everywhere, including the necessary tire changing equipment we needed. Nick also had a plan, he sent his teenage son to stay with a friend so that Michael and Lyndsay could use his bed. Offering Mary and my mother his own, he said the two of us could use the couches, once we'd finished fixing the tire.

"Perfect," I said, "But first let's have some dinner," and Mary nipped out to get some takeout. Changing the tire took a lot longer than we'd anticipated; just breaking the bead on the rim took an hour using hand tools. Once again I did battle with the notorious suicide rim and survived- then we finished things off with a bit of all-round maintenance and went inside to have a well earned rest.

To be honest, I can't say I slept very well that night, but at least I was rested and, the great thing was, we hadn't lost any time. We were still on schedule to meet Samantha and Dave in Kelowna.

The next morning we were all up with the sun determined to make a early start, but before heading off there was one more thing we had to do. Give Hammy a proper funeral. Nick found Lyndsay a nice spot beneath his front window, and together we held a small ceremony to say good-bye. We then thanked Nick for his hospitality and offered to pay him for his help, but once again our 'Knight in shining armour' refused. I did insist that we at least pay him the $60.00 it would have cost us for a Motel, and with a final kick of the tire we were on our way to Manitoba.

Finally leaving Ontario behind, we stopped in Winnipeg for a quick lunch and then continued on into Saskatchewan. Besides the fact that Mary and I had acquired sunburned left arms, we made it through both Provinces unscathed. 'But Boy' what a journey.

Everything we'd heard about driving across the prairies was right. Mile after mile of straight roads and talk about monotonous... once I ran out of gas and it took me an hour to realize I'd stopped. And flat, you better believe it, we watched a lightening storm in the distance and it was an hour later before we actually entered the rain. We stopped for the night, just inside the province of Alberta. Mary and I were exhausted, but at least we were now over half way, and with the truck and tires still holding out, we felt our troubles were behind us. YEAH RIGHT, AS IF!

Our next point of call was Medicine Hat, and reaching the town I pulled into a gas station to fill up. Mary, who was a little way behind me didn't need any gas, but pulled into a space at the rear of the building to use the washroom, the only space she could find. I was so busy filling the truck and checking the oil, I didn't notice her pull in and after paying, I became a little concerned when I looked around the parking lot and didn't see her car. Thinking that she might have broken down, I decided to drive back and look for her.

(Wrong decision #1.) When Mary and mom came out of the washroom, they were amazed to see the truck gone, and assuming that we'd continued on, they immediately sped off in the car to catch us.

(Wrong decision #2.) This meant Mary was now traveling in one direction, while I was going in the other.

About five miles from town I stopped at the place where I knew I'd seen her behind me. "Where the heck can she be?" I said to the kids, who like me were beginning to feel anxious.

231

Meanwhile, about eight miles on the other side of town, Mary had stopped to ask a group of pedestrians if they'd seen an old grey truck go by. When they said they hadn't, she also began to get a little worried.

Feeling perplexed and bewildered, we both decided to turn back. Mary drove back to the gas station, while I went to see if I could get any help from the local police station. "I've lost my wife and mother," I said to the officer, expecting him to bound into action and put out an APB on them. Instead he just sat there and did nothing, explaining that I'd have to wait 24 hours before I could file a missing person report. What a fat lot of help that was!

"Thanks for nothing," I said and returned to the truck, and there we sat for the next half hour, wondering if we'd ever find Mary and mom again!

Back at the gas station, Mary was in tears. She'd also tried to contact the police, but only got their answering machine. Without a cell-phone and having no home to contact, we were totally helpless. Believe me, mere words can't describe the utter feeling of panic we had. Poor Mary, not only was she worried sick; she also had the added bonus of my mother to contend with. Mom was constantly complaining, saying that we should have never left Ottawa in the first place and how she knew all along something terrible would happen. Not able to sit and do nothing I decided to take another trip through town, and as the gas station came into view, I could see someone waving frantically in the parking lot. "It's mommy," I shouted, and with tears running down my face I pulled the truck up alongside her. I don't think I've ever felt so relieved in my life. Then, laughing and crying at the same time, we all had one heck of a group hug.

After taking a few minutes to regain our composure, we hit the road again and made our way to Lethbridge, the last town before entering British Columbia. From there we made our way through the Rocky Mountains and into the town of Sparwood, British Columbia. Sparwood was a small town with a big attraction, 'The Largest Dump Truck in the World' and since the daylight was fading, we decided to stop there for the night. To the delight of the kids, I might add, who in a flash set out to explore the giant truck.

I'm not sure whether it was the fresh mountain air, or due to actually being in B.C., but the next morning Mary and I woke up feeling invigorated.

Consulting our map, we figured we had roughly another eight or nine hours to go before reaching Kelowna. 'Perfect timing indeed,' because Samantha, Dave and Leah would be arriving there at 2 p.m. that very afternoon.

Hitting the road at 8 a.m. we expected to arrive in Kelowna by five that evening. As we climbed yet another mountain I thought the stories we'd heard about crossing the Rockies had been vastly overrated. So far it had been a piece of cake and the truck had managed fine. Little did I know then that the worst was yet to come!

From then on each mountain seemed to be higher than the last, and as I started the long climb up another one, my mood changed to one of apprehension when the truck began to go slower and slower. I could barely maintain 15 kph in 1st gear! Any slower and I'd have been rolling backwards into Mary. Breaking-out into a cold sweat, I envisioned us all having to live in Sparwood, if we couldn't get our furniture over the mountains!

Inch by inch we clawed our way to the top, then the kids and I 'hung on for dear life' as I tried to stop from breaking the sound barrier on the way down, praying as I went that the brakes would hold out! Slowly but surely we continued like that until we reached a really steep slope going into Salmo. Noting the rate of incline, I warned the kid's to hang on tight, and manned the brakes as we began to go faster. We were about half the way down when Mary spotted smoke coming from the rear wheels, and as usual her first thought was to pass me. But since she could barely keep up with me as it was, her only other option was to flash her headlights and sound the horn in the hope of catching my attention.

Oblivious to Mary's plight, I was far too busy trying to control this hurtling mass of steel and furniture to notice anything, but when Lyndsay screamed out that a bee had stung her, I decided to pull over to the side of the road to attend to her sting. Mysteriously there was no sting? In fact, I couldn't even find a bee, and the three of us were busy looking for one when Mary pulled up alongside and told me about the smoke. Immediately, I ran to inspect the wheels and found the rear rims so hot, there wasn't a chance of us continuing until they had cooled down.

As luck would have it, I noticed that we'd stopped right next to a small creek and grabbing a bucket off the side of the truck I hopped over the embankment to fetch some water. Ten buckets later the wheels were cooled down and again we were able to continue our descent into the town of Salmo.

Well, what do you think? Considering the fact there was no bee, and we stopped without seeing Mary, right next to water, saving our brakes, do you think that our 'Guardian Angels' had intervened to help us again? 'We do!'

We arrived in Castlegar at 5 p.m., the same time we'd expected to be in Kelowna, so much for our estimation of 8 hours. It had taken us that already and we were only half way. After taking a short break to fix a leaking gas line and recapture Pye, (one of the cats) who had escaped and climbed up under the truck, we continued on our journey. Climbing up another steep slope, I wondered to myself if the rest of the journey had any other surprises in store for us.

It's true what they say… that the last part of the journey always does seem the longest. It took another seven grueling hours before we descended our final mountain and saw the welcoming lights of Kelowna ahead of us. Now approaching midnight, it had taken us over 16 hours to get there from the border of Alberta and British Columbia!

Thankfully, the real estate agent had faxed us a map highlighting the route to our house, so we had little trouble maneuvering ourselves though the now deserted streets. Then with a huge sigh of relief, we finally pulled up outside our new home. Upon seeing our lights, Samantha and Dave came running out to greet us, having picked up the keys from the agents earlier that day.

It was then I spotted our driveway. It rose up from the road over a hundred feet with a forty degree incline! To say the driveway was steep was an understatement, and along with the house keys we should have been given mountaineering equipment! (It never showed that on the photo they'd sent us).

Without a hope of backing the truck up there, and too tired to unload, we grabbed two mattresses out the back and everyone crashed in the lounge till morning. Tired and exhausted, it didn't really sink in that we'd finally made it, and I half expected to be back behind the wheel the next morning. Even in my dreams I could still see the traffic ahead of me, the never-ending roads disappearing into the distance. Thankfully, all that changed once the dawn broke and Mary, the kids and I got up to see the view from the window, and what a spectacular sight!

The morning sunshine glistened on the blue Okanagan Lake as it stretched langorously in front of us, surrounded by mountains as far as the eye could see. All around lay orchards overflowing with ripening cherries and apples, and there were vineyards full of grapes. The birds were singing, the squirrels were playing and high in the sky we saw our first baldheaded eagle gliding its way to the lake.

Mary and I hugged each other in celebration that we'd finally made it. Relieved that all the heartache hadn't been in vain, I thought to myself, 'Now I know why they call British Columbia, "God's Country."'

Before starting the arduous task of unloading the truck and carrying everything up that driveway, we grabbed some food and the kettle from the trunk of the car and shared some of our adventures with Sam and Dave. It was damned exhausting work doing the unloading in the heat that day, but what the driveway lacked, the house certainly made up for.

A beautiful, extremely modern five-bedroom split level, complete with a Jacuzzi on the rear porch, and even the house number gave us a feeling of new found optimism, 649. With the truck finally unloaded and everything neatly in its place, our next task was to find work. Dave was the first to succeed, getting a job with a local sawmill, though possibly not the best choice, knowing his bad reputation of being accident-prone.

I, on the other hand, had four fingers and a thumb and found things a little harder. First I tried some photographers, but once more my portfolio scared them off. To supplement our rapidly dwindling cash flow I decided to sell the truck, but first I had to get it safety checked again. Even though it had been done a month earlier in Ontario, it didn't count in B.C., and thankfully it passed first time. Ten days later we received an offer from a guy in Dawson Creek who assured us he wanted it, and would pay cash. There was just one flaw, he wanted it delivered to him. Oh well, how hard could that be, so we agreed… as if anything in our lives could be easy.

First of all, we rented a small car so that Mary could bring me back, then we set off as before, with me leading the way and Mary tailing my rear. The good news, the truck, now empty, was able to handle the mountain roads without a problem. The bad news, it took us over 17 hours, just to get there. Plus along the way I came down with the flu!

At least the guy was happy. However, the cash turned out to be a personal cheque, with no guarantee of being cashed. Since I was in no condition to drive the thing back, all I could do was accept the cheque and hope for the best. An hour later Mary and I set off on the 17 hour return journey home. And to make things a bit more interesting for us, it was 2 a.m. in the morning, pitch black and teeming with rain.

Mary had to drive and although she was tired, there was no way we were stopping. Miles from civilization, it took hours through windy, tree lined, muddy mountain roads before we hit what could be called a decent highway, and as dawn broke we stopped in Williams Lake for a hot drink and a snack before continuing on. To make matters worse, I broke out into a fever and the constant movement of the car was making me feel nauseous, aggravating my condition. Halfway home I couldn't stand it any longer.

"Stop the car," I said, and Mary pulled off onto some

wasteland. I crawled out of the car and collapsed on the grass, and then as I lay there I heard a rattling sound in the bushes and remembered in B.C. there are rattlesnakes.

"Ah' go ahead and bite me," I said. I couldn't feel any worse than I did. Closing my eyes, I managed to get a couple of hours sleep. Mary did the same in the car, then at midday we ventured out again and this time we actually made it all the way home. Thankfully, the cheque cashed three days later.

Once I was over the flu, I continued with my job search, but weird things kept happening. Letters and faxes I sent for jobs went missing; every time I followed up on a job they'd never heard of me and hadn't received my application. Even when I did get a job, the day I arrived to start, the person whose job I was taking also turned up. They hadn't left at all, and had been absent due to illness, so goodbye job.

Not wanting to get discouraged and remembering why we'd left Ottawa, Mary and I thought we'd attend some of the local churches, to see if we fit in anywhere, The one that we liked most was the Kelowna Centre for Positive Living, so we began to attend their weekly gatherings.

When people heard about the job I'd had and the celebrities I'd met, they began to take an interest in us and wanted to know more. One thing that fascinated them was the way we'd all chosen Kelowna by putting our hands over a map, and when I explained how it was due to my vision of the Pyramid, things really got interesting...

Someone introduced us to a Winery owner who was in the midst of constructing an authentic Pyramid right on his property. The funny thing was, we were living only three blocks away from it and didn't even know! The more people we met, the more they were interested in what I'd seen. It amazed me to see how little the people in the West knew about the things that went on in their nation's capital. It pleased me to see that these people really cared, and genuinely wanted to do something about it. Alleluia, this is great, I thought, and it renewed my faith in people. For the first time in my life, I came out of my shell and began speaking to small groups.

"You should write a book," everyone said, "People should know the truth."

Though I took their suggestion seriously, I first needed to find a job, and when someone recommended that I try the local Community Futures Centre, a Government sponsored organisation to help people start their own businesses, I thought I'd give it a try. At the first meeting I laughed to myself when the presenter explained to everyone that Government loans and grants were not available to anyone opening a business that had anything to do with, sex, religion or politics! Wow, I thought, could I tell them a thing or two, or what...

Anyway, my idea was to start up an 'Executive Sedan Service' between the Kelowna airport and the downtown hotels and businesses. This was something that I felt was desperately needed, since there was only a choice between the shuttle bus and a taxi, and I knew from past experience that many corporate types didn't like either. Getting through the preliminary interviews, my next task was to complete my 'Business Plan,' which I spent many hours compiling. I visited various hotels and businesses to get their response, and all were favourable, I might add. However, when the Community Futures committee reviewed it, they turned my idea down. "There wouldn't be enough demand," they said, and that was that! Who am I to argue with these experts... though I would like to add in my defense, that within a year someone did exactly what I had planned, and now they are the biggest limousine company in Kelowna. So eat my shorts, you bunch of know it alls!

It seems destiny had other plans in store for me.

Our good friend John Bailey, my assistant at the Night-Out and our chef at the G&D, visited us from England. In need of some R & R, his personal life had been nothing but one mishap after another since he'd left the St. George & Dragon. He was still a chef, and a good one; he'd won many awards for his work and could boast H.R.H Prince Philip as one of the delighted recipients of his culinary art. It was John's second visit to Canada, as he'd visited us before when we lived in

Ottawa. He knew from his last visit, that one of the things we missed most from England was a good Indian curry, and John decided to give us a special treat and make one.I should point out that Indian Restaurants are everywhere in England and curry has taken over from 'Fish & Chips' as the take-out food of choice.

John prepared a traditional 'Balti' for us that night. "What's a Balti?" I asked, and he explained that it was the fastest growing curry dish in Britain. Its origins came from Baltistan, and the cuisine itself blended the cooking styles of China, Tibet and Szechwan, combined with the aromatic spices of Kashmir. It was established in England twelve years ago in our hometown of Birmingham. Just from that first restaurant it had become England's greatest growing food sensation, with over ten thousand restaurants nation wide. "Impressive," I said, "Pity there's not any Balti houses in Canada."

'Then ping,' a little light flashed in my mind. "That's it, there isn't any here, so why don't we open one? While we're at it, we could combine it with a metaphysical centre and hold meetings to tell the public about some of the things I've seen! "

My idea wasn't as silly as it sounded, especially when John informed us that he had worked in one of the first ones and knew the cuisine inside out. Together we made a plan, John would apply for immigration as soon as he got home and I would do my part here by arranging the finances and finding a location.

My first task was to get investors, and surprisingly it was a lot easier than I'd expected. Once I'd explained my plan of incorporating a metaphysical centre with the restaurant, people became very interested. A lot of their favorite metaphysical shops had closed down, finding it hard to survive, so the idea of combining one with a restaurant made a lot of sense- one could help support the other.

Together with three investors, Harold, Flo and Tela, I managed to raise $15,000, with the promise of another $15,000 from a young lady in Alberta. She had heard of my idea from a friend and wanted to be part of our project, and although she was over 500 kilometers away, we spoke daily on the 'phone. She told me to go ahead with our plans, as she would be returning to Kelowna in a few weeks.

It didn't take long to find the perfect place. An ex-pizza restaurant on Bernard Street, not far from the beach and main tourist area, and across the street from a large hotel, with no restaurant of its own. The restaurant itself had a hundred seat capacity, a large fully equipped kitchen and small bar area, plus a second floor with three other rooms that could be used for meetings and workshops. One of the first things I did was pay a visit to the nearby restaurants to inquire about trade, confident that our opening wouldn't be a threat to them since the place had already been a restaurant. They were all tremendously helpful, and everyone told me the same thing. During the summer season they were extremely busy and the area was packed with hungry tourists. Just what I wanted to hear, and I arranged to meet with the restaurant's owners.

It took another week to sort out all the legalities, then I signed the lease and put down every cent we had as deposit. When I say every cent I mean every cent... I cleaned out all our bank accounts.

I wasn't too worried though, since I was on EI (employment insurance) at the time, and expecting my cheque the next day, and I still had $3,000 to come from one of the investors that I planned to use for the renovations etc.

When my EI cheque hadn't arrived two day's later, we had to go and get food from the local food bank, we were so broke... Ye gotta laugh at that, but at least it proves we were dedicated.

Luckily, it arrived the next day, which was the same day we got the keys to the restaurant. We descended on the place like a horde of worker bees! Julie and her new boyfriend Wes, had arrived from Ottawa a few weeks earlier, and this meant that the family was now at full strength, ready and raring to go.

Dave and Wes concentrated on cleaning the kitchen and getting it operational again, and Mary, Julie, Michael and Lyndsay took on the task of 'de-pizzaising' the interior. They repainted everything that didn't move, while Samantha and I renovated the decrepit bar area and dealt with the fundamentals of operating like stock, menus and pricing. One of my tasks was to obtain all the necessary certificates and licensing that we required to open: 'City, Business, GST, PST, Music, Fire, Food and Liquor' "Phew!" And although I don't drink myself, I must say I found the BC Liquor laws unbelievably archaic.

Wanting to make an impact from the word go, we engaged the assistance of a local artist to help us with the interior. She painted a huge Celtic design on the main wall from which emerged a spiraling Celtic knot boarder that encompassed the entire restaurant. Something that Julie was only too pleased to help her with, and then Julie continued to paint beautiful Zodiac signs on the glazed tiles around the bar, doing a wonderful job. Personally I think all our years of built-up creativity just burst forth, as we turned a mundane 'Pizza joint' into a mystical 'Medieval Paradise.' (fig.34)

In one of the front windows stood a large dormant water fountain, that I soon had repaired, and next to it I placed a replica suit of armour, that Mary had given me for my 40th birthday. Around the walls we hung an array of swords and shields, which I had acquired from my days in the shipping business. I purchased large poster's of, 'Knights and fair Maidens,' scouring the second-hand shops for old frames, and they too went on the walls. Using Dave's computer, I artfully copied old English quotations and sayings onto paper and Mary then used candles to burn the edges and age them to look like hundred-year old parchment. We placed them under protective sheets of plate glass on each table, which not only gave the customers something to read it kept the tablecloths clean. Mary also purchased some lace material of moons and stars and used it as a template to spray the older tables black and gold. This transformed them into beautiful works of art, and after adorning the place with gracious tall ferns and hanging baskets, our work was complete. Boy, did it look fantastic! (fig.35) A perfect mixture, inviting to the eye and cosy and comfortable to relax in, with the soothing music of artists such as, Enya, Sarah Brightman and Loreena McKennitt.

With three days left before opening, there was just one thing left to do and that was to get the supplies... but first we needed the money! Thankfully the young lady from Alberta arrived, just in the nick of time! It was her $15,000 that I was counting on to buy the stock and use as working capital.

Only once again I'd counted my chickens before they'd hatched, and sorry to say she had a couple of surprises for us.

First, although she loved everything we'd done, she wanted us to turn it into a 'Gay and Lesbian Restaurant,' and second, she had only $3,000 and not the $15,000 that she'd originally said! Immediately visions of Ella and Photogenic flashed through my mind. Was history repeating itself again?

It's not that I'm against Gays or Lesbians. On the contrary, what consenting adults do is up to them. I wanted this to be a 'family restaurant,' open to all, like my vision of the pyramid. I didn't want anyone to have an excuse not to enter; it was important for the meetings that the general public be involved. Anyway, why should the family and I consider letting her corrupt our dream for a measly $3,000!

"Thanks, But No Thanks," and we all agreed to go it alone, turning down her ideas and her money. Luckily for us, John Bailey arrived from England two days later for the opening, and he added an extra $2,000 to the pot, just enough to buy the stock we needed. 'The Millennium Cafe and Esoteric Centre' was ready for business!

With his immigration application still pending, John was able to stay for only two weeks, and immediately he got to work training Dave and me in the art of Balti cooking. Just to be on the safe side, he devised two menus, one temporary with just a few basic Balti dishes and a lot of traditional entrées that I knew from my years of being a Chef. The other a full blown 'Balti House' extravaganza, with other traditional classics like authentic British Fish & Chips, vegan and vegetarian dishes. These would be introduced as soon as he returned from England. John also prepared batches of the appropriate spices and sauce mixtures, to keep Dave and I going while he was away.

It was a real pain in the butt, him having to go back again, but at least he was able to be here for our opening. The night before we opened, John, or JB as we affectionately called him, worked through the night to prepare a virtual feast of Baltis for all to sample, and sample they did. We were packed! Heck, the aroma alone was enough to tempt people in. From mild, medium, hot, to inferno, there were dishes of every style and flavour, all accompanied by the appropriate kind of rice and the all important Balti bread, a flat bread similar to Naan but spicier, which JB also made himself.

It was the 3rd of March 1998, and what a wonderful day it was, Samantha commented that she'd never seen me so happy, and why not? I was surrounded by people I loved, the food I loved and doing what I loved, in a mystical paradise that was out-of-this world!

Our first week was fantastic and everyone commented on how delicious the food was and how beautiful the place looked. Then it was time for JB to leave again, so we changed to the temporary menu, and Dave and I held the fort until his return. Thank goodness it was only for two weeks, because I think some of our customers would have gone insane if they'd had to wait any longer. Right from the first day people were hooked on the taste, and having exhausted the few dishes Dave and I knew they couldn't wait to try more! I couldn't wait either as I still had a lot of renovation work to do.

The second floor hadn't been used for over thirty years and it was in a frightful mess. There wasn't even electricity, and when I wasn't working in the kitchen, I was busy working upstairs. In between those jobs I'd be buying stock, so it didn't take long before I was back working 15-hour days again though, I must admit, this time I was enjoying every minute of it. When JB came back I was released from the majority of the cooking, so I continued to fix up the second floor.

Being a little tight on cash, I was limited on what I could do. It had cost us a lot more to open than I'd expected, we even had to pay a $700 deposit to get the gas turned on. But the Millennium was a place of wonders, and once more heaven sent me an Angel in the guise of a waitress named Jackie.

Jackie wanted to join us in every way, and when she heard about the woman investor that didn't turn out, she eagerly offered to take her place. She could only raise half of the original amount, but it was enough to keep us going and enable me to start some of the other things I'd planned.

My goal was to make the Millennium totally unique, not just the food, but the entire operation. I was determined to break new ground in the way a business was run, and the first thing I did was pay everyone the same wage from the dishwasher to the manager.

I'd certainly seen enough things in my life, to realise that everyone needs and relies on others. The chef needed the dishwasher to supply clean plates for him to put his food on and they both needed the waiting staff to serve it and return the dishes.

As in life, no one could exist without the others.

Businesses need people to make their products, people need the businesses to earn a living, and part of that money is spent buying the products that the businesses make. It's the circle of life. Everyone needs someone, even if it's only to get their food, power and services, so why can't we all respect and appreciate each other and share the income equally?

I also wanted to get involved with the community. I willingly displayed work made by local artists. Not the normal mass produced stuff, but original items of art and crafts. I made sure that the mark-up was realistic too. I wanted to sell these things for the people and not have them hanging around for weeks just so I could make a fat profit. I didn't stop there; my next step was to put on live music, though I had to be careful with this one. The city bylaw allowed me to have people play, but I couldn't let my customers sing along- I needed a 'special license' for that! I wonder what highly paid bureaucrat came up with that one?

Here again, I specialized in local talent, and one great success was a group of high school kids that formed a 'Forties Style Swing Band.' They performed regularly on Saturday nights, and cost me a hundred dollars, but it was worth it and everyone loved them.

We had many other terrific entertainers, and one of my personal favourites were two banjo-playing brothers. On the night they played we had about 50 people in to see them. I only wish it could have been 500, they were that good! I also reincarnated some of the theme nights of my hotel years and one was a Moroccan Night complete with a sexy belly dancer, and there's a funny story connected to this.

The original drummer I booked couldn't make it and informed me at the last minute. What can I do, I thought, then I remembered I'd regularly heard one of the street kids playing a bongo on the beach. I grabbed Sam and told her to come with me to see if we could find him, and off we went to check out the area and, sure enough, there he was sitting under a tree playing his drum.

"How would you like to earn some money and have a good meal," I said, an offer he couldn't refuse. He wasn't too bothered about the money, as long as his girlfriend could join him for the meal.

"Done deal," I said, and away we all went. At the restaurant we found him a spare costume and he started to play. He was perfect, and even looked the part. Afterwards he and his girlfriend enjoyed some Moroccan cuisine, courtesy of JB and of course I paid him for his time anyway.

Well, I always was a sucker for anyone down on his or her luck, in fact, we all were! Every time one of the staff saw someone in the street asking for money for food, they'd invite them to come in at lunchtime and help themselves from our buffet table. A lot of them accepted, and the more colourful ones certainly raised a few eyebrows from our regulars!

Yep, we had quite a few regulars by then. News had spread fast, especially among curry lovers and metaphysical types, all of which were blown away by our ambience and décor. Most people found the place so relaxing they didn't want to go back to work, sometimes not even to their own homes. Many people commented that they'd been drawn inside as they were passing by, as if some invisible force was willing them in. This woman and daughter story will amaze you.

The mother and daughter had been in an argument that morning, about the girl wanting to pay a surprise visit to a guy she knew in Vancouver. Saying "No," the mother tried to appease her by taking her shopping instead.

As they walked down Bernard Street, on the opposite side of the road, the mother spotted our restaurant and asked the girl if she would like to try the Millennium for their lunch. Although they had never been inside before they opted to sit in a narrow area at the rear, usually reserved for smokers. Strange really, since neither of them smoked. Then as they sat there eating their meal, the girl looked around and saw a young man sitting with his parents a few tables down. Although the young man had his back to her, she thought she recognized him, and as it turned out she was right… it was the very guy she'd wanted to visit in Vancouver!

Well, you can imagine their surprise. It seems he'd decided to join his parents on a business trip at the last minute, and as they were passing through Kelowna they'd stopped to have lunch, and randomly picked our restaurant. Which meant if the girl had gone, he wouldn't have been there anyway. As things turned out, she not only ended up meeting him, her mom was able to meet him too. Was that a coincidence or what? Then again, considering the odds it seems more like a bloody miracle to me, but I'll let you decide.

Other mysterious events happened all the time. Customers would frequently bump into friends they hadn't seen for years, and others told us how they would be sitting there thinking of someone and the next minute that person would walk in. Sometimes not even knowing why they came in, as they weren't even hungry. "It was as if some invisible force coaxed me inside," they'd say.

Don't worry, we didn't always need the help of 'The Force,' or a 'Jedi Knight,' to get people through the door; our food spoke for itself. To say that people liked it would be another understatement. They rarely left a crumb, and regularly we saw people literally licking their plates! That was the great thing about Balti cooking, each dish could be tailor made to suite their individual requirements, both in ingredients and taste. I guess that's why it caught on so well in Britain. It's also the reason that Balti was so easy to franchise, because once you'd mixed the appropriate spices and prepared the special sauce, anyone could cook it.

To make a Balti, first you need to stir fry the basic vegetables in a small wok, to which you then add the filling of your choice: meat, poultry, fish or more vegetables. Next you add the prepared powder mixture of 14 to 28 different spices depending on the dish, Korma, Vindaloo, Rogan-Josh, Pasanda etc.

Once this has mixed, you then add one of four special sauce bases that, like the powder is already prepared, plus any other ingredients that may be required to suit the individual's personal taste. Finally, flame everything until it's properly cooked. Meanwhile, as the cook is doing this, the assistant would prepare the appropriate rice and bread to accompany the Balti, which is then served directly to the customer in the wok it was made in, piping hot, with an aroma to die for!

You see, any average cook can make it; the hard part is knowing what spices are needed for each dish, and what proportions of each to use. Once JB had prepared the sauces and mixtures, in advance, the actual cooking time of the meal is very fast.

"Someone should tell Oprah," because not only is it fast... all the ingredients are natural, making Balti the ultimate in healthy, fast food! (Anyone who's interested in franchising it can contact me!!!)

For those that didn't like stir-fry, JB created the Balti burger, 'the burger that bites back,' available in chicken, beef or vegetarian. - Anyway, that's enough advertising from me, so let's end the commercials and get back to the story.

Of course I'd be lying if I said that we didn't have any complaints. We did, though I must admit 99% of the few we did have, had nothing to do with the food. Mostly they were complaining about my window sign, the part that said, 'Esoteric Centre.'

Some people disliked it so much I'd receive weird phone calls from them accusing us of performing witchcraft or being part of an obscure occult group!

On one occasion when I was serving a table of four at lunchtime, a gentlemen asked what the word 'esoteric' meant and wanted to know if we were we all Wiccan's?

"Don't worry, I said, "Nothing happens until 10 p.m and then we all take our clothes off and run around chanting." Sorry to say, he wasn't amused and didn't appreciate my English sense of humour. We never saw them again.

Just for the record, the word esoteric actually means: 'A small group engaging in the pursuit of knowledge, wisdom and philosophy.' I put it there because I wanted the Millennium to be more than a restaurant; I wanted it to be a place of information as well. Which brings me to the other reason I opened the restaurant in the first place...

To inform the public about the things I'd witnessed in Ottawa, but not only that, I also wanted people to explore other issues that were affecting us and our world! I hoped to accomplish this, by holding what I called "Gatherings," and these gatherings/meetings would be open to all. Everyone and anyone who so desired, could talk there on whatever subject they wished. Not just spiritual issues, but anything that might be of interest to others!

With the vision of the pyramid centre still implanted in my mind, I didn't want to scare anyone away, so I changed the window sign to read 'Meeting Rooms' instead. I then made preparations for our first meeting. I decided to hold them on the first Sunday of the month, an ideal time since we were closed and could transform the restaurant's interior into theatre style seating.

On the morning of our first one I woke up a bundle of nerves, my mind churning over with all the 'What-if's,' and every disaster scenario imaginable.

"I can't do it" I said to Mary, "There's no way I'm going

to have the guts to speak out in front of dozens of complete strangers ... well' that's if any one bothers to turn up of-course."

By the time we arrived at the restaurant I felt even worse, convinced that what I was trying to do was stupid. Thinking to myself I thought, "Nobody cares about the things I've seen, and anyway why should they listen to me?"

"But what about all the posters I'd given out and the people I've asked to speak, I've come too far to turn back now, so I may as well see it through to the end. At least then I'd know for sure whether to continue or give up!" Getting the place prepared did occupy my mind, and while Sam and Dave arranged the chairs, Mary and I put out a small buffet of cakes, pastries and refreshments for people. All free of course, though we did have a donation box for those who wished to contribute. Luckily, I'd managed to find a great musician who was willing to play for us, and three guest speakers, covering topics on Reflexology, Tibetan Crystal Bowls and Alternate forms of Energy. They were the first to arrive, together with some of our friends who'd come to assist us with any last minute details.

Soon more people began to arrive and more and more, until there was over seventy inside.

"Not bad for our first one, hey." Only joking! Actually it was bleeding amazing, and double what I'd expected.

After the usual greetings and chitchat everyone took their seats and waited for someone to start things rolling, and 'OH-Crap' that someone was me. Grabbing the microphone and gathering all my courage I introduced myself and thanked everyone for coming. Still shaking in my boots, I then went on to explain what "the gatherings," were and what I was hoping to accomplish.

Amazingly once I got into my reasons for being there, my nervousness just disappeared, the words were still coming out of my mouth, but this time their source originated in my heart and not my mind! Being our first meeting, I concentrated on our journey from Ottawa and a few of the reasons why we left, not wanting to overpower them with too many details too soon. Even this was too overwhelming for some, and they found the intensity and passion of what I said so immense it brought them to tears, and the thirty minutes I'd allocated for my talk was over before I knew what hit me.

An hour earlier I'd wondered to myself how on earth I was going manage a full half hour, and now that it was over, I felt as if I could have continued for at least another week! Introducing the first speaker, I stepped aside knowing that my part was over.

Breathing a huge sigh of relief I returned to my seat and joined the others to see the rest of the day's presentations.

Between each display, there was a brief musical intermission for people to chat and partake of the buffet. Then, after the final presentation, we held a question and answer period where the microphone was handed to anyone who wished to speak. At first people were timid, not wanting to air their beliefs, let alone their problems. Then after hearing some of the others speak, they realized that there were many who shared their views or had gone though similar traumas themselves, all of whom were only too willing to help others though theirs. This segment later became an integral part of our meetings and literally changed people's lives.

The whole day was a tremendous success, far better than I could have ever imagined. For the first time in my life I began to see people in a new light. Deep down in all of us there's a willingness to help others, it just needs the right momentum to bring it out. If the meeting wasn't enough to amaze people, Mother Nature was about to put on a little show of her own, as if to confirm that what we were doing was right.

It had gone dark outside by the time we'd finished and one of the first couples to leave called us on their cellphone. "Quick, go outside and look up," they said. Which ofcourse we did, and there in the sky above us was a breathtaking display of the Aurora Borealis, or Northern Lights as some people call them. Even more strange is that they appeared to be centred right over our restaurant!

As you can imagine, this created a stir, and before long

there were fifty of us standing in the road, all-looking up. I can't really speak for the others, but it certainly sent shivers though Mary and me. It was even mentioned in the local newspapers the next day, described as "a most unusual phenomenon." Especially for that time of the year and, most unusual, it was seen only over Kelowna.

Whether it was by coincidence or not, it had an impact on us, because at our next meeting we had over one hundred people! News travels fast in a small town and our monthly 'gatherings' became a great success, and our range of speakers grew. We included topics such as Offshore Banking, Water Purification, Solar Energy, Immunization, Canadian De-Tax, Shamanism, Law Enforcement, Vitamin's, Channelling and Native Medicine Wheels. I'm sure though it was the open-mike discussions that generated the most help to people.

Besides the monthly meetings, we held smaller group sessions and workshops on the second floor, which I'm pleased to say, I'd finally got finished with the help of a 'certified electrician.' Turning one room into an office and the other two into meeting rooms, they attracted a variety of club's, support groups, Yoga workshops and even the occasional kids' birthday party and PTA meeting.

By the end of our fifth month we'd become pretty proficient at things and our 'customer comment book,' was full of compliments, including many from British tourists. The smell of the curry alone drew them in! We acquired several other Brit's as regulars, one of which was a local jeweller and his wife. His story is on a par to ones I mentioned earlier about customers meeting old friends... but this time I was the one to be blown away!

The jeweler's name was John, and like me, he loved a good curry, but we were to find out that we had a heck of a lot more in common than that. On his third visit, he and Mary got talking.

"Where are you from?" he asked.

"Birmingham," said Mary.

"That's funny, so am I, what part?" he replied.

Mary told him how she was from Erdington, and that I was from Yardley.

"What a small world," he said, since he was also from Yardley.

He then inquired if Mary knew the name of the street I'd lived in, and she answered, "Brays Road, his family had a grocery shop there."

"I don't believe it," he said, "I'm from Brays Road and I know that shop, my mom and dad were friends of the original owners, the Bells."

"That's amazing!" She replied, "They're my husband's parents." Then she ran to get me from the kitchen, so that I could meet them and find out more.

Upon hearing what Mary had to say, I was flabbergasted. Could it really be someone I knew from my childhood? Well as it turned out, it was and it wasn't...

It was certainly true that our parents were friends; in fact they frequently went dancing together. But sorry to say, John and I couldn't remember each other. He was a few years younger than me and since I was only eight when I left Brays Road, I never really knew him. We probably met once or twice, because I was a friend of his older sister, as we were in the same class at school.

There was one thing though that we both remembered, and that was the names of other people in the street, and we sat there naming each family and recalling what we knew about them. Mary and his wife Diane must have been bored stiff listening to the two of us rambling on about events that happened 40 years ago. There was still one more surprise to come, when I discovered that his mother was also in Canada, living in Vancouver!

"My mothers here too," I said, and when John told me his mother was coming to visit them soon, we couldn't wait to get the two of them together. From then on John and Diane became good friends and regular visitors. Although my mother was 89, she still had all her faculties and she was astounded when we told her about John and how his mother had been her friend in the 50's. You can probably guess she had quite an emotional day when his mother arrived a month later, meeting again after 41 years. That's one heck of a lot of gossip to catch up on, and although that year marked the 39th anniversary of my fathers death, I think their meeting rekindled a lot of fond memories for mom as she relived some of the good times they'd had together.

What an amazing scene, two dear old ladies sitting in a garden in British Columbia in 1998, laughing and drinking tea as they discussed life in Birmingham, in the late fiftys, remembering everything as if it were yesterday!

The restaurant had now been open for five months and I admit I was having the time of my life, even though it was hard work and long hours. When I wasn't in the kitchen cooking, I was renovating things, doing bookwork or out getting stock. And it wasn't just me; every one of us had pulled together to make it work. Mary, Jackie, Samantha and Julie, ran the restaurant; JB, Dave and I did the food and Julie's boyfriend, Wes, manned the dishwasher. Definitely a family affair. There'd been other affairs going on inside the family too, and Mary had some news for me, Julie was pregnant!

These are words a father of a teenage daughter dreads to hear, and I went nuts! "How can she be pregnant, she's just turned 17 for crying out loud. Hadn't they heard of birth control?" Putting it bluntly, I was not a happy man. I wanted Julie to enjoy her teenage years, and not have to worry about supporting herself and pay bills, as I had to do when I was her age. Now that she was going to be a mother, all her independence would be gone, and I think my relationship with her boyfriend Wes went down hill from there on. On the up side, I didn't have time to brood on it as the tourist season was in full swing and at last we were beginning to make money. I remember saying to JB, how even with a fraction of the capital required for such a huge venture, we'd managed to get this far and as long as things continued as they were, we'd end up with 'Canadian Balti House' franchises all over Canada.

Things looked even rosier when the local CBC Television

did a feature on us and JB prepared a 'Chicken Patia' live in the studio on their morning show. It was a terrific success and Mary recorded the program for us. Balti was becoming a hot commodity. But there was something even hotter about to happen some miles away near Salmon Arm, which was to change everything!

A forest fire had broken out and it soon became one of the largest ever to hit the region. Smoke and ash began to fill the air; so much smoke in fact that it affected your breathing. As the smoke increased the tourists decreased, and soon they were virtually all gone!

The news media were showing report after report on the blaze, which included film of the fire and details of the smoke filled air. Bad news travels fast; bookings everywhere were cancelled. As the local streets became empty, we realized then how much we and the other restaurants were dependent on the tourists. Without them in the local hotels there was no passing trade, and the large hotel across the street from us was one of the reasons I felt confident about renting our location in the first place. There was something else we soon discovered, few of the Kelowna residents bothered to visit the restaurants in our area. The reasons being, first, the restaurants were usually packed with tourists and second, they could rarely find anywhere to park due to the two Multiplex Cinema's (without car parks) that were near us.

Within days we had gone from being packed every night to virtually empty. Being from England I'd had no experience of forest fires and didn't really worry, expecting things to be back to normal within a few days. 'Hell, was I wrong.'

My first sign of things to come was when a 'For Sale' board went up on the hotel across the street. Then like dominoes in a row, other hotels and restaurants began to close. Things started to look a little shaky and our rent of $3,000 a month hadn't been a problem with what we'd been making, but now it loomed over us like a giant black cloud. This was just our first year, for crying out loud. We hadn't managed to build up any fat to live off. What were we going to do?

The tourists stayed away and things got worse. My first thought was for those who had invested in me. No way am I going to let them down, I said, and luckily JB and my family thought the same. We were all determined to do everything we could to survive, and we all agreed to half wages.

Something else we did was not renew our house lease and we decided to find something less expensive. We had only three days left before vacating our home, when I managed to find a house we could afford. It said, 'no pets,' but I managed to convince the owner that Tracy our Old English Sheepdog wouldn't be a problem as she was eleven and couldn't do any damage due to hip problems. (Paddington, by-the-way, had died back in Ottawa when he was also eleven). As far as our cats were concerned we only had Pye left. The other two had disappeared, we think coyotes got them. Anyway, Pye too was also getting on in years so I didn't even mention her, and on the 31st of July we moved again!

Moving house is bad enough at the best of times, but when it's 38 degrees in the shade, it's a nightmare. Even worse when you consider that moving into a new house should be an exciting adventure, but to us it was just a necessary evil as we were only doing it to save money. The new place was horrible compared to the one we were leaving.

Oh well, maybe things will improve now, we all thought as we staggered off to bed that night for some well needed rest.

We awoke the next morning to the realization that nothing had changed and we were deep in shit. Sorry, but I'm not swearing! The entire basement was flooded with raw sewage, and upon examination we discovered that the septic tank was full and all the toilets had backed up. The bloody stuff was everywhere... the smell alone was enough to make everyone want to throw up. It was three days before we managed to get the tank emptied, no one would come. It seems our new landlord was also having financial trouble and couldn't afford to have it drained. "Poor guy, at least we were still scraping by," I said to Mary! Me and my big mouth, as a few days later I received two unexpected bills.

The first one was for property tax, which I hadn't realized we were liable for (I should have paid more attention to the small print) and now had thirty days to find an additional $1,700.00!

The second was from the government demanding $1,200.00 for an EI overpayment. Although I had withdrawn from my EI on the day we opened, I'd been busy preparing the restaurant during the month prior to opening. Instead, it seems that I should have been actively looking for work, as they called it. They now wanted their money back, plus interest.

'Oh,' and for being a naughty little boy they were also coming to audit me.

You can imagine what I thought of that after all the money I'd seen squandered in Ottawa! After all I'd used that money to build a future for my family and myself, it wasn't wasted! For crying out loud, I'd seen politicians spend more than that on hookers in one night! Talk about kicking someone while they're down.

Personally, I didn't think the government should be asking me for money, instead they should be giving some to me and the other Kelowna restaurant owners, to get us through this disaster. Just think of the jobs they could save. 'But no,' they're too busy paying million dollar pensions to themselves for working all of four years.

Was I bitter? You bet I was, and this was only the beginning. I was about to find out the hard way, that there isn't half the amount of help out there that we are told, and what little there was, is so tied up in 'bureaucratic red tape,' you're lucky if you can get it at all.

The forest fire may have ended, but it had left more than burnt trees in its wake as over two dozen restaurants had closed. Some had been in business for years. Our pulling together had enabled us to ride it out, but now with these unexpected bills I dreaded to think what would happen if things didn't pick up and fast.

Working for $5.00 an hour wasn't for everyone and Wes was the first to quit, though I can't blame him. After all, he wasn't really one of the family. The rest of us decided to struggle on, but it wasn't long before we received even more bad news... Our landlord informed us that his bank was about to seize our home, and really he shouldn't have rented it to us in the first place. He also told us we must move out and quickly before they seized our furniture along with it. Only two months after moving in we were moving out again.

Luckily, one of our customers had a house for sale and they said we could live there until it sold. This time JB didn't join us; he had met a young lady, fallen in love and the two of them had secretly married. No one knew about it, not even Mary and I! Well, at least John was happy, which is more than I can say for the rest of us. To keep the restaurant going, Mary and Julie stopped taking wages altogether and lived off their tips. Samantha, Dave and I halved our wage once again, though I did my best to keep Jackie's wage as normal, because she was also an investor and had a loan to pay back. The city had become a ghost town and money was tight all-round, but once again our cutbacks paid off and we managed to scrape through to December. Things picked up again, thanks to the Christmas shoppers.

There was one thing though that the fire hadn't affected and that was the gatherings. They were better that ever and my goal of informing people had exceeded my expectations. Speakers came from everywhere and the Millennium became a virtual beehive of information, a lot of which I never knew existed. Though all our guests were fascinating, there were a few of note that I would like to mention here in more detail- the first being journalist Jean Manning.

Jean is the author of the book 'The Coming Energy Revolution,' and co-author of 'Angels Don't Play this Haarp.' Her talk was about the vast number of people that had invented alternate forms of energy and how powerful industry and government had quashed their research every time, forbidding them sometimes under fear of death from making their inventions available to the public. I would recommend her books to everyone as they certainly opened my eyes and put a lot of what I had seen and heard in Ottawa into perspective. I dare say her work could be considered controversial. Truth can be stranger than fiction sometimes, and the talk we received from the Canadian De-Tax movement definitely fits into that category.

Believe me, these guys had really done their homework, and everything they said made one heck of a lot of sense. Did you know that 'Maritime Law' controls our criminal courts and all the Judges are aware of it? This enables them to run under the protection of the 'Legal System,' and not the Law. There's a big difference between the two.

If in doubt, next time you visit a courtroom look out for a flag with a gold fringe around it. Canada and the United States, like Britain and elsewhere, are ruled by commercial law to enforce our compliance to the 'Legal System,' and bypass our rights as a sovereign individual under common law, and it doesn't end there; the driving license you hold also works under the same system.

That's why your name is always printed with the surname first, in BLOCK CAPITALS. By signing your signature on your driving license application you are agreeing to abide by the Government's legal requirements, and that's how they are able to issue you with speeding tickets etc. Whenever we sign a legal document we are giving our rights of law away, and again don't just take my word for this, but don't ignore it either. Find out for yourself. I know if you are anything like me, you'll be amazed at the things you will uncover.

Other speakers confirmed what others had been saying. These included an ex-high ranking RCMP officer, who had quit his job in disgust when he discovered what the government was really doing to the people. All anyone has to do is walk into any bookstore; the shelves are full of books telling us the truth. It's just that the media isn't promoting them and most of the time we can't be bothered to read them. Most people don't really want to wake up and smell the coffee;

they prefer to hide away in apathy hoping that someone else will save them.

Well, one person who is trying is David Icke, (pronounced Ike) author of over 15 books and videos. David is considered by some to be the most controversial speaker in the world! He's been accused of many things and mostly of being an Anti-Semitic, but I can assure you he's not. In fact, he is one of the nicest, most down to earth and genuine people you could ever wish to meet.

Like most of you, I had never heard of David Icke, until someone gave me one of his books to read, 'And The Truth Shall Set You Free.'

I'd never read anything like it; page after page of facts and figures that turned what I thought was reality upside down. I know it was all pretty controversial, but everything made so much sense, especially the section about Princess Diana. Everything he said I could verify though my years of experience driving such people. For one thing, her bodyguard broke every rule in the book.

I wanted to know more about David, and once more fate was on my side. David was booked to do a talk in Kamloops that very month, something unusual for him as he only comes to Canada once or twice a year and then it's usually only major cities. When I telephoned the promoter to get two tickets, something strange happened. The woman became fascinated by my accent.

"You sound just like David," she said, "Where do you come from?"

"Birmingham, in the West Midlands in England," I replied, and to my surprise she told me that David came from the same place! Then you could have knocked me over with a feather, when she asked if I would like to meet him as he always enjoyed meeting people from his hometown. "You bet I would!"

She explained how Mary and I could have dinner with him, and a few others at his hotel the evening before his talk. Wow, a week earlier, I'd never heard of the guy and now I'd read one of his books, was about to attend one of his seminars, and had been invited to have dinner with him. If that's not synchronicity, I don't know what is.

The day before David's seminar, Mary and I arrived in Kamloops around 6 p.m so that we could book in to a motel before meeting David and the others at 7 o'clock. I felt extremely nervous about meeting him, which is pretty strange when you consider how many famous people I'd met in my life. For some reason, I really wanted to make a good first impression.

We arrived at the hotel restaurant early to find the table and introduce ourselves to the other guests. David arrived shortly afterwards, a tall well-built man with a friendly smile. As soon as he opened his mouth I felt at home. Mary and I still have our accents, but when you hear it from a stranger it seems to have a different effect on you. We chatted on and off throughout the evening, mostly catching up on how much things had changed in England. It was just like talking to an old friend and I felt like I'd known him for years. When the night came to an end, David had to leave to do a sound check at the venue, and it was then that the organizers realized they hadn't arranged any transportation for him. Something that had never happened before, strange!

During the evening I'd mentioned my work in Ottawa, and they knew that I'd had a lot of experience with celebrities, so when I volunteered to drive him, they had no qualms about accepting my offer. Off we went to the venue, and it felt just like old times to be part of it all. After the sound check was done, we drove David back to his hotel and made arrangements to pick him up in the morning.

The next day we collected David as arranged and once he was safe inside the building, Mary and I joined with more than a thousand spectators who had come to hear him speak. People had driven many miles to be there, including some from Vancouver and Edmonton. It was worth the trip just to experience the atmosphere in the building alone. It was charged with a sense of togetherness and everyone got along no matter what their background. We all shared a common bond and a profound sense of purpose that is sadly lacking in everyday life. I know I'll never forget it. I suppose some would compare it to a religious gathering, but that's what made it so fantastic, a person's religious beliefs were irrelevant, it didn't matter. What did was that they were open minded enough to be there and hear what David had to say.

David was a tremendous speaker and had a great ability of finding some humour, even in the most serious issues, quite often using a Birmingham accent to embellish his point. During the lunch break, David preferred to disappear for a while so that the hordes of fans didn't confront him, as he needed to keep his mind focused on his afternoon talk. Again my past experience came in handy, and I positioned my car by the stage exit ready to whisk him away to a nearby restaurant. At the restaurant David was nice enough to buy me lunch, and as we sat there I thought to myself "How on earth did this happen?"

Talk about luck, I was probably the only person there to actually get David on his own. During our conversation I found out a lot about him, how he'd been brought up in 'working class' family in Leicester, a city not far from Birmingham. This was the town where my grandparents had lived, and where my uncle still ran a number of butcher shops called Bell's.

Bell was a name David knew well, because prior to his writing he'd been a professional soccer player for Coventry City and Hereford United. He had also played for England along with a cousin of mine, Colin Bell.

David explained how he'd had to leave soccer due to being plagued for years by rheumatoid arthritis, and ended up working in sports journalism, which became the turning point of his career as he then moved on into local radio and, finally, BBC television. Something opened his eyes and he became an activist on Environmental Issues. Subsequently, he joined the British Green Party and became their spokesman.

He soon discovered that the party was nothing more than old politics under a new name. Then, like me, he lost interest in life and went through some unbelievable upheavals. He found television itself to be an empty, soulless world in which insecurity and fear abounded. There was one thing, though, that always fascinated him, and that was the way the news was presented, a system called 'rip and read' whereby information was faxed into the studio and then read over the air.

"Where did this information come from and who compiled it?" he thought, and set out to find out for himself. It was what he discovered that prompted him to write his first book, 'It Doesn't Have To Be Like This!' From then on, every time David spoke out on issues he was inundated with letters from people who not only agreed with what he said, but informed him of their own experiences and pointed out even more things he should look into.

David detailed everything into book after book and his work is considered extremely controversial to say the least. He would be the first to agree! He told me even he had a lot of trouble believing some of the things he'd been told, and felt like leaving certain items out. But if he did that, he would be as bad as the Government by dictating what we were allowed to know. So rather then censor things David includes everything and lets us decide what to believe. Instead of losing readers the opposite happened. More and more people sent in evidence of even more outrageous things, most of which were being carried out by people and corporations that we were all supposed to trust! The more he writes, the more he uncovers; to the extent that there's not a publisher now that will touch his work, so he had to start his own publishing company. "Wow, what a story!"

After lunch, it was back to the seminar and this time I ended up on the edge of the stage myself, as I was recruited to operate the visual presentation system while Pamela, who had been doing it, went to organize a video presentation. The afternoon's performance was awesome, and I loved the way David introduced a spiritual aspect into things that appeared to be hopeless, making sense of it all. At the same time he diminished any fear that people may have had. It made us all feel privileged to be alive at this time to witness the awakening of humanity.

After the talk, David took time to meet and greet

people and many took advantage of having their photo taken with him. (fig.36) Then, after a quick dinner, it was off to the Airport to catch his flight to Calgary and that's where we said goodbye. I couldn't help but feel a bit envious of his work, and would have loved to have joined him, but I had a family to support and a restaurant to run. So home I went with Mary, determined to help him in any way I could, especially through our own gatherings. I never expected to see David again after that, so it was quite a surprise when David and Pamela walked into our restaurant three days later.

They were on their way back to Vancouver and had decided to visit us. I felt ten feet tall knowing that he'd made the effort to come. David also loved a good curry and was truly impressed with the quality of our food, and what we'd managed to accomplish in such a short time. Having him visit us put the stamp of approval on my work and our gatherings gained even more momentum from then on.

That was the magic about the Millennium; it brought out the best in folk, and there was always a feeling of tranquility and friendliness in the atmosphere. I've lost count of how many customers commented on how just by walking in through the door, it was if all their troubles and stress evaporated and a sense of calmness came over them. They felt happy, relaxed and at ease. Bernie, one of our staff, who had replaced Wes, loved the restaurant so much, he and his girlfriend Nicky got married there! Although things were tight financially, the comradeship between us was unbelievable. Flo, Harold and Tella, all loved the Millennium and were of course frequent visitors. Flo helped out on occasions and I'm sure she loved being in the thick of things.

With all the care, love and attention that had been put into the place 'there's no way we could fail' I thought, 'people cared too much.' Being honoured by David's visit invigorated me and made me decide to give a free traditional Christmas lunch for those in need on Boxing Day, complete with toys for the children.

I loved working in restaurants at Christmas. Putting

up the decorations rekindled the magic I'd felt as a child. I forgot the bills for awhile as again we were all busy, with office parties and festive entertainment. Unlike the St. George and Dragon, we were not recommended to be open on Christmas Day, so we decided to take the day off.

Just like previous years, Julie woke us in the early hours of Christmas morning, but this time it wasn't to open her presents, it was to tell us her water had broken. Within minutes everyone was up, and while Julie and Wes made their way to the hospital, Michael and Lyndsay got busy opening their presents so that Mary and I could follow later. I remember saying to Mary when we left that I had a feeling that Julie wouldn't be in labour long, and that the baby would be born about 11 a.m. I was eleven minutes out!

At 11:11 Christmas Morning, William was born, and both mother and baby were fine. "Merry Christmas Dad," Julie said when I saw her and then she presented me with my present, 'my first grandson!' What a Christmas Day that was, busy and full of excitement, but Boxing Day was to be a big disappointment.

Our customers had done a great job of donating toys, and I was really looking forward to playing Santa and giving them out to the children. The only problem was we only got eight, with about an equal amount of adults. In fact we gave out more meals to all the volunteers that turned up, than we gave to the needy. I hate to say it, but once again bureaucracy had got in the way. This time the bureaucracy of committees!

I had telephoned some local Churches and even the food bank to let them know what we were doing. I asked if they would let me put up a poster advertising the event, but sorry to say, they all said, no! There wasn't time to have it agreed to by their committees.

"Can you announce it then," I asked, but they couldn't do that either because we didn't attend their Church!

"Can you at least give me the names of some families that you think would like to come," I pleaded. To which they replied "Sorry we're not allowed to do that either, Merry

Christmas, good bye." Phew! You live and learn, I thought. There must be a lot of families that would have loved to come, if only they'd known, but because we didn't fit the criteria laid down by 'the committees,' we were not permitted to help them. Again it reminded me of my time in Ottawa, and the way people would change once the cameras were turned off and no one could hear them.

I must say, I couldn't give a 'rat's ass' about meeting their criteria. Christmas is supposed to be the season of 'good will' and all I wanted to do was share it with others, regardless of race, colour, creed or religion. At least, the ones that did come had a great time and the children received lots of toys; one of the volunteers had brought his accordion and everyone enjoyed a great sing along. 'OOP's' I hope I didn't need a special license for that.

With Christmas behind us it was back to reality. Although the income had been a lot better than previous months, the electric and gas bill soon gobbled that up and this time we could only pay half our rent. Still I was confident that we would catch up once the tourist season started again.

We scrimped our way through January, February and March and even though one of our customers helped me by giving me some money, (Thanks Raili.) it too was gobbled up by bills and we were now two full months rent in arrears. Our landlord wasn't too pleased about that, but in light of how many restaurants had gone under and how many were up for rent, he didn't want his added to the list. I suppose that he was a little more lenient because I had paid $11,000 towards the furnishings and equipment, so he did have that as security and anyway he and his family were good customers and loved what we'd done to the place.

I would now like you to cast your mind back to chapter six, and remind you of how Mary and I lost our jobs the same week as someone crashed into our car. Because what happens from now on, makes that seem like a picnic!

My role in life reversed. Instead of keeping my head while all around me lost theirs, here I was in an atmosphere of peace and tranquility, surrounded by relaxed people and I was the one who began to lose it! Many of the other restaurants in the area, had told me that if we could get through to April we would be okay. "That's when we start to get some tourists again," they said.

Well, we were now in the middle of April, and not a tourist in sight! I was definitely beginning to crack, and when one of the city's largest 'Buffet Restaurants' went under, I knew it was just a matter of time before we would follow them. If they couldn't survive, what chance did we have? I was up to my eyes in bills: GST, PST, Rates, Electric, Gas, Rent, Licenses, Wages, EI, Tax, Workers comp, and Bank fees and I still had to find the money to buy stock!

Knowing how severe things were my last hope was to put the restaurant up for sale. At least that way I might be able to retrieve enough money to repay the investors. I soon found out what a joke that was. The real-estate fellow told me that he had over thirty restaurants on his books already and the prices were so low I'd be lucky if I could give it away.

By the end of April things hadn't improved and I was rapidly losing the equity I had in the furniture. Once that expired, my landlord wouldn't have any security. But that wasn't all, I had been throwing every cent I had into the restaurant, and hadn't been paying my car payments so the finance company repossessed it. Goodbye car! I couldn't believe this was happening. "Why would God let us create such a wonderful place, filled with love and friendship, only to lose it all through lack of money?" Everyone had worked so hard, not one of us had put ourselves before the business. Both JB and I had drained every cent from our personal accounts to get through to this year. My neighbour, 'The Kitchen Cowboy,' had been in business for 15 years and had never seen the streets this empty. Even they were thinking of calling it quits. I knew that it was going to take a miracle to get me out of this mess and so when we received another surprise visit from David Icke, I thought he was to be our savior.

That was one visit I don't think he'll ever forget! I was so depressed with the prospect of losing the restaurant and the gatherings, that I constantly droned on and on about my problems, hoping that he would offer to invest in the place and save it.

Instead, David, like Brenda, told me that there is a reason for everything, and if it goes down, let it. Don't fight it, accept it. The restaurant had served its purpose and I must trust that there was another path waiting that would lead to even greater things.

How right he was, but at the time, I didn't want to hear it. In my mind I'd failed and I was about to let everybody down that had trusted me! After David and Pamela left I felt stupid and wished I could have turned back the clock. Me and my big mouth, why can't I be more positive? How many times in my life have things crashed only to change for the better. But in my life when it rains it pours.

Mary and I began to argue all the time; she couldn't stand seeing me like this. I had become nasty and bitter, because my dreams of changing the world had come to nothing. I went on and on about how we had no money to support Julie's baby and, if the restaurant fails, no employment for any of us. If that wasn't bad enough one of the customers tried to take advantage of my moodiness and hit on Mary, telling her that they had been lovers in a past life. One night he phoned the restaurant to see if I was working, and then drove to my house to ask Mary to go with him for a drive, as he might be able to help her with our relationship. More like his relationship, the conniving creep.

What he didn't count on was that Mary phoned me to tell me she was going. I left Jackie in charge and drove home like a bat out of hell, but I was too late, they'd already gone. They say time heals, but I'm not so sure. While I'd been driving home, thoughts from 22 years ago of how Debbie had cheated on me at the Swan Hotel drifted back into my mind.

When they returned an hour later, which to me felt like an eternity, I virtually attacked the guy and Mary and I ended up having the worse row of our lives. As it happened Mary wasn't interested in the guy and had genuinely met with him to talk about our relationship. The fact that I lost control only made things worse. I'd upset Mary more by not trusting her.

I had become so fixated on the restaurant failing and letting the investors down, I couldn't see clearly anymore. Like a person possessed by a demon I spewed out negativity about myself being a stupid and useless businessman, and I pushed my family away every time they tried to comfort me. I felt unworthy and didn't deserve their love. That's probably why I was so nasty to Mary. I was trying to punish myself by driving her away. If I fail and lose the investors' money then maybe I deserve to lose what I loved most, my wife.

I'm happy to say that I didn't lose Mary, but we had to say good-bye to Samantha and Dave, who had decided to return to their old jobs in Ottawa. Both of them were disillusioned with the way things were going. I must say I couldn't blame them, though I was going to miss them especially two-year old Leah. With eyes full of tears and a pain in my heart I waved them farewell, and wondered to myself "Why has it come to this?" In one way I was pleased they were now out of it, and knew it would just be a matter of time before things got worse.

I didn't have to wait long. On the morning of June 1st Mary, JB and I opened the restaurant as usual and we had been there about ten minutes when the landlord's assistant arrived. She was accompanied by a locksmith who proceeded to change the locks as she informed us that we were being evicted and had two hours to vacate the premises.

She also told me that if I signed an agreement letter, the landlord would release me from my lease and take no further action against me. This I did, though I must admit I had no idea of what I was doing as I felt like I had been hit by a freight train.

Next, Bernie arrived for work and after being told the bad news, he helped us grab whatever personal items we were allowed to take and load them into the car, an old Ford that Harold had given us. We were lucky we were able to take some of the perishable food as we were broke, and had been counting on that day's income to buy our groceries. Still feeling shell-shocked we arrived home. What a joke that was! It didn't feel like home to me; it felt more like a hole in which I could hide away from the world.

As far as I was concerned I'd lost everything! The business was bankrupt; I was now unemployed and $40,000 in debt. My car had been repossessed, I didn't have any money, we'd lost most of our furniture, I couldn't repay the investors or support my family and my marriage was on the rocks. "Oh well," at least I had my health! That was until my back went out, a few days later.

It was so bad I couldn't walk or sit down. I had to crawl around on my hands and knees. My only consolation was in knowing that this time things couldn't get any worse.

Or could they?

Chapter Eleven

The Silence must be heard

It's alright to sit on your potty of self-pity now and then; just be sure to flush afterwards.

What a bloody mess! The pain in my lower back was excruciating, and all the doctor could do was prescribe stronger and stronger painkillers. These actually made things worse as they ended up giving me constipation, and again I split my back passage. Oh crap! I wish I could. All I could do was lie there, flat on my back writhing in agony and feeling sorry for myself.

Poor Mary, if losing the restaurant wasn't bad enough, now she had to put up with me crying in pain and screaming with rage, but then, what could she do? She didn't have any money to buy medicine or creams to help me. Some of our friends suggested that I visit a chiropractor or acupuncturist, but you need money to pay for their services. Anyway, I couldn't even stand up to get there. Christ, was I sick and tired. Sick of all the agonizing pain and tired of being hounded by the Millennium's creditors. "We have nothing left to give you," we'd tell them. Nothing was putting it mildly; we were literally destitute.

Although the Millennium had gone, we still had to find the money to pay our rent, household bills and buy food, if only for the children's sake. Mary went to the food bank to see what she could get and returned with enough food to last two people for about three days, some powdered milk and a toilet roll. "That's it?" I said. "You better believe it," she said, "and we can't go again for a week."

Well, looking at the amount of food we'd been given, at least the toilet roll might last that long... Don't get me wrong, I know beggars can't be choosers and we were grateful for the little we did get, but how on earth were people expected to survive a week on this? Thoughts of parliament came into my mind and the lunch buffet they got, all you could eat for $2, and as many toilet rolls as you could use! Things they take for granted.

What do we do? I couldn't work due to my back and Mary was needed at home to look after me, and the children. Julie, Wes and William, were living somewhere else by then, and had enough problems of their own.

We had no money, no savings, no valuables, no assets, no income and, no hope. On the upside at least we didn't commit suicide; we couldn't afford to buy the poison.

There was only one place for us to go and that was "Welfare," and like visiting the doctor we had to go to them. It must have taken me an hour just to get to the car. Mary and Michael supported me while I held onto a walking stick, my hands shaking constantly through the pain. It took another half an hour to get into the office and there I stood gripping onto the counter while the receptionist examined our papers, checking for the slightest discrepancy. At least it was worth the effort and we were accepted. We were given a total of $1,030 a month ($650 for rent, $180 for utilities and $200 for luxuries). You know, food, drink, clothing, cleaning materials, toiletries and medicine. About the same amount of money that a Government minister gets to spend on lunch, not including the transportation of course.

No wonder people rob banks. Even if they got caught

they'd be better off than this. A single prisoner costs the taxpayer over $60,000 a year! We four sober and honest folk on the other hand, were worth a mere $3,000 a year each. Gee! Knowing that certainly does wonders for your ego.

We both felt terrible, and we soon lost whatever self-esteem we had left. Some might say it's money for doing nothing and all the people on welfare should get off their backsides and get a job. Hell, it's hard enough having an interview when you feel good, so imagine the confidence you'd have if you felt, desperate, worried and hungry! 'Like that's going to impress a prospective employer.'

Even now, while being 'down and out,' life was demonstrating to me again that 'you can't tell a book by its cover.' As I discovered years ago, working with the 'Rich and Famous,' a lot of people appear to be caring and considerate, when in fact they really couldn't give a damn. In truth, a lot of things are quite the opposite of what the majority of people think and the same can be said for those on welfare. Things are not always as black and white as they first appear.

Take our case for instance. On first glance some might think it would have saved the taxpayer a lot of money if Mary went out to work. She could earn around $8.00 an hour. But social services would have to send someone in to attend to me, as I'm covered by Healthcare. That someone would probably cost the taxpayer around $26.00 an hour. Furthermore, we would have to find someone to look after the children and the average childcare costs for two children are more than Mary could earn in a week on minimum wage, so this would have to be subsidized as well. Sure we could always put them into a foster home, until I'd recovered, but then the payment to the foster parents is $1,500 per month per child! After doing the math this means, Mary being on welfare and staying at home actually saves the taxpayer up to $4,000 a month! Just like the stretch limousines on Parliament Hill, things aren't always what they appear to be. Makes you think, doesn't it. I certainly did.

I was now seeing the other side of life. 'Thank God,' a

side that most people have no idea about. Unlike the regular Joe on the street, I had witnessed the other side of the coin, and I began questioning the whys and where-fors of what I was now discovering. Now, more than ever, the opulence I'd seen in Ottawa plagued me. I couldn't get that decadence out of my head. The two extremes between the haves and the have-nots were enormous and nothing seemed to make sense.

Why is it that a foster parent gets paid over $3,000 a month to look after two children, when we were given $200 a month to support them ourselves? Plus the usual family allowance, of course.

Why is it that people scream and shout when a prisoner doesn't get their benefits; like clean accommodation, heat, light, power, three meals a day, cable T.V., movies, use of a games room, fitness centre and free education, which costs over $60.000 a year. Then, say nothing about the single mother, who has to pay for everything the prisoner gets for free, while doing her best to bring up her child on a welfare cheque of less than $10,000 a year?

Who's the one being punished? 'Does anybody know, does anybody care?'

As I look back I realize I was at my wit's end, and felt like jumping off a bridge. Ironically, this act would also cost the taxpayer a fortune! They would have to send out fire, police and ambulance services to save me, costing thousands of dollars. If I'd walked into a police station first and asked them to lend me a few hundred dollars so that I wouldn't have to jump, they'd probably have told me to "Get lost," or even worse, "Go jump off a bridge!" Stupid, I know, so why do we allow it to happen? I'll tell you why, it's because the establishment keeps telling us how much they are doing to assist the less fortunate; poverty commissions, job creation, charity organizations and corporate donations.

Take it from one who knows, it's all smoke and mirrors, folks. Getting help from these people is like trying to get milk from a male cow, it's just…a load of Bull. Just as with a lot of our celebrities, charities only help when the media gets involved, then they have something to brag about to the public, who in return give them even more money!

Once, I overheard a group talking in the back of the limousine. They were saying something about what they were doing would raise around a million dollars, and they'd only have to give half of it to charity. Laughing among themselves they said, "Just imagine how many years a member of the public would have work to earn half a million and we're getting it in one night!" What made it so funny is how the public will then consider them heroes for doing it! "We can't lose, it's a win-win situation," they said. They'll certainly be laughing all the way to the bank.

Wake up people we're being conned- and as the song says- 'There's none so blind as those who will not see.' Though personally, I think we've not only gone blind, we've gone stupid as well. For instance what happened to our sense of value?

How is it that people can sit in coffee shops and bars, discussing how their favorite sports idol is worth the $200 million he's demanding for his 3 year contract, then toddle off to their own job, where they may earn $10 AN HOUR! What's wrong with them? Don't they think that their contribution to life is worth anything? Perhaps they think their hero gets paid in monopoly money or lives on a different planet, I don't know, but what I do know is that their idol is 'NO HERO.' In fact, he's just a 'GREEDY PIG' who wouldn't have a cent if it weren't for us poor schmucks paying to see him.

How many women reading this book can spend $500 on a pair of panties, as Brittany Spears does? And how many of you guys can spend a million dollars on gaudy jewellery just to look cool, like lots of the 'Rap Stars' do, while at the same time making millions singing about the poverty and oppression of their own race?

The money they spend on one wristwatch could stock a food bank for a year! If they really cared, they would channel some of their money back into helping the people who gave it to them in the first place, the public. Let's face it, these people are doing what they love to do and getting paid for it. How many of us can say that? I bet when they were young they would have given their right arm to be in the position they're in now, so what happened, isn't being 'famous' enough for them anymore? Now they want to be given extortionate salaries as well, more money than most people could earn in a hundred lifetimes. I think they should think themselves lucky that their dreams came true and stop being so selfish. I've said it before and I'll say it again 'we all need each other!' My conscience wouldn't allow me to demand millions while there's still homeless people and children going hungry, let alone spend $20,000 on dinner for four as I've seen these people do!

"Live simply, so that others may simply live," is a saying we could all learn from. Perhaps then the division between us wouldn't be so great. One solution is a cap on individual salaries, let's be generous and say 20 million a year; anything above that should be put into a Global Humanitarian Fund in their name. This non-Governmental fund would then be distributed to wherever it was needed. Each year we could then hold a Gala event similar to the Oscars, where we would honor the individuals who have contributed monetarily and physically to the fund. That way they'd get the respect of the world's population, as well as their 20 million, becoming a real 'Hero' to those that they have helped through their endeavors. On no account, would this earnings cap end the development of people like Bill Gates and other corporate and entertainment figures, because these individuals love what they do. With this system they not only live well, they get commended for their talents and contribution to society.

In any case, my failure as a working class hero had stripped me of my will to live. I would lie in bed praying to die. At least then I could release Mary from the chore of looking after me. I was selfishly absorbed by my plight. I didn't consider how upset she and the children would be. The only thing that stopped me from suicide was I knew she wouldn't be able to pay for my funeral.

The pain didn't help. I had to crawl on my stomach to get to the bathroom, not able to support myself on my knees. Once there it was like passing razor blades and my knuckles would turn white as I gripped onto the sides of the toilet trying to hold myself into position. Like an idiot possessed I'd scream out to Mary to grab a hammer and put me out of my misery. On retrospect it was a good job she and I weren't getting along well. Imagine the pain she must have felt hearing someone she loved asking her to kill him, knowing at the same time there was nothing she could do to ease my suffering. You always hurt the one you love, they say, and after all the things I said and did to Mary, it's amazing that we're still together. Such was the test of a good mate.

Slowly I slipped further into depression and like my namesake 'St. John of the Cross,' I entered 'The Dark Night of the Soul.' Wallowing in self-pity, not trusting anyone or anything, the guilt of losing the money that my friends had invested in me was eating me alive. The endless calls from creditors didn't help and the stupid thing was, Mary and I couldn't even declare personal bankruptcy, as we needed $1,500 to do that.

I was convinced that everyone hated me for failing and losing the restaurant. How on earth could anyone like a horrible bastard like me, who couldn't support his family and had nothing to show for his life? I didn't own a house, a car, I had no money, no investments, no possessions and even the little furniture we did have was decrepit like me!

Needless to say, I was not a fun guy.

I had a family with a beautiful wife and healthy, considerate children who loved me; my problem was that I couldn't see beyond my condition.

I became withdrawn, and wouldn't go out in case I saw anyone I knew. I couldn't come to terms with what had happened and knew we'd have to leave Kelowna. When eventually my back recovered, Mary and I helped out at a community event in Salmon Arm, and it was from that I received a job offer in Nelson, some four hours drive to the east, nestled on the shores of the west arm of Kootenay Lake.

Packing what little we had left, the family and I moved again, our fourth move in two years. Sorry to say, the job only lasted a month, and soon we were back on welfare. I ended up repainting the house we were living in to equal our monthly rent, since welfare could only pay half. In between recurring bouts of depression I was able to get the occasional job, but I was honest enough to declare every penny and our welfare cheque was reduced accordingly.

My health went up and down like a roller coaster. Sometimes my back would slip out again, and on other occasions, I'd collapse with an inner ear problem that made me dizzy and nauseous. Thankfully, Mary managed to get a job at Wal-Mart at minimum wage, not much but at least it was a start.

I'd lie on the couch thinking of the money I'd seen squandered by the government in Ottawa, millions and millions of dollars paid out to people who didn't need it. I'd think about the people I'd driven about, like the man who worked for Indian Affairs. The guy was miserable. He owned a beautiful house in the suburbs, a boat and two new cars, but every time I drove him he'd complain the whole time, and always about his job. His main gripe was being a government-employed lawyer. He got a hundred dollars an hour. This depressed him because the government paid freelance lawyers three hundred dollars an hour. I'd nod and appear sympathetic, as if I could relate. A hundred dollars an hour! Strewth, if Mary and I earned an extra hundred bucks in an entire month and didn't declare it, the authorities would have descended on us like a pack of hungry wolves.

I was consumed by hypocrisy. When we couldn't pay a $150 electric bill, I went to the Hydro office to ask for extra time and they told me that if I didn't pay on time our power would be cut off. We would then have to pay an extra $50 to have it put back on, plus a deposit of $500 to guarantee the account! I explained that if I was having trouble paying the $150,

277

then how on earth could they expect me to find the $700($150 + $50 + $500) needed, if they cut us off.

"Don't know, don't care, just doing our job" was their response. "You'd better find the $150 soon or you will be cut off!"

Again, no wonder people end up robbing liquor stores! What's a father to do when confronted with attitudes like that? Luckily for us I had a couple of old swords that I'd managed to hang onto for over 30 years, both over two hundred years old. I sold them for $150, a pittance of what they were worth, but at least we managed to pay the bill on time.

The story gets worse. A few weeks later we were broke as usual and didn't have a scrap of food in the house. Mary was working but her next payday was three days away. 'I've got nothing to feed the kids,' I thought, and tried telephoning the 'Red Cross' food bank, but there was no answer. They had closed down and were in the middle of building a new location. I tried calling some other places, but no one could help me, so I dug out all the empty bottles I could find and took them to the recyclers to get money.

I managed to raise $7, and went to a local supermarket to see what I could buy. I knew the kids liked poutine (cheese, fries and gravy), and decided to buy that, but we also needed milk and I couldn't afford to buy all four items. I looked around for a small piece of cheese and put it in my pocket, then went though the cash and paid for the rest. I nervously walked out of the store and was accosted by a man who was the store detective. He asked me to empty my pockets, which I did, showing him the piece of cheese.

He went ballistic at me, swearing and calling me every f'ing name in the book, I tried to explain that the food bank was closed and I was just trying to feed my family, but he wouldn't listen and continued swearing at me while he telephoned the police. When the officer arrived he took a look at the $3 piece of cheese and phoned the station to see if I had a record. "You're squeaky clean," he said, and took me to one side to listen to what I had to say. Luckily for me he knew that the food bank was temporarily closed and understood my predicament. After the store detective took a Polaroid of me, he informed me I was banned from the store for a year and the officer escorted me out- through all the on-looking customers, of course. Once outside he decided to let me off with a warning, and gave me his card and told me to call him if ever I needed help again.

'Thank my lucky stars,' he at least understood and I went back home, without the cheese.

Looking back, I guess my lack of expertise in shoplifting must have made me stand out like a sore thumb. But desperate times call for desperate measures and I don't regret what I did. The store detective became a lesson on how people over react today and have no compassion for the needs of others, even when their only crime is trying to feed their family. Sounds like something out of 'Oliver Twist,' but at least I didn't end up on Tyburn Gallows. However, as usual one lesson wasn't enough for me.

We received a telephone call from Alan in England, one of Debbie's ex-husbands. Debbie had died in her sleep! She was only 49 and it appears she died from a degenerated heart condition. She was living with Mr. X at the time, and they'd had a bad argument the night before her death, which may have contributed to her heart failure. If you remember, Debbie had left me for this guy, and I didn't want to tell you his name for a reason, but now that Debbie's at rest I'll explain why.

During our years at the St. George & Dragon, Samantha would occasionally go to stay with Debbie and Mr. X in Sheffield. Every-time she returned she seemed strange and distant. We put it down to the trauma of not having her parents together and learned to live with it. Many years later when Debbie and he had split up, we eventually found out the truth.

We were living in Canada and Samantha who was then 16, was having extreme stomach pains. They were so bad the doctor was considering giving her a hysterectomy, but before making his final decision, he recommended that Sam try some counseling, and that's when the truth came out. Mr. X had been sexually assaulting her for years, convincing her that if she told us we would cast her out for being dirty and then she would have to live with Debbie and him all the time! He also made other threats of harm to her, Mary and me!

"Oh my God, that explains her attitude after each visit," I said. No wonder she always acted so strange. We thought of informing Debbie, but decided against it as they were no longer together and Samantha didn't want to give her any more guilt. Sam then continued to see the counselor and thankfully her stomach pains went away, but the memories of her ordeal didn't and it's something that will never truly heal. Now upon hearing this news of her death, I wish we had told Debbie, perhaps then she wouldn't have gone back to him, but she did and now she's gone.

Sam took the news of Debbie's death pretty hard, and I remember how it had been when my father had died; she needed the closure that I never had. Neither Sam or Dave could afford to go to England, as they had spent what little money they had returning to B.C. (Sam wasn't happy in Ontario and missed the family too much). Debbie's father in England couldn't help either, he was broke too, having just buried Debbie's mother, who had died a few months earlier.

Then I discovered that Air Canada had a plan to help people attend family funerals. All we had to do was pay the airfare up front and they would refund the money in full, when Samantha returned with a copy of the death certificate. All we had to do was find the money for the initial airfare. Hey, what a perfect opportunity for a charity organization to help us, after all it's only a loan and they would get the money back.

All excited, I grabbed the phone book and started calling around and explained our position. One by one they all declined to help. I decided to try the churches and again I was given the old excuse of not being a member of their congregation. Mary was working at Wal-Mart and we knew they did community work, so Mary asked there, but again no luck.

Regrettably, no one would help us, and Samantha never made it to say good-bye. Honestly, I feel that if only one of them had helped us it would have rekindled my faith. Instead I just went even deeper into depression, convinced that I was a terrible father for not being able to help my daughter when she needed it. 'Thank goodness' my mother was in a home by then, as she would never let me forget this.

Samantha, Dave and Leah had moved back to Kelowna, since there was a lot more work for them there than in Nelson. Still it was only four hours away and it cheered me up a little knowing that the family was together again. Even that was short lived, as Julie dropped a bombshell! She, Wes and William were moving back to Ontario, Wes was homesick and the two of them were having problems. They thought that moving back might help them save their relationship, plus Julie didn't want William to lose his father. So, back they went and of course I blamed myself for that as well. But life goes on, and so did we, scrimping and scraping our way though.

The next two years would follow the same script. My back would seize up every few months, and between bouts I managed to get a job doing shuttle driving to and from the airport. Mary eventually acquired a full-time position at Wal-Mart, and we were able to say a final good-bye to welfare! Though by then we were only getting $200 a month, after declaring our income.

I did such a good job of repainting our house, our landlord recommended me to some of his friends. Once again I took on a 'career' change, and started doing house renovations, getting recommendation after recommendation. Slowly but surely, my self-esteem returned, and then instead of getting angry each time my back went out, I'd use the time to write and reflect on my life. I no longer felt imprisoned by my emotional body. Slowly, but gradually, a healing was taking place.

Gathering up the notes I'd made over the years, I realised what an amazing life I'd had and I started to look at things in a different way. Perhaps, I wondered, there was a reason that fate pushed me into arenas where I didn't belong.

Maybe I was there to be an observer, someone who had to experience these things so that they could pass on their knowledge to others. Knowledge is a funny word for it. Then again, I suppose it's not when you consider how many years of my life it took to acquire this information. Some might say I'd been a witness, that in learning to become a witness and not a victim, I had come closer to the truth.

I know there are some of you that will find the truth a difficult pill to swallow, but if we can stomach it, it could well be the medicine we need to heal this planet. I, for one, think it's worth the effort.

I began writing letters and articles, sending them to newspapers, magazines and radio stations, some of which received a media positive response. I got a front-page biography in the Nelson Daily News and was featured on the CBC radio programme 'Workology'. One letter in particular was a great success; it was printed in a newspaper, a magazine and read out on CBC radio. Strangers telephoned me to comment on how good they thought it was, and how they agreed with the sentiment. It was entitled "Apathy. The Eighth Deadly Sin." and can be found at the end of the book.

I wrote a letter to the Prime Minister Jean Chretien, concerning his so called "Government Employment Incentives." After all, I had personally driven him; perhaps he'd remember me? A few weeks later I received a letter from an assistant saying that my letter had been forwarded to 'the appropriate Minister,' and that's the last I heard of it. "Oh well, it was worth a try!" My adrenaline also shot up after being interviewed three times on the local radio station. I would have loved to have done more but my back went out again!

This was the third Christmas in a row that I'd had to endure back pain over the holidays, though we still made our usual journey to Kelowna to spend Christmas with Sam, Dave, Leah and my mother.

Now I even saw the positive side of back pain. All that lying in bed gave me plenty of time to read. Not the main stream stuff and glossy magazines, but books that pushed the buttons of conformity. Written by people who weren't afraid to challenge what they'd been told to believe about our history. Books like, 'Bloodline of The Holy Grail' by Laurence Gardner, 'The 12th Planet', by Zacharia Sitchin, 'Joining CLUB FED' by Nancy Tatum and 'Conversations with God' by Neale Donald Walsh.

The latter blew me away; it detailed channeled information given to Neale in the early nineties, written at the same time that I was writing down my thoughts while waiting in the limousine for clients. When I read it I couldn't believe my eyes! There in front of me was everything, I'd written, some of it literally word for word. I was flabbergasted! Here were my thoughts printed for all to see. Was it just a coincidence or were he and I tuned into the same frequency? However it happened I may never know, but one thing for certain it meant there were people out there who believed as I did and they too were prepared to 'tell it as it is!'

I think we've all pussyfooted around so long it's become a habit. So many people go around in fear, complaining about the amount of crime and violence in the world today, then go home and spend the evening watching programs filled with anger, rape and murder and call it entertainment. Lets face it, if we really want to change our world; we have to change ourselves first, what we read, watch and eat.

Did you know that when the World Trade Centre collapsed the price of gold virtually doubled and investors everywhere made a fortune, including the US Government? Then when the Gulf War started the price of oil went from $13 a barrel to over $40 and again investors made a killing. Even as the Americans went into Iraq, investors in the U.S. were cheering and hoped that Saddam's troops would put up a good fight so that the price of oil would go even higher. (Regardless of how many people got killed on either side). Everyday

'We the People' are pouring our blood, sweat and tears into situations that are creating millions of dollars for a select few. WHY? Because we're told if we don't, the sky will fall! "Bollocks!" We could end all hunger, stop child pornography and have world peace tomorrow, if we knew the real truth and worked together!

"If we really want to change our world; we have to change ourselves first!"

It wasn't Hitler that took Germany to war, it was the millions of people following him that did all the work, and if people working together for WAR could do all that, imagine what they could do if they put the same amount of effort into creating PEACE!

Let's face it, we deserve what we get! For instance; If someone conducts a presentation on 'Saving the Rain Forest,' or 'Free Alternative Forms of Energy,' only a handful of people bother to attend. But, if the presentation was to see two boxers beat the crap out of each other or a hockey final, over sixty thousand people would turn up! And we say we want world peace! Isn't it about time we started practicing what we preach?

"If we really want to change our world; we have to change ourselves first."

Since the beginning of recorded history, civilizations have been ruled by leaders who've controlled their subjects by fear, threatening wrong doers with jail, violence and death, and what has it accomplished? Nothing but war after war, and crime continues everywhere! At least now we have over twelve thousand years of proof that ruling by 'Fear,' doesn't work. So why don't we try the opposite and rule with compassion, love and consideration. You never know, it might succeed!

I let the smoke from the forest fires cloud my vision and destroy what I'd accomplished, and when the Millennium closed down I gave up on my quest and slipped into depression. Believing I had failed, I let the negativity in my mind take over instead of looking at the bigger picture.

For thousands of years people who are the backbone

of this world have been taken for granted- their hard work, sweat and tears being used to create a utopia for an elite few, and it's about time they got the credit they deserve. This is that time and we are the people we've been waiting for to make it happen.

Everywhere around me people are waking up. That's why governments all over the world are tightening up on security. They're watching us and restricting our movement, using the threat of terrorism to disguise the truth. They're finally losing their control over us, and the only people that they are trying to protect are themselves.

Question; who pays the wages of our police force? We do.

What is the purpose of the police? To serve and protect us. The public!

Who pays the wages of our Government? We do.

What is the purpose of our Government? To maintain and care for the country and it's people. Us, the people they work for.

So why is it, that our Government uses our police force as their own private army in any conflict between them and us! Are we not allowing the employees to beat up their employers?

But that's nothing compared to what they have in store for us in the future. Currently the U.S. military is working on a weapon that can control rioters from two kilometers away; it's called PEP's, pulsed energy projectiles. This weapon fires a laser pulse that generates a burst of expanding plasma, that when it hits a person will inflict temporary pain in their nerve cells, enough to knock them off their feet. It should be fully operational by 2007, unless we put a stop to it. There are thousands, of environmentally friendly energy patents, and amazing medical cures sitting on shelves gathering dust, all hidden away from the public for one reason only …and that reason is *control*. The governments and large corporations of the world must maintain at any price our dependency on these archaic resources to ensure control over the economy. That way, it keeps the select few rich and the masses poor.

Isn't it time we removed the blinkers from our eyes and took hold of the reins of life? For far too long, we've allowed this power hungry bunch to hoodwink us, concealing important information from us! Treating us like little children, they think that we, the people, aren't responsible enough to handle our own affairs. But they're wrong. Thanks to people like you who've read this book and others like it, the time has come for these greedy manipulators to be the concerned ones, because, believe me folks, the kids are growing up.

The End   - Or is it?

Epilogue

Reflecting over my life, I consider myself an extremely lucky man. If reality could be compared to an 'Organic Universe,' where manure creates growth, then I've been in enough s**t to manifest a bleeding forest, and if love equaled money, I'd would certainly be a multi-millionaire. I may not have much in the way of material possessions to show for the past fifty-five years, but I'm surrounded by people that love me for who I am, not what I have. In fact, I feel sorry for those power mongers who think money is the be-all and end-all of existence. They're so busy making money, they've forgotten how to make a life. Their millions might buy them the illusion of happiness during their lifetime, but they can't take it with them... LOVE on the other hand, will always prevail, and is probably the one and only thing you CAN take with you when you die.

I'm happy to say that the problems Mary and I had in the past few years didn't damage our relationship; actually, we both grew from it and we are now closer than ever. Two years ago we celebrated our twenty-fifth wedding anniversary, and even though we hadn't any money at the time, we still had a fabulous night out. Lyndsay who was then twelve wrote a letter to the manager of the Prestige hotel in Nelson, asking if she could reserve their Egyptian suite for us, and pay for it by doing work for them. Amazingly, the manager agreed, and then the rest of the family pulled together to buy us dinner in the restaurant as well. Afterwards, Lyndsay, Michael, Samantha, Julie, little Leah and William worked on various days de-weeding the grounds to pay for the room. Bless their hearts. They say it's the thought that counts, and it's the thought that went into that, that made it such a unique gift. They managed to show a lot more sincerity this way than if they'd had the cash to just buy something.

You're now probably wondering what the heck Sam and Julie are doing here in Nelson? Well, sadly Samantha and Dave separated, and she moved in with us. Then a few months later, Julie returned back from Ontario; her relationship with Wes didn't work out either. So here we are again, one big happy family. Only this time we have the addition of grandchildren Leah and William. Thank God we all get along...

Luckily for everyone I managed to combat my depression and considering that three years ago we were living in a trailer, on virtually nothing, we've accomplished an outstanding comeback. Today we live on a hill in a five bed-room house adorned with beams, overlooking the west arm of Kootenay Lake, coincidently like the one described by the psychic, Mrs. Becket, 20 years ago in England.

For the past few years, most of my time has been spent compiling this book, in between bouts of employment where my hodgepodge of work experience once again comes in handy. From looking after the rental properties for yet another millionaire to working as a part time handyman, housekeeper and occasional chef at the beautiful Blaylock Mansion, which, by the way, is the most unique Tudor style Manor house in B.C., I manage to keep busy, stay positive and pay the bills!

It's said that everything happens for a reason, and it's with that in mind that I accept the experiences of my past and look towards the future. No matter what lies ahead, I continue my journey through life with an open heart and mind, secure in the knowledge that I have been able to share my experiences with others- in the hope that one person can make a difference.

I don't know any fancy words and didn't achieve any

higher education. At 15 I was enrolled into the university of life itself, where the professors were my employers and the homework never ended. Although I've had my fair share of bullying, I managed to stay the course and graduate with a degree in reality! This book has been a compilation of all my learning experiences, some of which may be considered unconventional, but no matter what I did I or how I did it, my quest was to find the truth. It's the results of that search that I'm passing on to you. What you do with this knowledge is up to you, but I am determined to continue informing humanity of what I, and others like myself have discovered.

As an incentive, I wear a thousand year old coin from the crusades around my neck to spur me on, because the 'King Richard,' in me is off on a final crusade. We've all kept silent for far too long and now– 'The Silence Must Be Heard!'

I love and thank all of you who were concerned enough to read this book.

John St. John

Apathy. The Eighth Deadly Sin!

Appeared in the Nelson Express, Alternative Insight and read on CBC morning radio in January 2003.

What a world of moronic hypocrites we all are, constantly moaning and groaning about everything and everyone, myself included.

Most people sit around complaining about their Governments and Leaders as if they are powerless to do anything about it. For crying out loud, people, you're talking about your employees. If you don't think them worthy of the position, 'Fire Them!!' Or better still, don't vote for them in the first place.

I know we have the right to vote, but let's pull together for the right to choose. Presently we begrudgingly pop down to the polls to vote for the party or person we dislike the least, instead of the one we really want. The reason being, we again allowed the election to become a matter of who has the most money to campaign, instead of the most ethics. If we the people can't get our act together and demand what or who is best for us, then how can we expect the Government to be any better?

If President Bush wants to go to War, good for him, let's give him a gun and a packed lunch and send him on his way. Remember this… unless we do his fighting for him, he can't have a War!

Come on people, we are now in the 21st Century. Are we going to act like it, or go back to the Middle Ages and hide our heads in the sand once more? After all, we are the ones that always pay for it in the end, with our blood, sweat and taxes, not the Government!

So how is it they get away with it? They rely on our APATHY, that's how!

John St. John
Nelson, BC.

Some books and other sources of information that might be of interest

And The Truth Shall Set You Free   David Icke

Webs of Power   Erik Fortman.

Take Control of Your Health   Elaine Hollingsworth.

The Crucifixion of Truth   Tony Bushby.

The Coming Energy Revolution   Jeane Manning.

Conversations with God   Neale Donald Walsch

Web sites

davidicke.com

hiddenmysteries.org

surfingtheapocalypse.net

theuniversalseduction.com

For those of you who might be interested,
here is a list of all the entertainers that I had the
privilege of meeting in England.

This will rekindle some memories for you Brits out there.

Dave Allen
Ward Allen
The Black Abbots
Tony Blackburn
Joe Brown
Marti Caine
Jasper Carrott
George Cole
Billy Connolly
Peter Cook
Ronnie Corbet
Dana
Windsor Davies
Roger DeCourcey & Nooky Bear
Lonnie Donnagan
Val Doonican
Ronnie Duke
Ivor Emanuel
Dick Emery
Don Estelle
Anita Harris
Herman's Hermits
Vince Hill
Noele Gordon
The Grumbleweeds
The Hollies
Mary Hopkin
Hot Gossip
Billy Jay
Danny LaRue
Lulu
Kenny Lynch
Madness
Nicky Martin
Eric Morecambe
Robert Morley
Bob Munkhouse
Tom O'Connor

Michael Parkinson
Cliff Richard
Clodah Rodgers
Tammy Rodgers.
Ted Rodgers
George Roper
Freddie Star
Tommy Steel
Diane Solomon
Carl Wayne
Ernie Wise
Mike & Bernie Winters, and Schnoubitz
The Wurzels
Frankie Vaughn

Made in the USA
Middletown, DE
28 May 2019